SHERLOCK'S LOGIC

SHERLOCK'S LOGIC

William Neblett

BARNES
&NOBLE
BOOKS
NEW YORK

This edition published by Barnes & Noble, Inc.,
by arrangement with University Press of America.

1993 Barnes & Noble Books

ISBN 0-88029-723-9

Printed and bound in the United States of America
M 11 10 9 8 7 6

ACKNOWLEDGEMENTS

I wish to express my appreciation to Grace Allen and Luisa Reyes of the Word Processing Center at Occidental College for their conscientious preparation of the manuscript.

DEDICATION

This work is dedicated to the logicians at the University of California at Los Angeles with whom I had the opportunity to study: Rudolf Carnap, Alonzo Church, Donald Kalish, David Kaplan, Richard Montague, and Abraham Robinson, and to students in my logic and critical thinking courses at California State University at Los Angeles, and Occidental College.

TABLE OF CONTENTS

SHERLOCK'S LOGIC: THE MYSTERY STORY

THE TEXT

1. Modus Tollens: A Deductive Operation of Thought
   The Disconfirmation of an Hypothesis
2. Modus Ponens: A Deductive Operation of Thought
3. Universal Instantiation: A Deductive Operation of Thought
4. Disjunctive Syllogism: A Deductive Operation of Thought
5. Validity and Invalidity; Truth and Falsity
6. Inconsistency: A Fallacy
   Reductio Ad Absurdum: A Technique for Exposing Inconsistency
7. Tautologies
8. Equivalent Thoughts
9. Summary
Study Aids
Study Materials for Chapter I

SHERLOCK'S LOGIC

Sherlock Holmes, the Third, was indeed the grandson of the legendary detective, Sherlock Holmes. He had been blessed, and cursed, with a legacy that he would never escape — at least, not until his death. I looked at him now pacing about his room at the university, excited and intense, surrounded by a cloud of smoke from the cigarette he constantly puffed, and I must confess that I felt sorry for him. I thanked God that I had not been born into such a predicament.

"Dr. Watkins, I presume," he said and laughed, re-affirming his ancestral curse, but with a sense of humour.

"Sherlock. Good evening." Immediately in response to this innocuous greeting he grew intense.

"It is not a good evening. No! It is not a good evening at all. Do you realize, Watkins, that tomorrow I will come of age, and that I am obliged to settle upon my life's endeavour. You have almost completed your medical studies and are well along in your career. But I . . ." He stopped abruptly, pushed his glasses with his forefinger back upon the bridge of his nose, and looked at me expectantly. I was flustered.

"You are only twenty-one."

"I am not only twenty-one. You know very well that I believe that excuses attributed to youth are illogical."

"You are a difficult taskmaster, particularly upon yourself." He glowered at me as if I was pretending to be a fool.

"Is there any other way? But you are side-stepping my question. Please. No more pettifogging and circumlocution."

"Side-stepping what question?" He had the unfortunate habit of presuming that what he had thought, he had also said. He knew of his bad habit, but still he pressed me.

"You're just feinting. Whether I explicitly asked you or not, you know that I need your advice. You know me better than anyone else. My time is running out. Tomorrow I will be twenty-one. Twenty-one! What am I going to do?"

"I don't know, but whatever it is, it'll be different."

1

"Don't joke with me. I may be smiling, but I feel like a man facing the guillotine. I am dead serious." He did seem serious.

"You are a logician."

"Yes. That is my talent, and the focus of my studies here at the university. But now that my mind has been lathed into a refined logical instrument, I do not wish to study logic further, I wish to apply it!"

"You have attempted to apply it to the understanding of history and theology."

"Yes. But to this date, with only marginal success." He had seated himself now and was gazing transfixed out of a window of his room. I decided to go directly to the heart of the matter.

"Of course, you could apply your logical talent to the detection of crime."

He bolted upright, twisted round to face me, and pretended to be totally taken aback at my suggestion. I, in return, looked him squarely in the eye and began to laugh. My laugh was infectious and he laughed too. While he was thus helpless, I decided to take the opportunity to get myself off the hook.

"Stop pushing your problems off on me. Besides, you don't have to decide the entire course of your life's history by sunrise tomorrow morning. You have at least until the end of the week."

Fortunately, he continued to laugh, and I was reminded again of the power of humour to relax. I pressed on while I had him at bay, for I knew that this would not last for long.

"In the meantime, why not apply your logical talents to crime detection in your spare time? Why not attempt to develop as a hobby, what might or might not develop as a profession? Be a detective. Incorporate yourself as a consultant. Get yourself some business cards. Solve a few crimes."

"You make it sound so easy."

"It is."

"If I am to solve a few crimes, then I must have a few customers."

"Then do what anyone else would do in a business that needs customers. Advertise. Put an ad in the newspapers and hope for the best. London is a big city. What can you lose?

2

"Alright. I'll do it." And he did it.

It amazes me even now when I think how rapidly events transpired from that evening to a time not very long thereafter when the young Sherlock's name had become a common household word, although he was naturally viewed in the shadow of his never-to-be-outmatched grandfather. The public did not know that the science of reasoning had progressed by quantum leaps in the one hundred years intervening since the original Sherlock Holmes had matched wits with that great master of crime, Professor Moriarity. But they would soon learn.

In any event, the new Sherlock did take out an advertisement in the London Times, and his first respondent was a stroke of good fortune for any neophyte detective. On the Saturday evening before our conversation, a shocking murder had reverberated through the West End. Mrs. Laura Anderson, eminent socialite and wife of the distinguished surgeon, Phillip Anderson, had been brutally murdered in her home some time around the hour of midnight. In fact, because the murder had been so highly publicized, it had come to Sherlock's attention. The body had been discovered draped with a cloak highlighted by a specially designed crucifix. This curious and bizarre feature of the murder had aroused as much comment and controversy as the murder itself. Perhaps the murder was a ritual act of some demented witch cult or the handiwork of some lone psychotic religious fanatic. Such eccentric murders had been known to occur in the United States, but I myself doubted that they could occur here in England. Sherlock had been struck by a photograph of the cloak in the headlines, and had commented that the design of the cross had some special significance. I myself had almost forgotten the case, when Sherlock rang me up, terribly agitated, and almost demanding that he see me. He had been hired as a consultant in his first case.

I am certain that I was as excited as he, and my emotional state must have shown as I entered his private dormitory room. He laughed at my entrance.

"I have never observed you to respond to one of my calls with such efficiency."

"I am naturally curious about your first case. Beside, I have some of the detective's instincts in me too."

"Don't we all," he said, his eyes alight and almost on fire. He leaped from his chair and firmly gripped my hand.

"We've done it! I have been hired, or at least been asked to contribute to, the mysterious murder of Mrs. Laura Anderson."

"That's bloody marvelous," I said, although I quickly flushed with

3

shame over the realization that our delight was possible only because of some poor woman's death.

"Don't feel guilty!" the observant young Sherlock shouted at me, "You didn't kill her. Besides I need your mind to be lucid and alert. I have arranged a meeting, which we must keep shortly, with Detective Kemp of Scotland Yard, the best of their personnel in homicide, and the investigator in charge of the case. It wasn't easy, but he has allotted us some of his precious time since I have been retained by one of the leading suspects in the case."

He grabbed my arm and we headed out to flag a taxi to Scotland Yard. On our way there Sherlock explained how he had so fortuitously become involved in a highly publicized case of murder. It seems that the nephew of the Andersons, a young medical student named Sylvester, had been intensively interrogated by Detective Kemp, and although no formal charges had been advanced, Sylvester feared that special circumstances surrounding the case were so incriminating against him that he might indeed be charged with the crime. He had already arranged for legal counsel, but the law could be of genuine assistance to him only later in mounting a defence. And he was convinced that his innocence could be proved by someone astute enough to do so, thereby avoiding the embarrassment, the publicity, and the lingering suspicion associated with a criminal trial. Sylvester was particularly distressed because he had recently become engaged, and all of his optimistic plans for the future now seemed in jeopardy. It was for this reason that he had sought the assistance of an independent detective, and had lighted upon young Sherlock's advertisement in the Times. He had heard of young Sherlock through acquaintances at the university, and was aware of his outstanding reputation as a logician. Thus an arrangement followed in which Sherlock was retained to investigate the case.

The taxi pulled into Scotland Yard and with a few proper inquiries we were soon ushered into the office of Detective Hilary T. Kemp. Detective Kemp was a large man. He had a square and powerful jaw, a properly coiffeured but thick moustache, and alert green eyes that peered out from spectacles that lent him an intellectual air. He wore a tweed jacket and was seated straight upright at his desk, apparently studying some notes. We were introduced.

"So the young Sherlock is following-in-the footsteps." There was a patronizing, though not in any way hostile, grin on his face. The young Sherlock, of course, got right to the point.

"Is there a special significance to the cloak draped over the victim's body?...Since it was worn by the medieval monastic order of the Knights Templars." Detective Kemp's condescending grin disappeared at once.

4

"Perhaps. Perhaps not." He was cagey, but then, that was his profession. Sherlock just gazed at him for a few moments and then continued.

"Do you have a prime suspect for the murder?"

"We have narrowed our suspects to two."

"Eleanor the chambermaid and Anderson's nephew Sylvester?"

"Yes."

"And Sylvester's fiancee, who accompanied him during most of that Saturday evening?"

"At most an accomplice, but almost surely not even that."

"Because she has no motive?"

"Correct."

"But then, from your line of thinking it follows that both Sylvester and the chambermaid must have a motive."

"Murderers do have motives." Kemp was becoming annoyed, and this began to show in his voice.

"True. If one considers all of the various extended senses of 'motive.' But in the garden variety sense, when we speak of revenge or greed as a motive, not all murderers have motives. The thief who, when surprised in the midst of a crime, fires and kills his apprehender without really wanting to. Or the religious fanatic who commits some bizarre crime and who selects his victim at random." He added, laughing and easing the tension, "That's the Daily Mirror's analysis of the crime." I laughed, and Detective Kemp, who wasn't an unlikeable fellow, but who preferred to be viewed as a mentor and not as an equal, laughed too. Kemp then took responsibility for the conversation and proceeded with the business of presenting his analysis of the case.

"The chambermaid deeply resented her mistress. As far as I can tell it was because her mistress was wealthy through the coincidence of birth, whereas she had not been nearly so fortunate. Moreover, as far as we know, only she, besides the mistress, had a key to the mistress' bedroom. When the doctor was out of town, the mistress upon retiring, always locked the bedroom door. She was a cautious woman whose caution, unfortunately, failed to save her. The young Sylvester, on the other hand, has been a surrogate son to the Andersons, who have no offspring of their own. Laura Anderson — whose maiden name, by the way, is Fairchild — was independently wealthy in her own right. Her will, a totally separate document from her husband's, directs the executor to divide her wealth equally between certain charitable organizations and her solicitous nephew, Sylvester."

Sherlock had been listening very intently, but upon this last revelation he seemed stunned and puzzled. Detective Kemp, keenly observant, and anxious to take the advantage, asked innocently;

"You were unaware of the contents of Mrs. Anderson's will?"

"On the contrary, Sylvester himself informed me of it." This was news to me. I realized that the suspicions directed toward Sylvester were more cogent than I had thought, and I hoped that Sherlock's first client was not guilty. As for the will, Sherlock had obviously not considered it sufficiently significant to comment upon to me. Kemp continued:

"And it is your opinion that Sylvester is innocent?"

"Yes."

"Which leaves us with Eleanor, the chambermaid."

"Only if we accept your original assumption that the murderer is either she or Sylvester, which I do not." Detective Kemp was naturally chagrined at this retort.

"And whom may I ask is your prime suspect?"

"Personally I have none. And I must add that I think you have astutely analyzed the case, given the limited facts we have before us."

This compliment mellowed Kemp temporarily, but he abruptly rose from his desk as if remembering some other pressing responsibility, thereby signaling his desire to bring the discussion to a close.

"I merely have two brief questions to raise before Watkins and I depart."

"Yes?"

"Was everything in Mrs. Anderson's will, including her jewelry, for example, left either to Sylvester or to charity?"

"Yes. And her jewelry is a small fortune in itself."

"And none of it is missing!"

"No. That we thoroughly checked."

6

"Well. My final question, and then we will leave you to your many duties, is about your reasoning in this case."

Kemp now seemed more composed and in control, I suspect because we were leaving momentarily and would cease to be a bother to him. He smiled and said:

"The famous 'powers of deduction' of your illustrious grandfather...."

Sherlock continued as if Kemp's comment had never been made.

"It is important in your mind in identifying the chambermaid as a prime suspect, that she had a key to the mistress' bedroom?"

"Absolutely."

"But you would not go so far as to claim that she could have been the murderer only if she had that key."

"I do not understand."

"Well. Suppose, just hypothetically, that she did not have the key, that she lost it or that Mrs. Anderson had lost hers and had temporarily borrowed the chambermaid's key until her own could be replaced."

"Yes? So? Suppose that to be true."

"Would you still consider the chambermaid a prime suspect?"

"No. I would not!" Kemp responded with conviction, but he was obviously fearful that he was being led into some sort of logical trap. And he was right.

"But Sylvester did not have a key either, and by the same reasoning should not be identified as a prime suspect. But you do identify him as a prime suspect. And that, of course, is a contradiction."

Kemp was now very, very much displeased. He leaned forward looking Sherlock squarely in the eye, glanced menacingly at me, the guilty accomplice, returned his glare to Sherlock, and said in a nasty tone of voice:

"Did it occur to your logical mind that it would have been a very simple matter for Sylvester, in his constant comings and goings in the Anderson's home, to have taken one of those damned keys and for a measly three shillings, had a duplicate made?"

7

"Of course! Your're quite right! It did occur to me. And there are any number of people, for example, the chef, who could have done the same. That is one of the reasons I could not accept your initial assumption that Sylvester and the chambermaid ought to be singled out as suspects!"

And with that comment Sherlock turned on his heel and started for the door. I hastened after him, and we almost collided when he turned back for a moment to say to Detective Kemp:

"Thank you very much for the information. Let us all hope that the true culprit of this awful crime is brought to justice."

And with that last comment, our interview with Detective Hilary Kemp of the homicide division of Scotland Yard, came to an end.

CHAPTER II

DETECTIVE KEMP IS A WINNER

The next event in the mysterious murder of Laura Anderson, in which I was personally involved and can report as an eye-witness, occurred only a few days after our interview with Kemp. All of the members of the Anderson household had agreed to meet together during the late morning at the Anderson home at Detective Kemp's request. Kemp had also consented to Sylvester's insistence, supported by Dr. Anderson, that Sherlock and I be present. I was mildly surprised that I had been included, but obviously Sherlock and I were now viewed as a team. Naturally, I did not protest. Although I was in my second and final year of internship in a medical clinic with a very busy schedule, I did not face the psychological pressures of entering into private practice, since I had long ago decided that I would be employed with the state's social system of medicine. Moreover, I had already pursued with Sherlock the idea of diagnostic logic, a logical method of inquiry by which to traverse with rigor from symptoms to disease, and Sherlock had agreed that there was something to it. Indeed, he was convinced that there was an investigative logic proper to detective work, but similar in kind to doctors identifying the cause of an illness. When we had discussed these matters we had quickly moved to the conjecture that all inquiries intelligently engaged have a common pattern of logical thinking. And if that were true, we further conjectured, that common pattern could in principle be displayed. And although it would depend upon the natural intuitive logical talent that we all have from birth, it could be taught and was highly perfectible as a skill.

In any event, it is obvious why I was pleased to be included as Sherlock's assistant, and I made every effort to participate actively in the investigation. I arranged to be away from the clinic on the morning of the meeting, joined Sherlock for an early morning tea, and together we traveled by taxi to the Anderson home in Knightsbridge.

When we arrived at the Anderson's home, Dr. Anderson himself greeted us at the door. He was a distinguished looking man, greying in a becoming manner, and obviously in the best of health. He was quite tanned from his recent vacation in Torquay. I was startled to see such skin tone even during the summer, since Londoners are known for their bleached out complexions. His face looked tormented. I supposed at the time that he was not only feeling grief, but also guilt over enjoying a playful vacation, while his wife was having her life and consciousness forcibly wrested from her by a fellow human being.

He led us to a small library at the rear of the home where Kemp was already seated at a gaming table in the corner, with notebook and pen in hand. He looked up at us and smiled a greeting without leaving his chair. Sylvester and his fiancee Cassandra, a very young lady with black hair and black eyes, were seated on a couch and rose to greet Sherlock and to be introduced to me. I did not at the time suspect what an intriguing person Cassandra would later prove to be. The chambermaid, whose name was Eleanor but who was called "Miss Ellie," was standing, as were the chef and the butler. They awaited a signal from Dr. Anderson, who politely asked them to be seated.

Miss Ellie was petite with a modestly attractive but childish face for a woman well-advanced in her twenties. Her most striking feature, and it was striking, was her sinuous figure. She walked and moved as if she knew it, and I'm certain that men's eyes always followed her around. I even found myself looking at her repeatedly and once she caught my eye and we smiled politely at one another. I reckoned that such an event must have happened to her hundreds, or more likely, thousands, of times.

The chef, Louise-Phillipe de Molay, was a curious mixture of French on his father's side and Welsh on his mother's. I could immediately discern that his was a dynamic personality, although he kept himself subdued during the course of Kemp's interview. The butler, Richards, was tall, portly, with deep jowls, a reddish bumpy nose, and an unhealthy complexion. Being an aspiring practitioner of medicine, I could tell at once that he was an alcoholic.

Eleanor, Louise-Phillipe, and Richards seated themselves somewhat uncomfortably around the room. It was evident that they felt awkward taking a seat, as a guest might do, in the household in which they were employed. Dr. Anderson opened the conversation.

"It is important to me that everyone here be aware that under English law there is always a presumption of innocence. Detective Kemp assures me that he agrees, but, of course, at this point in the investigation, he cannot rule out anyone as a possible suspect. Those of us here know that it is not one of us. We are a family, and I have personally vouched for the integrity of each person in this room. We are proceeding informally today. I have not requested legal counsel. And Mr. Kemp has assured me that the purpose of today's meeting is to gather further information that might assist in tracking down the murderer's identity. That, of course, is a goal common to all of us here." Anderson smiled reassuringly at everyone, and gestured to Kemp, "Inspector Kemp. The floor is yours."

"I appreciate your meeting with me this morning, and I guarantee that the time spent here will not be considerable." Kemp remained seated and casual in his manner. "As you are well aware, this is a particularly difficult case to bring to a resolution. Almost a week has transpired and

10

my office's investigation has hardly progressed at all. Although each of you has been interviewed thoroughly, I have asked you to gather for one further and final interview of that tragic evening." He glanced at Anderson. "I know that this is particularly difficult for Dr. Anderson, but I must insist that it is necessary to the investigation."

Kemp now rose from the gaming table. His actions were studied, and I was certain that he viewed himself as an actor staging a performance. I had to admit that those of us there did constitute an audience.

"Miss Ellie." He addressed her by her name within the household. "You reported that on Saturday past you retired at approximately 8:30 to view television, that you went briefly to the kitchen for a snack at 10:00 P.M., and then returned permanently to your room for the evening."

"Yes, Inspector. That's correct."

"Your room is here, near the rear of the house, is it not?"

"Yes sir. It's just down the hall from the library."

"So that if someone entered through the front door, and proceeded immediately up the stairs in the front hallway, it would be unlikely if you heard them at all."

"That's true."

"And you neard not a thing after ten P.M. on that evening."

"No, Inspector. Not a thing." Kemp had been shifting from foot to foot in the center of the room, but now he drew himself up dramatically and looked at her eye to eye.

"Would you indulge me for a moment Miss Ellie? I would like you to close your eyes to determine whether you can identify a certain sound."

"Why, of course, if you wish, Inspector."

Miss Ellie closed her eyes and squeezed them tight. Kemp stepped towards the French doors standing behind him.

"I can hear footstep sounds of someone walking." Miss Ellie blurted out proudly.

"Fine! Splendid!" said Kemp, a bit distressed and impatient, glancing in the direction of Sherlock, who was only partly successful in restraining a grin. Kemp took hold of the French doors, which were slightly ajar, and

11

opened them slowly. They emitted a definite grating, scratching sound of metal on metal.

"Oh! That's the French doors." Miss Ellie spoke out again quite proudly. Kemp appeared embarrassed at his game, but seemed satisfied that it had some genuine point. Miss Ellie kept her eyes shut tight.

"You can open your eyes now. And I want you to think very carefully, trying your best to remember, whether on last Saturday evening some time after you retired, you heard that sound."

"No. I'm sure. I didn't hear that sound. I would have suffered a fright if I did. I would have thought somebody was sneaking into the house."

"Ah! Then you've never heard that sound late at night before?"

"No. Well. Just once." Miss Ellie was a little flustered and began fidgeting in her seat.

"And when was that?"

"Oh! Quite awhile ago. One night when Sylvester was staying over for the week-end. I joked with him about it the next day." She was now embarrassed, but obviously believed that she had to tell the truth. "He had forgotten his key, and instead of waking up the household, he came round the back."

"But the door was locked."

"Well. It was and it wasn't. You see, it doesn't latch on the top or the bottom, so that if you shove it hard right in the middle, it'll spring right open."

Kemp was quite pleased with himself, as he now turned to Sylvester, eyeing him with a deadly serious demeanor. This was a moment of encounter.

"Is all that Miss Ellie has reported true?"

"Why. Yes it is. Of course, it is." responded Sylvester.

"And on how many other occasions did you find it necessary to use those French doors to gain access into this home."

"None."

"None whatsoever?"

12

"That's what I said. None!" Sylvester's reply was harsh and antagonistic.

"You had your door key with you last Saturday evening when you went out?"

"Yes. I was again staying for the week-end. As I earlier informed you, I returned around 1:00 A.M. and was totally unaware of anything that had happened until the next morning when Dr. Anderson arrived from Torquay."

"You must be patient with my detective's persistence. You heard nothing after your return?"

"No! Nothing. If the autopsy report is correct, the crime was committed very near the hour of midnight, a considerable time before I returned."

"And no one heard you come in either?"

"No. Unfortunately no. Or I wouldn't be subject to your grilling now!"

The psychological temperature of the room had risen sharply. I was surprised at this other, very aggressive, side of Sylvester's personality. It was clear that he did not like Kemp and it was clear that Kemp lost no love on him either. Kemp had worked his way up in the world, and Sylvester, in his mannerisms towards Kemp, always made evident his superior class background. I knew that Kemp resented that.

"You may call it 'grilling' if you like. But, of course, I am just doing my duty!"

"Well! Get on with it then." responded Sylvester, still condescending, and obviously confident that Kemp's queries were leading nowhere.

"I have only one further question to ask you."

"Yes."

"When interviewed, you claimed that you arrived at midnight at Waterloo station from the evening you spent with friends in Sussex, and that you recall distinctly, that as you walked through the station, the large station clock was exactly on midnight. You then proceeded to walk leisurely from there the considerable distance to the West End, arriving around 1:00 A.M. or thereabouts."

"That's correct."

13

"My question is simply this: Are you aware that there is no train scheduled to arrive at Waterloo from Sussex at the hour of midnight, on Saturday or any other evening?"

Kemp was concentrated on Sylvester's eyes to see his response. Sylvester, of course, was completely taken aback, as were we all. Kemp continued, now on the offensive.

"Let us be frank with one another! You have been contemptuous of me throughout the course of this investigation, resenting me as an intruder and as a person of less noble background than yourself. If you look at our family histories more carefully you will discover that my father as a young barrister, joined the commandoes at the beginning of the war when my mother was pregnant with me, and was killed in a raid on the French coast, coast, leaving us with very modest means indeed. On the other hand, your father was a thief, who embezzled money left and right and finally killed himself. Secondly, you are one of a few obvious suspects for this murder: You have motive. You have access. And you have no alibi that is supported by witnesses. In carrying through with my duty I have had to pursue you as a suspect! And I might add, that in doing so, I have discovered that your alibi isn't worth a straw in the wind! What do you have to say?"

I personally will never forget that moment in my life. The situation was so intense that it has visually imprinted itself upon my memory forever. Sylvester was overwhelmed. Dr. Anderson was totally confused, and Kemp was at the absolute height of his powers. To my total amazement — and this I will never forget either — Sherlock was smiling. He was smiling. And I thought: 'He's insane! He is absolutely insane!'

And then, still smiling, Sherlock stepped up to Kemp, patted him in a friendly way on the arm, and said:

"Excellent! Sylvester certainly deserved that, even though he is my client."

And I thought that Sherlock was a traitor to the core, and that I would never trust him as a friend again. But, of course, I had not grown accustomed to his pose as a detective. For he immediately followed his congratulatory remarks to Kemp with a defence of his client.

"But nevertheless, he is obviously innocent. Isn't that true, Sylvester?" Sylvester, of course, nodded heartily. "Sylvester is clearly intelligent. If he were guilty of the murder, he would never have proposed an alibi that would fall apart so easily — a train arrival totally at odds with the train schedule. So he must be innocent! Admit it, Detective Kemp. You know that I'm right. He must be innocent."

A sly grin stole over Kemp's face as he responded.

14

"Perhaps Sylvester is not as intelligent as you think."

Sherlock was quick to reply, but I would swear that he was smiling inside:

"That is uncalled for."

"No. Maybe it is called for. He hired you, didn't he?"

"Yes. That's why I must insist that he is intelligent. And if he were the murderer, he would have designed an intelligent air-tight, or very close to air-tight, alibi. Since he didn't do so — his alibi is bloody awful — it must follow, and you must agree, that he is positively innocent!"

"No! I think that he is probably innocent. And I have thought that all along. But in my years of experience in the detection of crime, I have more than once been surprised to find someone guilty whom I all along thought to be innocent."

"So you still retain a genuine doubt about Sylvester?"

"Yes. Indeed."

"And are you aware that there is a train that leaves Crawley in Sussex at 9:50 and is scheduled to arrive at Waterloo Station at 11:40?"

"Yes."

"And are you aware that on this past Saturday evening that particular train was late in departing and consequently only arrived in Waterloo Station at just a minute or two before midnight. There was an emergency. A man had suffered a heart attack"

"Yes. I am aware of all that."

Sherlock was surprised.

"You have known this all along?"

"Of course! What sort of detective do you take me to be? Use your grandfather's famous powers of deduction. If Kemp is intelligent, he has investigated Sylvester's alibi, and if he has investigated Sylvester's alibi, then he has known these facts all along. It's obvious that you under-rate my intelligence."

"I see your point."

"But do you? Do you see my point about Sylvester? Are you aware that an underground car leaves Waterloo at midnight precisely arriving at Knightsbridge at 12:18, and that the coroner put the time of death at midnight given twenty minutes on either side?"

"That's cutting it awfully close."

"Yes. But what evidence is there in the first place that Sylvester even traveled on the delayed train to Waterloo? That hasn't been confirmed. You assume that Sylvester was on that train, because he's your client, and he told you that he was on that train."

It was obvious to everyone that Sherlock had been outwitted, and it seemed to be the mood of everyone to view him now as young and naive, as an unworthy participant in the league of the likes of Detective Kemp. He did regain some of his lost estimation in our eyes by pressing Kemp to admit once again that Sylvester was "probably" innocent. Moreover, Sylvester did seem pleased and relieved that Sherlock had extracted that explicit admission. But I myself was experiencing the sinking feeling that Sherlock's career in crime detection had terminated before it had hardly begun. I was depressed. And I recalled that it was I who had given him his first encouragement. I began to rationalize excuses for myself when my thoughts were abruptly interrupted by an announcement from Kemp:

"I still have a few questions remaining for Monsieur de Molay, and perhaps Mr. Richards too."

We all re-directed the focus of our consciousness to these two gentlemen who heretofore during the conversation had remained inconspicuous.

"Monsieur, you reported that on last Saturday evening you retired to your room early to read, and that although your room is near the front of the house, you heard no one enter, and certainly no one ring the doorbell, after 9:30 or so."

"Yes, Mr. Inspector. That's true."

"And naturally you heard nothing from the back of the house, the squeak of the French doors, for example."

"No, Mr. Inspector."

"And when Miss Ellie came into the kitchen around 10:00 P.M., and you went in, and you and she talked over coffee and croissants, did you hear anything then?"

"Why!...I..." Louise-Phillipe glanced furtively at Miss Ellie.

"You did have coffee, or was it cafe au lait and croissants, with her

16

that evening, didn't you?"

"Yes. He did." Miss Ellie spoke up, and I was certainly one who admired her for her frankness. She smiled at Kemp and asked:

"The cups and plates were still unwashed in the sink the next morning?" Kemp smiled back, and then turned to Louise-Phillipe.

"And how long did you converse, there, in the kitchen, on Saturday evening?"

"Oh! for quite some time."

"Until as late as one or one-thirty when Sylvester returned, or at least, alleges he returned?"

"Oh! No! It was not nearly so late."

"But you talked at least until midnight or twelve-thirty."

"Yes. I Believe that it was quite near to twelve-thirty."

"And you heard no one enter the front door?"

"No. No one."

"If no one entered the front door, and Sylvester was not yet home, and only you, Miss Ellie, and Mr. Richards, and Monsieur De Molay were within the house..." Kemp now paused for effect, looked at each of them individually, and continued with his voice lowered to a conspirator's whisper, "Do you realize? Do you fully realize that one of you must be the murderer?"

"Oh! No. Monsieur Inspector. No one. No one of us is the murderer. I am sure."

"Do you have a key to the mistress' bedroom Monsieur Molay?"

"No. I do not."

"And do you, Mr. Richards?"

"Certainly not."

"And Miss Ellie, what about you? Do you have that key?"

"Yes. I do. You know I do. But I am innocent, and can prove it."

"By Monsieur Molay's testimony you mean?"

17

"Yes."

"That sounds convenient."

"It is. But someone could have come through the front door."

"And not be heard by you and Monsieur Molay? Were you talking so animatedly?" Miss Ellie looked sheepish.

"After the coffee we started drinking cognac. It was Saturday night."

"So you weren't hearing sounds so well."

Louise-Phillipe had been shifting and squirming, and he now spoke up:

"Inspector Kemp, may we pass into the next room for a moment and have a word."

Kemp agreed and we waited impatiently. Cassandra took the opportunity to excuse herself to seek out the bathroom facilities, and as I was watching her leave, out of the corner of my eye I caught Sylvester watching me watching her leave. His eyes then shifted to Sherlock who was watching Cassandra too.

She shortly returned and was immediately followed by Kemp and Louise-Phillipe. Kemp seemed satisfied.

"Well. I believe I have asked all of the questions I need to ask. Perhaps Mr. Holmes has a question or two he would like to have answered."

"Yes. I do. Just one. I am curious about one detail of the circumstances under which Mrs. Anderson was discovered on Sunday morning. Mr. Anderson, when you knocked and no one answered, and then entered the room, you instinctively yelled, and at once Mr. Richards, who was already up and about, came into the room too."

"Yes."

"Do you, or do you Mr. Richards, recall the exact location of Mrs. Anderson's key to the bedroom door?"

Anderson was the first to answer:

"Why yes. It was on her dresser near the bed."

Kemp added, nodding.

"Yes. That's where we discovered it when I arrived."

18

"Does anyone know whether that's where she usually left the key on those occasions when she locked her door from the inside?"

Miss Ellie was quick to respond.

"No, I don't think she ever did, at least not that I recall. She left it in the lock in the door."

"And when her key was in the door, could it be opened by a key from the outside?"

"Why. No. Once she overslept. I didn't realize she was in the room when I went to clean it, and my key would not work. I couldn't even insert it."

Sherlock smiled.

"Thank you very much. That's all that I have to ask. Anything further, Detective Kemp."

"No. Nothing further. Ladies and gentlemen, let us adjourn."

CHAPTER III

WORLD'S END

Our meeting at the Anderson home had taken place on Thursday morning. On the Saturday evening immediately following, exactly one week from the date of the crime, I was invited by Sherlock to meet with him at the World's End Pub in the South-West corner of Chelsea, where Kings Road terminates and is joined by Old Brompton Road, in a area not unsurprisingly called, "World's End." I was uncertain why Sherlock had selected this spot for a meeting, although I was aware of the fact that the World's End Pub a few hundred years ago was a famous rendezvous of the fashionable young gay-blades of London.

Sherlock wished to discuss some features of the case, and had informed me that we would be joined later in the evening by Sylvester and Cassandra, and by one further guest whose name he thought it best not to divulge. I was curious that Cassandra had been included, even though she and Sylvester did seem to be inseparable. But when I had hinted to Sherlock that he had invited her because he was infatuated, he had sharply rebuked me:

"Watkins. I am always correct in my dealings with others. It is only logical. For your information and to dispel any further suspicion on your part, Cassandra — whom I must remind you is betrothed — has been included because her discipline is history. She will report to us on the Order of the Knights of the Temple. For we must begin to ascertain the significance of the Templar Cloak, so purposively draped over the victim by the murderer. And Watkins. Do remember not to confuse my personality with yours. You erred in projecting your attention to Cassandra upon me. The very first fact that you must affirm about human motives, if you are to excel as a criminal investigator or as a practitioner of medicine, is that they admit of an extraordinary variety." I must confess that I remained unconvinced by this apologetic outburst, but I let it go at that.

I arrived at the World's End Pub very close to the hour of 9:00 P.M., and in the midst of the Saturday night clatter, sought out Sherlock, who was seated at a small booth with a cigarette in one hand and a glass of cider in the other. I ordered a large Watney's ale and relaxed in the atmosphere of the pub. Saturday was always our busiest day at the clinic.

Sherlock, however, was extremely agitated, and I was not destined to find a moment of relaxation until the early hours of the morning when I

21

finally made my way to my flat and collapsed exhausted, both mentally and physically, into my bed.

"Watkins, I am very pleased to see you! I can tell that you have had a busy day ministering to the sick."

"Indeed, I have. But I have also had time to reflect upon the mysterious crime before us, a crime, I am beginning to think, that is so complex it will not admit of resolution."

Sherlock laughed. "Pessimism, my dear Watkins, is only attitude. I prefer to be optimistic."

"And you have no more rational grounds on which to be optimistic than I do to be pessimistic."

"True. That is very true. But optimism is better for one's disposition, and at least has that one clear practical advantage." We laughed and he continued. "But enough of this idle banter. Please tell me. Why do you think this particular crime is so complex?"

"There are two reasons. First, unlike you, I cannot eliminate even one suspect. Miss Ellie, I think, is far more shrewd than she appears. And so is Louise-Phillipe. And they may be in conspiracy together. The butler Richards is an alcoholic, and thus unstable. For all we know he suffers delirium tremens, and is capable of anything in that distorted state. Sylvester is sometimes mild and nice-mannered and at other times his arrogant temper completely carries him away. He is a moody pendulum that swings in one direction and then, abruptly, in the other. Finally, there is Dr. Anderson. I do not trust him. He seems to be all action and pretence, never revealing what is truly inside. Perhaps he hired someone to commit the crime while he was away. Perhaps he hated his wife. And for all we know, this damnable crime was just as likely committed by someone who is not even from the household."

"And the second reason?"

"The details of this crime are so extraordinary. I am convinced that the guilty party is so eccentric and so deviously brilliant that we will never succeed in un-masking his, or for that matter her, identity."

"Your intuitions, Watkins, I think are very good, but we must make them more explicit. Taking your second reason first. You claim that the crime is extraordinary. All murder in my mind is extraordinary, but I understand that you mean "extraordinary" in another sense, as this murder is compared with others."

"Yes."

"But let us be specific. The agent of this crime must be capable of murder. But you wish to say that this is an unusual murder as murders go, and that the murderer must in some way be unusual, as far as murderers go. But why? You must be specific. We can't assume that merely because you and I, and Kemp, have failed to solve this murder, that it must be unusual."

"You're right."

He laughed. "Of course, I'm right."

"Well." I continued, "Consider the fact that there was nothing stolen, no jewelry, not a thing."

"But many murders, undoubtedly most murders, are committed from a motive other than theft."

"Well then! What about the Templar Cloak? How often do murderers drape their victims' bodies with a religious object?"

"Sometimes, but not often, I would assume. And I do believe that you have a point about the cloak. That is the purpose of our gathering here tonight. And what else?"

"All of those doors and keys. The front door, the bedroom door. The murderer had to have a key to the front door and a key to the bedroom door. Or for all we know, he entered through the French doors around the back."

"So what do you conclude?"

"Not much. I don't believe that the murderer was a professional criminal, someone who could pick the locks, including the lock to the bedroom door, but who was discovered by Laura Anderson, and forced to silence her. If it were a professional, he would have quickly gathered up some of the valuable jewels before departing."

"Unless, of course, he became flustered at being apprehended, or something of the sort."

"Yes. But that's not the likely response of a true professional robbing a wealthy home in Knightsbridge."

"But perhaps it was not a true professional, or perhaps it was a true professional, but there to murder not to rob."

"Yes. Both of those are possible. But why would a criminal, either a professional or not, drape a Templar's Cloak over the body?"

23

"Well. There are a variety of possibilities, but I do agree that they are improbable. So! Go on. What further do you conclude?"

"I suppose, that the murderer is someone from within the household, who is familiar with its layout, and all of the doors, and all of those bloody keys."

"Yes?"

"And that whoever it is within the household is very eccentric indeed."

"Excellent! That is absolutely excellent!"

Sherlock seemed genuinely impressed with my ramblings, and I took a long draught of ale while beaming with pride inside. I was startled abruptly back to reality, however, by the pressure of a hand placed on my shoulder by someone standing behind me — a hand I knew at once to possess extraordinary strength. But before my body could register alarm, Sherlock looked up smiling and I heard the sinewy voice of Louise-Phillipe:

"Doctor Watkins. Monsieur Holmes. *Comment allez-vous?*"

Holmes quickly responded, rising to greet him.

"*Bien, Monsieur de Molay. Je vais bien. Et vous?*"

I joined the exchange of greetings with perfect English:

"Monsieur de Molay. Welcome to the World's End Pub."

He smiled broadly and asked:

"So this is the World's End? I have often wondered what it would be like, the World's End."

"Oh! It's pretty much like any other place, at any other time," I replied.

"But there are no barbarians here. I thought that at the end of the world there would certainly be barbarians."

Sherlock now engaged in the banter:

"Oh! The barbarians are here, and they are everywhere. Aren't we all, everyone of us, barbarians, Monsieur de Molay?"

"Yes. But some of us believe in the dignity of humanity. I, for one, believe in that dignity. That is the reason why I could never commit

24

murder. You can eliminate me from your list, Mr. Holmes and Dr. Watkins. I did not murder Laura Anderson." And with that surprising announcement, he seated himself next to me, laughed heartily with his head thrown back, pounding his head against the back seat of the booth. Sherlock remained standing and asked:

"What may I get you to drink, Monsieur de Molay?"

"Please. Call me Louise-Phillipe. I believe in equality for all. I am a true Frenchman."

"And thus could not murder one of your equals."

"Brilliant, Monsieur Holmes, you understand me well. That would be like murdering myself." He laughed at the thought.

"Which a true Frenchman would never do either."

"Of course not!"

"So in France there are neither murders nor suicides?"

"Oh! Unfortunately yes."

"Then not everyone in France is a true Frenchman."

"You see my point exactly, Mr. Holmes."

"Let my name be "Sherlock," and I will call you "Louise-Phillipe," and we will both call Watkins, "Watkins." We all laughed. "And I will order you a drink. Whiskey?"

"That would be a pleasure."

As Sherlock stepped up to the bar, Louise-Phillipe turned to me and said intently:

"I should have more seriousness about this tragic crime. I was truly saddened at Mrs. Anderson's death, committed right under my own nose. A brutal act, murder. Even more brutal that she was smothered to death, with her own pillow. But my weeping will not return her from the dead." He began to smile again. "Life goes on. But you must know that. Every day you deal in life and death." He nudged me with his elbow and I was again impressed by his unusual physical power. "And you are paid a handsome sum, whether your patients live or die." He began laughing again, and although I felt at that moment more like a mortician than a physician, his infectious laughter caused me to laugh too. Sherlock, returning, overheard these last comments, and added, laughing:

"Indeed Watkins. Yours is the only profession in which you are paid to tell someone that they are going to die." He lifted his glass and we all toasted one another in greeting. And Louise-Phillipe, his face turning intent again, spontaneously began reciting in a dramatic and resonant voice:

"Death is the net that catches all.
Death is the hand that snatches all.
All she holds she keeps.
Death serves all men equally.
Death bears every secrecy.
Death makes every bondsman free.
Death makes serfs of pope and king.
Death is the net that catches all.
Death gives poor men back their purse.
Death takes back what rich men stole.
Death weighs all with tested scales.
Death avenges every wrong.
Death is the net that catches all.
The hand that snatches all.
All she holds, she keeps."

He ended the poem and then informed us:

"That, gentlemen, is a poem by Froidmant, poet to the King of my namesake, Louise-Phillipe, a half-hearted crusader in the Holy Land, in Outre Mer."

Sherlock, in usual form, was quick to the point.

"The Order of the Knights of the Temple was garrisoned and fighting in the Holy Land at that time too, was it not?"

"Yes. But it was there a very long time before Louise-Phillipe, and stayed a very long time afterwards. The Knights Templars were the very last to depart when the Saracens finally defeated all the Christians in 1300. Louise-Phillipe's crusade with Richard the Lion-Hearted was one century before."

I was curious and joined the discussion.

"You know the history very well."

"Yes. Of course. It is part of my family's history. Jacques de Molay was the Grandmaster of the Order in 1300, just at the time when the Order was destroyed by Phillip the Fair and the weak-willed Pope Clement."

"And what was the fate of Jacques de Molay?"

26

"He was burned alive at the stake for recanting his confession after several years of imprisonment. But let me not deceive you. I take no pride in Jacques de Molay, nor in the Order of the Knights Templars. I dislike both." He looked squarely at Sherlock. "I Have nothing to do with an order of monks of the Christian Church, the Church's own army, devoted to murdering Saracens in the name of Jesus Christ. And I have nothing to do with Jacques de Molay who betrayed his own order when threatened by the Inquisition with torture. And I have nothing to do with the Knights Templar cloak found on Laura Anderson's body!"

Sherlock now re-entered the conversation with a series of questions:

"But there is a striking connection between the cloak placed there by the murderer and you. How do you explain that?"

"How do I explain that? I am not the detective. That is for you and Kemp and Watkins to solve. I am merely a chef. I can explain to you why your souffle did not rise," He was smiling now, "but I cannot explain a murder."

"You realize that it looks very bad for you."

"Yes. I can only think that the murderer put the Templar cloak over the body to throw suspicion directly upon me."

I added:

"And if that's so, the murderer is aware of your name and connection with the Knights Templars."

"Yes. You must be right."

Sherlock smiled at me and pursued my line of thinking:

"What persons whom you know are aware of that connection?"

"Some friends."

"Some friends who are also enemies?"

"No."

"And within the household?"

"Everyone."

"Everyone? Even Miss Ellie?"

"Yes."

"Dr. Anderson?"

"Yes."

"Richards?"

"Yes."

"And, of course, you yourself."

"Yes. But Sherlock, if I did commit the crime, for what reason would I wish to throw suspicion on myself? I would be a fool."

Sherlock's reply was immediate:

"There is a possible reason."

"What do you mean? What reason could there be?"

"To make it appear as if someone else committed the murder and placed the cloak there to cast suspicion upon you. And that is not the action of a fool."

"Sherlock. Your young mind is too devious. It trips itself up."

"Perhaps. But that is just the point. Suppose, just for the sake of argument, that you are the murderer."

"I do not like that suppose. But go ahead."

"You know that a detective's mind is subtle. Everyone knows that."

"Yes."

"Kemp — Let us use Kemp as our example — finds the cloak. The cloak immediately points him towards you, like an arrow, singling you out as the obvious, the prime, suspect. But, Kemp thinks: Why would a murderer intentionally leave evidence that would lead directly to him? Why would Louise-Phillipe do a thing so bloody stupid as that? He would not. It is much more plausible, Kemp would think, to believe that someone other than Louise-Phillipe committed the crime, and attempted to mask his identity by directing the suspicion to Louise-Phillipe."

Louise-Phillipe was now extremely intent. He was grasping the table with his powerful grip, his body was strained forward, his breathing was fast, and I would swear that I saw in his eyes the terror of a man whose very life is threatened. Curiously, I too felt fear for him.

28

"Yes! Yes! Go on. And Kemp would be right in his thinking."

"But my point Louise-Phillipe, is just that you could have committed the crime, and placed the cloak over the victim's body, predicting that some detective like Kemp would reason to the wrong conclusion that the murderer put the cloak there to cast suspicion on you!"

These last words of Sherlock devastated Louise-Phillipe. His robust and charismatic air abandoned him and he slumped back into his seat dejected and defeated.

"Then you believe that I am the murderer after all?"

"No, I do not believe that. To tell the truth, I do not have the vaguest idea who the murderer might be. I only know that it is not Sylvester."

Louise-Phillipe began to take heart again and to revive his spirit. Sherlock continued:

"But I am convinced that the cloak is our main clue to the murderer's identity. So let us begin once again. Let us suppose that you are innocent."

"Ah! That is a suppose which I can easily live with."

"There are two alternatives: Either the murderer draped the Templar Cloak on the victim's body to cast suspicion upon you, or the murderer has some independent connection with the Order of the Knights of the Temple. So let me ask: Do you have any enemies?"

"No,"

"You're sure. No one in the household with whom you do not get along?"

"Well. Richards and I do not get along very well. He does not approve of my relationship with Miss Ellie. But we have adjusted to one another, and I am certain that he does not wish me to hang for a murder." Louise-Phillipe shuddered at that thought.

"And Miss Ellie?"

"No! Never!"

"Are you certain. Absolutely certain?"

"I am absolutely certain."

"She has never shown a romantic interest in Richards, or in Dr. Anderson?"

"No! Your mind is too devious."

"Yes! It must be. The murderer is devious, and I must put myself in his mind, into his—or her—thoughts. And has Richards or Dr. Anderson ever shown a romantic interest in Miss Ellie?"

This question caused Louise-Phillipe to pause. When he responded, I must confess, I was very surprised. Sherlock, on the other hand, was not.

"Both of them in one way and another — it is true — both of them have shown an interest." He was reflecting now, his mind racing through thoughts he had never thought before. "But neither of them, I am sure, would commit a murder, and the murder of an unusual woman, in order to clear the way to Miss Ellie."

"Probably not. But it is possible that either of the two committed the murder for other reasons, but were happy enough to use you as the scapegoat?"

"That is possible."

"Now. The second alternative. Is there anyone besides you who might have a connection with the Knight Templars, and who might also have a connection to Laura Anderson?"

"Mrs. Anderson was devoted to charity work. She may have had contact with the Order of Freemasonry, whose members are obligated to the widowed, the orphaned, and the poor, and who have, as one of their highest degrees, the Knights Templar Degree. The Order of the Knights Templar itself some claim to have survived to the present in France and in Portugal."

"Yes. That I know. But what about here, specifically, in London, in the West End?"

"I do not know. There are Masonry organizations, and perhaps Templar organizations all over Europe and America. Some are secret, some are very powerful. Perhaps there is one that meets just around the corner."

"But as Christian organizations they would not engage in the business of murder."

"Who can know? To defend the faith by murdering the infidel was the first occupation of the Knights Templars."

At this point I was finally able to contribute to the conversation.

"I have read somewhere that some of these chapters of freemasonry

30

aren't strictly Christian, that they only believe in one supreme God and not the trinity, that some are pantheistic, and even a few are atheistic humanists."

"That is absolutely correct," confirmed Sherlock. "And believe it or not, I have been informed by Kemp that there is one such organization, a very small one made up solely of scientists, that gathers every fortnight in Kensington. Indeed, according to Kemp they were meeting on last Saturday evening. And earlier on that same evening they were visited by none other than Laura Anderson!"

I was extremely excited at this information, and Louise-Phillipe was ecstatic. It seemed to be the first general breakthrough in the case. I was impressed with Kemp, who had obviously been exploring many alternatives. Sherlock, however, was matter of fact. He looked hard at Louise-Phillipe.

"Watkins believes very firmly that the murderer is someone from within the household. If he is correct, then this connection will lead us nowhere." Louise-Phillipe was naturally taken aback, and I the culprit, felt shamed to the core. "That is why I must ask you, and you must be honest with me, whether you, Louise-Phillipe, knew of the existence of this group."

Louise-Phillipe was clearly flustered. But he replied with conviction:

"No. I did not."

"And Mrs. Anderson took her dinner in on that evening, prepared, I assume, by you."

"No. She said that she would be eating out, that she had an engagement. She was not in the habit of telling me the details of her social life."

Sherlock smiled as if he were satisfied, but I had already learned that in his new role of criminal investigator, I could not tell when he was pretending and when he was not. Still he continued smiling.

"You can see, Watkins, how vital it is to determine the significance of the Templar cloak." He glanced at his watch, and I knew that it was nearing the hour of 10:00 P.M. "It is almost time for our rendezvous with Sylvester and Cassandra. I have arranged for them to meet us a mere few blocks from here in a favorite spot of mine alongside the Thames, where we can sit quietly to absorb what Cassandra has to report on her research into the Order of the Knights of Temple. We will need all of our powers of concentration, for we must try to determine the relationship between the murderer's motive for placing the cloak on the victim's body

31

and the Order of the Knights of the Temple itself. So let us drink up, and be on our way. Perhaps this night will reveal to us the secret to this murder."

CHAPTER IV

THE RIVER THAMES

We stepped out into the street and the chill of the night air abruptly startled my mind alert to the beauty of the night all around me. My mind, and all of our minds, were still racing, as we shuffled, laughing, the few blocks towards the River Thames. But our laughter ceased as we rounded the last corner and stepped into the street directly facing the River. For we were greeted by one of the most extraordinary visions I have ever witnessed in my life. The moon was perfectly full and cast a brilliant umbrella of white light displaying the River below. We stood there muffled in awe. The River was still, a quiet home to the houseboats moored at her banks and their reflection on her surface. The only sound was the light lapping of waves against the sea wall. It sent a thrill quivering through my body.

Sylvester and Cassandra were standing on the sea wall, waiting, their bodies close together, silhouetted now with the houseboats against the glimmer of the River. I looked at Sherlock and he too was overcome. He moved next to me. He looked pale and I thought that he might faint.

"It's a still life. A still life before us. The clicking has stopped, the scales are in balance, and everything is, just as it is."

He put his hand on my shoulder for support. He turned his head, I could tell, to listen to the quiet lapping of the waves. And then he said to me in a voice almost at a whisper:

"Sometimes. Sometimes I hear sounds from outer space, in waves, reiterating rows of rhyme, ad infinitum. And Being is just as it is. Sometimes. Sometimes I hear the symphony of creation, ever-changing, each present universe-event a cataclysm. Sometimes I feel I am alive in sound, at one with Being's organism."

He started to walk forward and although I started forward too, I could feel his hand falling from my shoulder. I reached out to grab him, when Louise-Phillipe stepped quickly up and girdled him with one strong arm around the waist. We continued to walk, slowly, without words, to the sea wall, and there we collapsed on a bench enveloped within the scene. Sherlock began to regain his senses.

"This is why I wanted us to meet at the World's End Pub. This is a favorite spot of mine, especially when the Night is clear and can draw us near to it, and the moon is full."

We sat there for some moments quietly. Sylvester and Cassandra unselfconsciously embraced, and then stepped down from the sea wall to greet us. It was Cassandra who finally broke the silence.

"I have been asked by Sherlock to report on the Order of the Knights of the Temple, which I shall do."

She took out a small notebook from her purse, put on a pair of reading glasses, and began to read by moonlight. Sylvester stood to her side, proudly. It was obvious that he was very much in love with her, or at least, very infatuated. I personally felt envious of him and didn't think he deserved her at all. In fact, seeing him there in his weaning pride, I had the sudden urge to strike him in the jaw. Naturally, I restrained my impulses, and fortunately Cassandra began her report.

"To understand the religious and military Order of the Knights Templars, and the brethren who were its members, we must, as far as possible, imagine ourselves within the world of Medieval Christendom. The universe is conceived in the Greek image, with the celestial sphere of stars in constellations permanent and unchanging, but encircling in perfect motion the fixed earth at the very center. The planets are different in kind. They are imperfect. Their change in rotation in regard to the fixed celestial sphere and to one another, is erratic and puzzling. Although if one believes Ptolemy, they move in perfect circles within perfect circles. The universe in which we live, we must imagine to be inhabited with a host of extra-terrestrial and terrestrial beings other than animals and humans. Of the extra-terrestrial beings, there are angels, archangels, saints, the Virgin Mary — who is often worshipped more than any other being — God the Father, God the Son, and the Holy Ghost, whom I suppose also frequents the Earth. On the Earth itself, there are demons of various kinds, and there is Satan himself in the underworld of Hell somewhere beneath the surface of the Earth. You and I have been baptized by a priest of the Christian Church, who has the power in that ritual act, to transform our nature from that of a member of the highest animal species to a completely different world of existence, the eternal kingdom of God. Remember that we live in a feudal world, that we believe in kings and kingdoms, Dukes and Duchies, Counts and Counties, and oaths of fealty to our Lord. God the Son is the King of Kings, that is, the King of all the terrestrial kings. The terrestrial kings have a second baptism in which they assume the authority and the duty to rule a Christian kingdom. It is their responsibility to secure and defend the Christian faith in their dominions. The papacy is secondary and assumes whatever power it can get, which is sometimes a lot. You, the male nobility, are knights, that is, persons trained and devoted to the art of warfare and to its highest virtue, prowess in battle, or in tourneys and tournaments.

34

Now, within our society, the Knights Templars have existed since circa 1100, and they will continue to exist until circa 1300, when they are destroyed by King Phillip the Fair of France in collusion with Pope Clement, whom Phillip hoodwinks and browbeats into submission. These two centuries span a truly brilliant period of architecture, theology, philosophy, music — all modern music has its beginnings here —, and even logic." Cassandra glanced at Sherlock and then turned her focus to Louise-Phillipe. "The great and most robust culture, of course, is France. The Franks are dominant among the Templars, as they are in general in the crusades. But it is a mistake to think of the Order of the Knights of the Temple as a state within a state, if by implication, that means solely within the French State. For the Order has chapters and thrives vigorously in several different countries, including England and Germany. Indeed, many of its members reside for most of their lifetime in the Holy Land. The Order, it is true, is strictly independent of any state and exempt from taxation. For it is a monastic order of the Christian Church under the direct authority of the Pope. It is so wealthy and powerful, however, that its grandmasters sometimes act in opposition to the Pope's wishes. These Knights Templars in our midst, all from the nobility, take the traditional monastic vows of poverty, chastity, and humility. As knights of the Church, in a rigorously circumscribed military organization, they also vow to defend Christianity with their lives against all of its enemies, particularly the Saracens."

Louise-Phillipe had been growing more and more uncomfortable with Cassandra's dissertation, and he now broke into the conversation with a huff:

"They kill for Christ! They pervert the morals of the Christian Faith, the true teachings of Jesus!"

Cassandra looked up expecting more, but Louise-Phillipe seemed satisfied that he had made his point. She then responded:

"In our era, all of the nobility are knights, and all good knights are willing to take up arms for Christ. Richard the Lionhearted carries the true cross on which Jesus was crucified before his army in his battles in the Holy Land. The Knights Templars are no different."

"But they are different! They are monks of the Christian Church! They are an army of the Church that lives by the sword!"

"And I suppose that you also hate the crusades in which they and many others participate."

"Yes! Of course, I do!"

"And the French Revolution that comes later?"

That caught him off guard and made him pause. Cassandra took the advantage.

"Your feelings on these matters are clear. I think that you lack historical perspective. But my thoughts, like your feelings, are at this moment beside the point. May I proceed?"

"But, of course."

Cassandra smiled in return.

"I realize you have a personal stake in the discussion Monsieur de Molay."

"In more senses of 'stake' than you imagine, Mademoiselle."

Cassandra flushed red, realizing that it was Jacques de Molay, Louise-Phillipe's distant ancestor who had been burned alive at the stake. Louise-Phillipe, ever full of surprises, threw his head back and laughed heartily. We all began to laugh, and even Cassandra could not help but join in too, even though the joke was at her expense. Sherlock, however, interrupted our joviality.

"Why was the Order destroyed?"

"That, Detective Holmes, is one of the great mysteries of history. There are various theories, but I am hardly knowledgeable enough to venture an opinion for one theory rather than another. The facts do show that they were destroyed mainly at the hands and because of the wishes of King Phillip. Phillip was a strong king who manipulated the papacy and who desired the Order's possessions in France for himself. The great mystery is whether they were or were not guilty of the charges brought against them, which ultimately convinced Pope Clement to disband them altogether and to transfer their great wealth and vast properties to the Order of the Knights Hospitallers. I can report to you the charges brought against them."

"Please do."

Cassandra flipped her notebook forward several pages.

"Let me quote directly, but selectively, from the official bull of Pope Clement, Faciens Misericordiam, to the Archbishop of Canterbury in 1309:

That at their reception and sometimes after, they renounced Christ, or Jesus, or the person crucify'd. Or sometimes God. And sometimes the Blessed Virgin. And sometimes all the Saints of God.

36

That they said he had not suffer'd
For the Redemption of Mankind.
Nor been crucify'd but for his own crimes.
That they obliged those there they receiv'd
To spit upon the cross.
That they caused the cross to be trampled under foot.
That at the reception of the brothers of the said Order
The receiver sometimes and the person received
Now and then kiss'd one another's
Mouth, Navels, Bare Bellies.
That they told the brothers they receiv'd
That they might have carnal copulation with one another.
That it was lawful for them to do so.
That they were to do this to one another and be passive.
And it was no sin among them to do this."

Cassandra allowed us time to ingest the devastating nature of these charges, and then she added:

"Tied to their alleged renunciation of Jesus, obviously the most serious charge, were other charges that made them out to be a secret and bizarre heretical cult that worshipped idols. As you may know there were several vigorous heresies in the Middle Ages, and it was the duty of the Christian Kings, once the Papacy had given the determination that a sect was heretical, to ruthlessly stamp it out." She continued reading from her notebook.

"That they ador'd a Certain Cat
That appeared to them at their assemblies.
That they did this in contempt of Christ
and of the orthodox faith.
That the brethren themselves
Had Idols in every province, viz. heads
Some of which had three faces and some one
And some had a man's skull.
That they honour'd it. That it was as a God.
That it was as their Saviour."

Cassandra ended and looked up intently at Sherlock. But Sherlock turned his attention to Sylvester:

"Sylvester. What do you think is the significance of the Templar Cloak?"

I was taken aback that Sherlock would draw Sylvester into the analysis of the crime. I had assumed that he disliked his client and thought little of his intelligence. But I was wrong, and I now realize, having come to know his personality better, that there is no one whom he truly dislikes.

He is too understanding. And he also believes that everyone is intelligent, if only they would properly attend to perfecting their intellectual skills. In any event, Sylvester rose to the occasion.

"The cloak is a cloak to mask the murderer's identity. It is a clever device intended to divert us. It is irrelevant."

"That is the only intention of the murderer, to divert us?"

"In his use of the cloak. Yes."

"You say, 'his'."

"Yes. It must be a man."

"But why?"

"Because it's obviously not a woman."

"Why are you so certain it is not a woman?"

"It's obvious. Would a woman commit this murder, I mean this murder, entering the household, leaving a Knight Templar's cloak?"

Sherlock completely surprised me by answering, "No." Sylvester continued.

"Whoever committed the murder had a specific motive for doing so. The cloak is a sham."

"But it is a Knight Templar's cloak."

"That's what the murderer happened to have available to use as a diversion."

"But then the murderer must somehow be connected with the Knights Templars."

"I suppose so. Somehow."

"And we must interpret that connection, because it may be a clue to his identity."

"And then it may not."

"So you think the murderer is very devious, with a very subtle mind."

"Correct."

"Does Richards have that kind of mind."

"No."

"Does Louise-Phillipe?"

"No. I don't think so. He is intelligent, but not devious."

Louise-Phillipe smiled. And then Sherlock completely surprised me again, by turning to Louise-Phillipe and asking:

"Does Sylvester have such a mind?"

Louise-Phillipe paused, and then said:

"Yes. Very definitely, yes."

Sherlock then turned to question Cassandra:

"Do you agree?"

Cassandra was unsettled by the question, but still replied:

"Yes. Sometimes in regard to some things. But why do you ask?"

"Because if Sylvester is correct that the murderer is a man, and if Watkins is correct that the murderer must be from within the household, then we're left with Louise-Phillipe, Dr. Anderson, and Sylvester as the three prime suspects, whether we like it or not."

"But you know very well that Sylvester is innocent."

Cassandra's voice was beginning to show irritation.

"That's what my instincts tell me. But I..."

"But what. He's your client and he's innocent, and you know it. Yet you're pretending that he might be guilty. What's the point?"

Sherlock was very embarrassed, but not completely without words.

"We need Sylvester's thoughts on the crime. He is familiar with the persons, and the situation, of the crime, like none of the rest of us."

"Except for Louise-Phillipe."

"Yes."

"Who in your devious mind is still a prime suspect too."

39

"Unfortunately, yes."

"Even though you know very well that he's innocent too."

"I believe that, but I can't claim to know that."

"Know or believe, I don't care. They're both innocent, and you believe they're both innocent. So they're not prime suspects."

"If that's true, then there only remains Richards, Miss Ellie, and Dr. Anderson, as prime suspects."

"Not Miss Ellie. You just agreed it was a man."

"Yes. But I must keep alternative hypotheses open."

"Not true. You told Sylvester when you called that you thought Watkins was right, that it was someone from within the household."

"But I could be mistaken, the murderer could be a stranger."

"Then Sylvester and Louise-Phillipe are clearly off the hook."

"Well. If they are, that means that either Richards or Dr. Anderson is the murderer."

Sylvester, quick to his Uncle's defense, added:

"Since Dr. Anderson was in Torquay, it follows that it must be Richards."

This conclusion seemed totally implausible to me, so I objected:

"But what motive could Richards possibly have for murdering Laura Anderson. It doesn't make any sense to me."

Sherlock nodded in agreement. He was obviously relieved that the argument had taken a turn away from his indictment by Cassandra. I was now even more convinced of his infatuation for her, which I believe prompted him to envy Sylvester. I thought that it was humorous that Cassandra didn't see it. In any case, it was Sherlock who responded to my objection.

"The murderer's motive must be linked somehow to the Knights Templars. And in that regard I have something important to report, of which Watkins and Louise-Phillipe are already aware. A small group of scientists calling themselves a Knights Templar Guild, meets regularly in Kensington. Laura Anderson had some sort of relationship with them. In fact, she visited them in the early evening on the very night she was murdered."

40

This took Sylvester by surprise, but it only seemed to irk Cassandra more.

"Why didn't you tell us this, rather than stringing us along?"

"I wasn't stringing you along."

"But this means that the murderer certainly was not someone from within the household and that neither Sylvester, nor Louise-Phillipe, nor even Richards or Anderson, fit in as suspects at all."

"Not necessarily."

"What do you mean, not necessarily?"

"You and I interpret the significance of the cloak differently. You see it as pointing to a murderer outside of the household, someone in some way connected with this Guild."

"Obviously."

"Well, what is obvious to you is not obvious to me, and indeed may not be true."

Sherlock was fighting back. He would not let his guilt get the best of him, even though he knew he had wronged Sylvester in treating him as a genuine suspect. He continued.

"In my mind, Sylvester is on the right track. The cloak is an intentional diversion. But it could be a diversion that gives the murderer away. In any event, Kemp has arranged to interrogate the members of this Guild tomorrow, Sunday evening. Watkins and I are to be present, and, in fact, I will have a few minutes to speak with them prior to Kemp's arrival."

Cassandra's curiousity was piqued.

"Would it be possible for Sylvester and I to attend?"

Sylvester had to interrupt.

"I cannot. I am too close to my examinations. I just cannot take the time. This murder mystery has side-tracked me from my studies already too much."

"Then could I attend without Sylvester?"

Sherlock was cool and detached, but he replied positively.

41

"Yes. Here is the address. We will meet this Guild of Knights Templars promptly at 10:00 p.m., after they adjourn their own meeting."

As I recall, it wasn't long after these words from Sherlock that the group began to break up. Cassandra had the habit of kissing everyone on the cheek when she said her good-byes, and her doing so this evening washed away some of the uneasy feeling that lingered in most of us over her disagreement with Sherlock.

CHAPTER V

THE ARGUMENT FROM DESIGN

Sherlock and I arrived together at the Templar Guild address in Kensington and discovered a nondescript building with a bakery at street level and a stairwell to the left. The meeting place was obviously on the second level, immediately above the bakery. We waited outside for Cassandra and idly watched the bakers inside who were beginning their night's work. Since it was already a few minutes before 10, the bakery had long since closed to the public. Kemp had promised to arrive some time between 10:15 and 10:30, after fulfilling a social obligation to which he had been committed for some time.

Sherlock paced about the sidewalk smoking a cigarette. He looked up, and we could see lights from behind shades on the second story. His eyes then returned to observe the bakers, although I know the expectation was killing him. We were both very curious about scientists who conceived themselves to be present-day Knights Templars. Kemp had already interviewed their leader, a Professor Hawkins, and had explained to Sherlock that the Guild was very secretive and very small. It maintained no official relationship with other Knights Templars organizations or with the body of Freemasonry. And its membership was restricted to exactly four scientists, each of whom was engaged in some facet of biochemical research. One of its members, a brilliant young chap named Caldwell, was quite familiar to us. He had received a number of scientific prizes and had already established an international reputation in the field of mathematical genetics.

Cassandra finally arrived a few minutes after 10:00 P.M., smiling and slightly apologetic, and the three of us went up the stairs together to the most extraordinary and unsettling experience I have ever had in my life.

On the second floor landing Sherlock put out his cigarette and rang a buzzer to the right of the door. We were greeted by Professor Hawkins, a kindly gentleman in his middle to late forties, who introduced us to the three other Guild members: the young Caldwell, an aging Professor Stevens, and a decidedly old, but very spry, Professor Perkins.

The room was odd. It had one large table, a number of oddly assorted chairs, some bookshelves with a few books, a fireplace at one end, and a small bar. We were offered and took a glass of sherry and and each found a seat. Everyone seemed formal and tense. Hawkins then surprised us. He asked us to sit quietly while he observed the street below. We nodded

43

our agreement and he immediately extinguished the lights and stepped to the window to peer intently through the shades. He continued with this unusual behaviour for at least a minute or two, and then, seemingly satisfied, turned the lights on and proposed an informal toast.

"Shall we drink to a better future for humanity, gentlemen?" He noticed Cassandra and added, "And ladies." We drank the toast, still sitting about stiffly. I sensed that these gentlemen were quite incapable, and probably uninterested, in social small talk. I believe Sherlock sensed this too. For after the exchange of a few awkward comments about the weather, he spoke up. I knew he had designed a plan for the discussion, and, that he intended to subject each of the members to some sort of test. I was therefore quite surprised when the began as follows:

"Gentlemen. All of you here assembled are scientists, and therefore, objective inquirers of truth. For you, belief must be grounded in, and confirmed by empirical observations of nature. While we await Detective Kemp's arrival, I beg your indulgence to assist me in grappling with a problem."

Now that he had their attention, he rose to take a commanding position in front of the fireplace, fishing for his pack of cigarettes as he did so. Fortunately, it dawned on him that he was in a closed room with men of science, and he put his pack of cigarettes away.

"I have attempted to apply my logical studies to theology and in pursuit of this endeavour I have often reflected upon a famous theological argument, the Argument From Design, which alleges to prove the existence of God from an empirical observation of nature."

An immediate and uncomfortable stir came over those present, a communal frown at the very idea of a scientific-like proof of God's existence. But the young Sherlock, performing at his best, persisted:

"I expected a skeptical response from such learned and critical minds, and indeed I am confident that your objections to the argument will roundly defeat it. But it is exactly for this reason that I have requested your assistance, since I have never finally convinced myself of its refutation. Certainly, many of the most brilliant theological minds have found the Argument From Design persuasive, and it has been advanced by many Christians as the most important rational argument in support of their faith. Undoubtedly, some of the knights of the Order of the Temple invoked it in debates with Saracens during their long occupation in the Holy Land."

This last comment understandably created another uncomfortable stir. It succeeded, of course, in raising the level of respect and attention to this young upstart who had presumptuously — or as those present would

44

now think precociously — taken over the situation.

"The argument from design, at least under one rendition, can be stated as follows: First assumption. The universe, though fragmented in myriads of parts and replete with an extraordinary variety, nevertheless exhibits a remarkable structural design. Second assumption: A machine too is fragmented in parts, has variety, and yet reveals the imprint of a structural design. Third assumption. A machine is made by an intelligent being. And finally the conclusion: The universe too was made by an intelligent being, namely, that being we call 'God'," He paused briefly and then added, "The intuition behind the argument, of course, is that the structural design of the universe could not have originated merely by chance, but like a machine, must be the product of an intelligent designer and creator."

"Hogwash!," the aging Professor Perkins blurted out, as everyone turned to focus upon his face, now flush with indignation.

"That's not a logical proof and from it nothing whatsoever can be concluded! Not one whit of mathematical or deductive reasoning is employed in it! And one can only prove what logically follows from incontrovertibly true premises — and that's not much!"

Sherlock, as one might expect, was at first startled at the vehemence with which Professor Perkins had lashed out. But he proceeded in a calm and controlled voice, retaining his mastery of the situation. I conjectured at the time that logicians were quite familiar with, and perhaps even enjoyed, the expression of anger during the heat of a logical debate.

"The reasoning in the argument is indeed not deductive, and the conclusion therefore does not with necessity follow from the assumptions. However, the argument does employ analogical reasoning, and I thus feel obliged to continue to press the question whether it is rational to accept it or not."

"It is still hogwash!," rapped Perkins, as if his ears had been grated by the very sound of Sherlock's words.

"But why," Sherlock continued to press, "It employs reasoning so convincing it even bewitched the brilliant medieval churchman Saint Thomas Aquinas, in the opinion of many, the greatest Christian Theologian of all time."

Perkins grumbled and muttered to himself something about "empty heads" and "church doctors," but was joined at this point by Dr. Hawkins, who, with a winning smile, and friendly manner undercut the harsh tension that Perkins had introduced into the room.

"The brilliant St. Thomas was obviously lacking in analytical talent.

Even a half-witted logician would refuse to accept the argument and its conclusion."

"But!," replied Sherlock, "Using their full wits, detectives have often employed analogical reasoning in identifying persons guilty of criminal action. Therefore, one cannot reject the argument simply on the grounds that the reasoning it employs is not deductive."

"Of course, you're quite correct. I have myself fruitfully employed analogy in my micro-biological studies into the genetic coding of the aging process. Nevertheless, the conclusion of the argument from design is not properly related to the assumptions from which it begins."

Perkins, who seemed to be still quite engaged in the discussion, added:

"It certainly is not — which was just my point!"

Hawkins continued:

"Even if the analogical reasoning the argument employs is worth serious attention, it does not prove the existence of God. And I don't think that I am prejudiced in this matter. I think the existence of God is quite possible."

These last words prompted some worried expressions, until Hawkins added:

"I said that I think that the existence of God is quite possible. I did not say that I think the existence of God is quite probable."

Sherlock was obviously pleased at the course the conversation had taken with Dr. Hawkins' entrance. He smiled broadly at Hawkins, stuck his two hands into his coat pockets, probably fiddling with his pack of cigarettes in one of them, and then looked around the room expectantly for a response to the question he would now raise:

"Then if the reasoning in the argument is cogent, there is some conclusion which the argument warrants."

"Yes," responded Hawkins, "That some intelligence of some sort is responsible for the structural design of the universe."

I had noticed that Cassandra was intensely concentrated on the debate, and now, to my surprise — although I'm not at all sure why I was surprised — she joined the fray."

"But then, isn't that a proof, of some sort, of God's existence?"

Hawkins, still smiling, returned her question with a question:

"Is God in your meaning of "God" benevolent and just?"

"Yes. Of course."

"And eternal and immutable?"

"Well. Eternal, but I've never been sure about immutable. I always thought that never-changing was rather boring."

"Still. Leaving off the trait of being immutable, the argument certainly doesn't prove a being that's benevolent or just, or eternal, or perfectly powerful for that matter."

"I see. The conclusion is far too immodest."

"Indeed it is. Only someone first gullible enough to believe in the existence of God will be gullible enough to believe that the argument proves the existence of God." Hawkins laughed good-naturedly to give a proper tone to the jibe he had cast in Cassandra's direction, and she responded in the same spirit.

"My goodness! That's double-gullibility. Can they try you twice for that? And if you're guilty, do they send you immediately to hell?. . . ."

There was a lull in the conversation as we enjoyed the humour and allowed Hawkins' point to settle into our thinking. It was Sherlock who took up the conversation again.

"And I suppose, Dr. Hawkins, that you do not think that the conclusion of the argument shows a single intelligent being as contrasted with a plurality of beings?"

"I hadn't really thought of that. But, of course, you're right. Machines are usually designed and fabricated by more than one intelligent being. In fact, the more complex the machine, the more likely several intelligent beings are involved in its design and fabrication. Yes! If you follow through the analogy, the conclusion should be, 'made by some intelligence, either singular or plural — and more likely plural'."

At this point the young mathematical-chemist Caldwell entered the conversation for the first time. We had all along been curious about this already world-renowned young scientist. In fact, we had wondered whether he would comment at all. For he was very unusual, to say the least, in both brains and looks. He was as thin as a rail, and had a beard and moustache and hair all over his face, so that only his eyes were visible. He was somebody's — perhaps his own — stereotype of a scientific genius.

He also seemed shy, but now when he spoke his words were crisp, and carried an antagonistic tone:

"By the same reasoning, the argument from design must conclude that the makers of the universe possessed eyes and fingernails."

Cassandra, I could observe, sensed an error, and instinctively went on the offensive. Her black eyes were flashing and she was perched on the edge of her chair very tense and very alert.

"But intelligence seems relevant to conceiving and making structure, whereas having fingernails does not."

"Nevertheless," continued Caldwell, not to be put off, "By precisely the same reasoning which concludes that the universe was created by some intelligence, one must conclude that this intelligence also has fingernails, because machines are made by intelligent beings with fingernails."

"And I suppose the same is true for sex," added Cassandra, thereby prompting a defensive blush from Caldwell; "I mean," she continued, "a division of beings by sex."

"Yes." responded Caldwell, now confused and still blushing.

"And the universe must have been made by a group of persons numbering in the billions?"

"Yes."

"And by a group of persons, whose descendants include someone who is a brilliant young scientist, and whose names is 'Caldwell'."

"Yes. I admit it does sound absurd. But that is just the point. The argument reduces to absurdity."

"I don't agree! I can't agree! If you're correct, then every argument that uses an analogy in its reasoning can be reduced to absurdity by your technique!"

Caldwell jerked in his seat, his eyes blinking wildly, and then, to our surprise, he smiled, regained his composure, and admitted defeat:

"I suppose you're right. You've shown that the technique of reducing the argument to absurdity, itself reduces to absurdity. We could certainly use you in our laboratory."

As one might expect, we were all amazed at this interchange between Caldwell and Cassandra. Sherlock beamed, and everyone else seemed

48

impressed. I sensed that Sherlock was about to continue, when at precisely that moment Kemp arrived, explaining that he would be indisposed for a minute to wash up, but would join us shortly. Sherlock immediately turned to Professor Stevens. I was reminded, since I had long since forgotten, of his original intent of engaging the persons now gathered in the drawing room. Of course, I could not for the life of me comprehend what the argument from design had to do with the murder of Laura Anderson.

"Professor Stevens. You have not commented." Naturally, Sherlock would leave no stone unturned. Stevens readjusted his frail and aging frame, and responded courteously:

"The inconclusiveness of the debate is its own point."

"And that point!"

"If we place high demands upon the grounds and reasons for our beliefs, which I, like Professor Perkins, certainly do, the Argument From Design should not alone persuade us of the existence of God."

"Should it more modestly persuade us of the existence of some intelligence as responsible for the design and the creation of the universe?"

"No. It shouldn't even persuade us of that. Personally, I doubt whether something can come from nothing, and thus it is more plausible to me to conceive of the universe as existing ad infinitum from the past, and as never having been created. The Argument From Design trades on an ambiguity in the way machines are "made" and the way the universe in some popular conceptions was "made." Machines are made from pre-existing stuff, whereas the argument strives to prove that some intelligent God created it, ex nihilo, out of nothing..."

Stevens' comments were never to be completed, because at this moment Detective Kemp entered hurriedly into the room.

His attitude was very stern, very severe. I confess that I was startled to witness him so indisposed. When he spoke, his tone was harsh and indignant. He began his interrogation immediately.

"Professor Hawkins. You described the Templar Guild to me as willing to go to any extreme to achieve its goals."

"Yes. That's true. But I did not mean any extreme."

"Then why did you say any extreme, if that's not what you mean?"

"I wanted to impress upon you our willingness to sacrifice personally for our ideals."

"Then would you describe the Guild as extremist? Does that word fit?"

Hawkins fumbled over this question, and when he responded it was with considerable reluctance.

"Yes. I suppose that I must answer, Yes. The profound changes human society now faces demand in response extreme plans of action."

"And these extreme plans of action, you have already insisted to me, are secret, and must be kept secret, no matter the cost, even from an officer of the law?"

"No. Not exactly. Our over-all plan is no secret: To keep the results of reseach into the aging process within the hands of a small group of scientists."

"Namely, the Templar Guild."

"Yes."

"And you are confident, it would seem, that your research will succeed, that you will develop the understanding and the technology to delay the aging process?"

Hawkins paused. He glanced inquiringly at his compatriots, and then proceeded in a quiet voice:

"Our research goes far beyond delaying the aging process, Inspector Kemp. Far beyond."

That thought settled into the room, overwhelming us all. I was stunned. My mind groped anxiously to fathom the implications of Hawkin's quiet comments. Kemp was bewildered, but his habit as detective and his moral anger made him relentless. He pressed on with his questioning.

"And making the results of your research public, you are convinced presents a grave threat, not a glorious opportunity, to mankind!"

"If it is handled incorrectly — Yes."

"And you therefore abrogate the authority and power, and indeed, the right, to withhold these results, and to keep them secret."

"Yes. Until the time is opportune to reveal them."

"And I would like to ask you, Professor Hawkins, I would very much

50

like to ask you, whether you think you are God! Whether you and your fellow knights have the prerogative of God to give and take life as you will!"

"No. I do not — we do not — think of ourselves as God."

Kemp was now vehement. He had worked his moral anger to the point of rage. I thought: 'He will lose control.'

"But you are willing to act like God!"

"It may appear to you that way."

"It does appear to me that way, because it is that way!! Anyone listening to you and your plans to control mankind. . ."

"I must insist! The Guild does not desire to control humankind, only to benefit it."

Kemp was now completely beside himself. His inflamed anger and resentment had overcome his will. He stepped threateningly towards Hawkins.

"And would you kill? Would you murder to achieve these benefits you have stored for mankind, that you expect shortly to have within your power to distribute at your whim? Tell me! Would you kill?"

"No. I would certainly not kill. No one of us would kill. We believe in a reverence for life and for all living things."

"And I say that you are a bloody liar! If you have the power to continue life, and do not, you are a murderer! What thrills you is the power, the power of life over death. I know your kind! I have seen you before! You want to control the destiny of man!"

Kemp was now screaming. He reached out to grab Hawkins, as Sherlock, interrupting his concentration, shouted his name. At the same moment, distracting him further, old professor Stevens rose abruptly and walked towards him, commanding:

"Detective Kemp! Restrain yourself! We did not agree to this meeting for the purpose of being physically attacked and berated by you, but to explain our position, and to make perfectly evident that we were in no way involved in Laura Anderson's murder."

Kemp was momentarily shocked out of his frenzy, and he now found himself embarrassed at having lost control. Stevens pressed his advantage.

"You have bombarded us with questions, all of them misleading.

Because your mind is made up. Well! Turn about is fair play. Let me ask you a few questions. Perhaps we can finally clear up the misunderstanding between us."

"You may ask whatever questions you wish."

He was trying to regain his composure, to restore the position of authority he had earlier occupied, at center stage, commanding everyone's attention. His look at Professor Stevens was defiant.

"Suppose that you discovered a cure for a fatal illness that claimed the lives of ten thousand persons a year, but only one person could receive that cure. How would you proceed?"

"I am confident I would not keep my cure secret, that I would set about to save that one person."

"But how would you select, or who do you think ought to select, that one person?"

"The young would have priority over the old, that's for certain."

"And among the young? How would you distinguish among the young? Would you take the youngest?"

"No. There would be other factors that would have to be taken into consideration."

"For example?"

Kemp hesitated. His instincts warned him of a trap. He did not respond.

"And would you personally decide these factors?"

"No. That would not be for me to decide. I would not play God like you."

"And I take it that you would not sell the cure to the highest bidder?"

"No! Of course not. No!"

"But you said you would publicize it. So suppose the cure was frightfully expensive, say tens of millions of pounds. Would you allow those who could afford it to have it?"

"It would be far better than no one receiving the cure, although I wouldn't like it."

52

"Well then! Why wouldn't you take the highest bidder, and put the excess monies into research towards a less costly cure, or into some charity?"

"That's not a bad idea."

"But what if the highest bidder is the government, which, of course, it would most likely be?"

"I do not see the point in your line of questioning."

"That is because you are out of your depth, Detective Kemp. If some government, say the British government, had the technology to transform one thousand of its citizens to the first human beings to attain de facto immortality, do you think they would select those one thousand by random lottery?"

"I can see that you distrust all governments, including your own."

"In this matter, yes! But that is not the main point. You have not registered the main point."

Kemp was very flustered. I myself vowed to remember the dialogue, particularly Steven's devastating comment, "You have not registered the main point!" I intended to use it the next time I found myself in a tight spot.

"Can't you see the main point, Detective Kemp? You yourself made it to us earlier. No one should have the power to play God."

"And so you won't allow the government or the rich to play God. You reserve that right for yourself."

"No! No! Our role is merely to keep everyone, including ourselves from playing God."

"But you play God if you can extend life, but refuse to do so."

"No. Exactly the contrary. We would play God if we extended immortality to some and denied it to others. You do value human life as a right, don't you, Detective Kemp?"

"Of course! That is my main point — which you have altogether failed to register."

"But you value human life equally for everyone, do you not?"

"Yes. I am not a Hitler if that's what you think"

"Well! I was uncertain for a moment there when you began to select criteria for the one person to receive the cure. But let us be clear in our understanding of one another. It seems to follow from your comments that you believe in the right to live indefinitely, assuming indefinite life is possible."

"Yes. If it is possible."

"And this right is an equal right for all human beings?"

"Yes. It must be, I suppose."

"You suppose. We ardently believe that it is. Can't you understand that our aim is simply to make indefinite life available to all, only when it can be distributed to all persons fairly, that we are not selling out to the highest bidder, to the rich, or to governments in belligerent conflict with one another."

Kemp had now been overcome by Steven's battery of questions. The full significance of the new micro-biological technology upon the destiny of human life had finally dawned upon him, as it had upon all of us. I found myself wondering out loud.

"But if everyone were de facto immortal, the effect would be devastating upon birth and re-creation of human life in human offspring."

"You grasp the point clearly, Dr. Watkins. Human life as we know it is about to be transformed fundamentally and permanently. The extraordinary impact of the new micro-biology will make the revolution of modern science upon which it is based, pale in comparison. We are faced with a goliath, with the most momentous juncture in human history and in the history of all life on this planet. Do not forget that the new micro-biological technology will apply to all forms of life, and to both the animal and the plant kingdoms."

Young Professor Caldwell now intervened to add the following thoughts:

"At precisely the moment we resolve the problems of world hunger, we attain de facto immortality! Very poor timing I would say. And perhaps the even more important point, we will shortly have the ability to eliminate any species of life that we desire, and to create any viable species of life that we desire. In other words, we will shortly take over the course of the evolution of life! We, the most intelligent of life's offsprings, will achieve autonomy from our parent. We will determine the future destiny of all life, both human and not. And do not let yourself think indulgently, Detective Kemp, that it is all extremely unfortunate. For even if it is extremely unfortunate, it is irrevocable! Nothing will stop it! The future

54

is exploding upon us now!"

These last thoughts were too weighty for Kemp to ingest. He retreated to the chair at the gaming table, and looked around at us all inquiringly. A quiet settled over the room. Only Sherlock in a muted voice spoke up, and his words have remained indelibly imprinted in my memory forever.

"It follows from your comments, professors, that Life itself has now achieved consciousness of itself and is about to assume control over its portion of the universe through time."

There was a pause and Sherlock added:

"And if evolution is true, it follows that we are the physical universe becoming conscious of itself, and now assuming autonomy over its own destiny at least through some portion of its body and through some portion of time."

CHAPTER VI

VIVE LE FRANCE

A stillness settled into the room as each of us was thrust into the interior of his private consciousness, ingesting as individual human beings the profound effects soon to transform our entire race. The stillness was finally shattered by Sherlock, who rose and moved again to stand near the fireplace. The eyes of everyone following him.

"Gentlemen." He turned to Cassandra. "And ladies. The matter of Laura Anderson's murder still lies before us unresolved. You have presented us with general philosophical reasons why no one of you would have a motive to murder anyone. But that is altogether unsatisfactory in elucidating the particular matter at hand. You must be more specific! If we are to be satisfied that you are innocent, and can then be on our way, you must tell us first, the exact time Laura Anderson arrived at her meeting with you. Secondly, you must tell us the exact time she departed and her state of mind at that moment. And thirdly, you must tell us the exact nature of the conversation you had with her."

Sherlock's business-like conciseness shocked us back one again into group awareness. Some of us nervously readjusted our bodies. Hawkins, however, leaned forward, looked intently at Sherlock, and responded.

"There is only so much that we can tell."

"Then tell us that and we shall see whether it is sufficient."

"Laura Anderson had agreed to, and did meet with us, at about 8:00 P.M. on the evening of her murder. She left some time shortly after 9:30, and certainly no later than 10:00 P.M."

"And how late did your meeting continue after she had left? Or did it continue?"

"Yes. It did."

"Until what time?"

"For another hour or hour and a half. I'm not sure exactly."

"Then any one of you could have followed Laura Anderson to her home and arrived there before midnight."

"Yes. But not one of us did. In fact, I took a taxi with Professor Stevens, and Perkins went home with Caldwell in Caldwell's car."

"Did you and Professor Stevens arrive at home by midnight."

"Yes. But we live in the same apartment complex, and we remained talking until at least 1:00 A.M. in the morning."

"So you are each other's alibi."

"Yes."

"Or possibly you are lying."

"Yes. Possibly. But not actually."

"And Professor Caldwell. At what time did you drop off Professor Perkins?"

"Some time before midnight."

"Making it possible for you to drive to the Anderson home in time to commit the murder, and even conceivably, for Perkins to take a taxi there too."

Caldwell smiled.

"Or a third possibility. We are both lying, and we drove together to the Anderson home and commited the murder."

"But you did not do that?"

"No."

Sherlock looked around the room at each of the professors individually.

"Did any one of you return to a wife who can verify your story?"

Hawkins responded.

"No. No one of us is married. It is part of our vow as a Templar Guild member never to marry, indeed, never to have a liaison."

We were shocked at this revelation, though perhaps we should have expected it. It seemed unnatural, and I looked at these four men with renewed curiosity, and I must confess, with renewed suspicion. Sherlock was obvoiusly curious too.

"What is your reason for vowing never to marry or to have a liaison?"

"Isn't it obvious?"

"Is it the risk and the danger?"

"Of course. The endeavour in which we are engaged, Mr. Holmes, is fraught with many dangers. There are numerous parties who would sacrifice almost anything to pierce our Guild."

"For example?"

"The British government for one. Other governments. Pharmaceutical Corporations. Wealthy individuals."

"Aren't you a bit paranoiac?"

"Do you define paranoia as disproportionate fear?"

"Yes."

"Then no. We are not paranoiac. The British government has already threatened us. A friend scientist acquaintance of Caldwell's — a very attractive lady, I might add — turned out to be a CIA operative. We have evidence that the Direction de la Surveillance du Territoire, the French Secret Service, is trying to infiltrate us. Professor Perkins was offered thirty million pounds — thirty million pounds — by a large Pharmaceutical complex. Need I go on?"

"No."

"You see that it is imperative that each of you keep even the existence of our Guild a secret. The public does not know us yet. Those whose business it is to know us, of course, do."

"I am beginning to understand."

"Good. Perhaps you can now see why we are modeled on the Knights Templars. We have taken a vow of chastity. We have taken a vow of poverty, that is, a vow never to profit, in any manner whatsoever from our investigations and the knowledge confided in us by others, even in applying the new technology to ourselves. And we have vowed to be willing to die, rather than to be defeated by our enemies."

"And your enemies, like the enemies of the medieval Knights of the Temple, are the enemies of Christianity."

"They are the enemies of Christianity as we perceive it. But that means for us that they are the enemies of humanity, and its proper future destiny."

"And Laura Anderson?"

"Laura Anderson was our one, and our only one, trusted contact to the outside world. Among other things it was she who was entrusted with the contingency plans in the event that we all suddenly met an untimely death."

"So. According to this account, her death is a great loss to you, and puts you in a terrible predicament, at least for the moment, unless somehow or other you and she disagreed, or you came to believe that you could no longer trust her."

"That did not happen. We trusted her more than any other person on earth. She understood. And like us, she was a humanist."

"And the content of your conversation with her?"

"That I cannot make public."

"Even though she is dead?"

"Yes."

"You say that you cannot make that conversation public. Can it be communicated in confidence to Detective Kemp, and to me?"

"Perhaps you could be trusted." He looked at Kemp. "But I feel uncertain of Inspector Kemp. He does not trust us."

Kemp rose to the remark.

"I do not agree with all of your methods. But I now understand what you are attempting to do. And I certainly would not betray you."

"We are very relieved to hear that."

Kemp directed his regard to Professor Stevens, undoubtedly because he seemed to Kemp the wisest.

"Perhaps one of the other members of the Guild could reveal to us the content of the conversation." Kemp was dogged, that I had to admit. If you can't get something one way, try another.

Stevens returned Kemp's look.

"No. No one of us can, at least without Hawkins' permission. He is our Grandmaster, and we are a para-military organization, Mr. Kemp, with a strict hierarchy of command, like our mentors, the Knights Templars."

Sherlock returned the questioning to Hawkins.

"Is the conversation with Laura Andrson germane to her murder?"

"It could be."

"In directing the focus of suspicion on someone other than yourselves?"

"Yes. And in further verifying the relationship we have described between Laura Anderson and ourselves."

"Then it is to your advantage to have it known, specifically to Kemp, and perhaps also to Watkins and me."

"Yes."

At this point Professor Stevens collected his fragile body, rose, and addressed the group.

"I propose that this grand meeting be brought to an end, that we all vow never to reveal any part of it, and that all of us depart, with the exception of Hawkins and our three visiting detectives. We will leave it to Hawkin's discretion to impart whatever he thinks appropriate to do so."

Hawkins smiled.

"That is acceptable. That is what we will do. Friends. Our gathering is adjourned."

It was clear who was in command, even if that command was benevolently exercised. We all said our "Good Evenings," and I smiled perhaps too profusely from the pompous feeling I felt from having been included as a detective. I was also naturally piqued with curiosity at what Hawkins would have to say. Finally everyone had departed and Hawkins and the three of us were alone.

"Gentlemen. On the Saturday evening in question, Laura Anderson met with us to discuss the matter of her successor, or stand-in, in the eventuality she were to die, whether from natural, or more likely unnatural, causes. By the time of our meeting with her, we had narrowed our selection to two persons, both of them from within the Anderson household, the only household outside of our guild with which we have had close contact."

Kemp, now re-settling into his ordinary role, asked:

"And these two persons?"

"Dr. Anderson and Monsieur de Molay."

Sherlock and I looked at one another with surprise. We could perhaps understand Dr. Anderson, but not Louise-Phillipe. Hawkins read our minds, or at least our faces.

"Monsieur de Molay is both a humanist and a person with an original relationship to the Order of the Knights Templars — or at least, so it first seemed."

I blurted out quite childishly:

"It only seemed?"

"Yes. de Molay had been highly recommended to us by Laura Anderson, but we naturally investigated him independently. We discovered that he is not Louise-Phillipe de Molay at all, but rather Phillipe Moreau, an undercover agent for the Direction de la Surveillance de Terretoire. He is a French spy in England."

I need not describe to you our amazement at this startling revelation. Hawkins smiled at us and continued:

"If the matter were not of such momentous importance, I would be chuckling heartily. We, of course, were naturally suspect of him because he is French."

"You are suspicious of the French and do not like them?"

This question was from Kemp who was still prodding.

"No, Gentlemen. I personally like and admire the French. But you must be aware that the French Government and the French business community are determined to regain their former international eminence through the means of technology. This great ambition, which is their great strength, could be their Achilles Heel. So we must be very cautious."

This final revelation of Louise-Phillipe's true identity brought our private interview with Hawkins to a close. We took our leave, parted with Kemp, and flagged a taxi. Sherlock had originally planned to return to his dormitory, but he was anxious to discuss what had transpired, and instead stopped over for a tea at my flat. It was late but he was very agitated. As I was preparing the tea, he informed me that he felt much of the same hostility Kemp had expressed towards the Guild. He too believed they were enamoured with power, that they enjoyed the role of playing God. He too believed that underneath their gentlemanly and gentle exterior, each was experiencing a euphoria of self-importance. He respected them, he believed them to be well-meaning, and he even liked them. But he did not

62

trust them. When I asked what alternative course to theirs he would pursue, however, he had nothing to offer. I chided him with a look which said, 'If you can't recommend an alternative course of action, then your objections are worthless,' and he responded to my look by saying:

"Watkins. There are genuine dilemmas where every course of action that can be pursued is unfortunate. Theirs is perhaps the least unfortunate, but it is unfortunate nevertheless."

He then abruptly changed the subject, and reported that the four members had passed his test of their humanism, and that no one of them appeared to be a secret religious fanatic capable of committing crimes against humanity — such as murder — in order to save humanity from itself. I expressed relief at now understanding the rationale for his theological discussion. But he laughed heartily and confessed:

"To be honest, Watkins, I thought it would be presumptuous of me to interrogate such men of distinction. I had to do something, since the time was allotted to me until Kemp arrived. I have always been curious about the Argument from Design. And besides, I thought the discussion might reveal something about each of them, which, indeed, it did."

We continued our discussion of the evening with some observations of the Guild members' differing personalities, when quite suddenly we were startled by the ring of the telephone, even though it was by now very near the hour of midnight. It was Caldwell of the Templar Guild calling in a fit of great anxiety. It seems that Hawkins had just rung him up to tell him that when he returned to his flat he became aware of being watched by a man seated in a car below. The man had but a moment ago disappeared, but his car remained, and Hawkins feared he would force entry into the apartment building and soon be at his door. He was adamant about not involving the police. Caldwell was about to rush over when he realized that my flat was much closer to Hawkins' than his, and he wanted me to hurry over too. Before I could even complete my report of this conversation to Sherlock, he interrupted me:

"Take off your coat, Watkins, we have a nice sprint before us." And with those words he was out of the door. I followed immediately after him, running down the corridor to the front entrance. We hit the night air, and he settled into a fast steady pace. I prayed that I could keep up with him, for he was in excellent physical condition, and he had always been a good runner. I caught up to him and ran at his side.

"Damn!" He yelled. "I shouldn't smoke." And he turned the corner to the right for a straight run the ten or so blocks to Hawkin's flat. I tried to keep pace with him, and fortunately the streets were empty. There was an occasional car, but certainly not a single taxi. That run, I must report, seemed to me endless. For some reason, I truly feared for Hawkins' life, and almost, by sympathetic feeling, felt my own life to be in jeopardy. I also feared that I would arrive too late. And so we ran and ran. Finally, when I was on the verge of collapse, my breath wheezing and whining, and a sharp pain like a dagger stabbing my side, we came up to Hawkins' apartments.

"You go inside," Sherlock shouted at me, as he stopped at the front entrance. He pointed to a chain of outdoor fire stairs that wound up the side of the building. I ran straight to the front entrance. The door, which I am certain was ordinarily locked, was ajar. It took me a brief moment to check the mailboxes for Hawkins' number, and I was up the stairwell headed for the fourth floor and flat 402. The pain in my side was killing me, but I raced up the four flights leaping several steps at a time. I flung myself into the fourth floor hallway, saw 402 immediately to my left, and threw myself at the door, knocking loudly. I heard sounds from inside and called Hawkins' name, but there was no response. I knocked vigorously on the door again but to no avail. Finally, I turned the knob — I was about to break the door in — and to my total surprise the door opened. It had been unlocked all along, and I felt like a fool. I strode quickly into the flat, and although the lights were on, I saw Hawkins nowhere — that is, until I stepped around the couch while headed towards a small bedroom, and bumped, almost tripping, into a body on the floor.

I was aghast! It was Hawkins, there on the floor, face up, perfectly still, as if in a deep sleep. I confess that I choked with sorrow and anger in my traumatic encounter with his absolutely lifeless body. His existence was over, his consciousness gone forever, and I felt his death as a terrible tragedy. He was a gifted and honorable man, struck down in the prime of his life. Although, it was true, he did know that he was playing a very dangerous game.

My senses awakened to sounds coming from where I could not tell, and I was reminded of the sounds I had heard at the door. In a split-second I thought, 'The murderer may still be here.' 'In the bedroom.' And I was overwhelmed with a rush of fear. My eyes lighted on a window facing the street and I lunged to it, opened it, and finding the screen unhinged, climbed out onto the landing of the fire-escape. Below, a car had just started up and was quickly accelerating away. Sprawled on the sidewalk was a body, alive, collecting itself. It was Sherlock. He looked up, gave a gesture of defeat, and started into the building. I climbed back in the window, realizing that the terror that had seized me was gone. But I did not enter the bedroom. Instead I waited for Sherlock, and stood gazing around at the room. It was quite small and practically bare of furniture — only the couch, a writing desk with a telephone, a filing cabinet and a sink with a mirror above it. Hawkins lived a stoic existence. The full awareness came home to me that he was truly a monk, his entire existence pinpointed on one religious aim, the betterment of humanity. And as a warrior monk he had made the supreme sacrifice, the sacrifice of his life.

I moved a few steps so that I could see his body in full view, and at that moment Sherlock entered the room. I gestured with my head towards Hawkins' body, and Sherlock, without looking, intentionally not looking at the body, went directly to the telephone and rang up Detective Kemp. As he placed the receiver down he glanced at the small bedroom and then at me inquiringly. I shrugged with the gesture, 'How should I know?," and he stepped into the bedroom and briefly looked around. He then came to the couch, collapsed into it, and lit a cigarette. Never once did he look at Hawkins' body.

"I think we can now determine Laura Anderson's murderer, and, of course, Hawkins' murderer too; not because of my brilliance, mind you, but because of the coincidence of participating in this sordid event."

"So you saw the murderer?"

"Just before he struck me down. But his face was masked, and I'm sure he wore some sort of disguise...Perhaps a wig."

"So you didn't recognize him?"

"No. But he was certainly male, and fast, and physically fit."

"That description fits millions."

"Yes. But it enables us to narrow the identity of the murderer to only two suspects." Curiously, he stated this as if he were disappointed. "One murder helps to solve the other, that is, to solve them both. You and I only happened to be here because Caldwell called. Thus, Watkins, I am a dunce. I didn't prevent the murder tonight, and I didn't even have sufficient wit about me to apprehend the murderer when he ran right into my arms."

"But that was smart of you to wait outside while you sent me in."

"It was brilliant." he replied sarcastically.

I smiled. Sherlock was always more open and honest than me. I confess that I never did tell him or anyone else of my continued rapping on an unlocked door while the murderer was still undoubtedly inside. But I had to question him.

"How can you claim that the suspects are narrowed to two? I don't understand. We can't even be certain the two murders are connected.

Even if they are, they could be the acts of some obscure agent for the KGB or the CIA, or some religious fanatic who got wind of the Templar Guild."

"The answer, my dear Watkins, is the convincing case you yourself made supporting the hypothesis that Laura Anderson's murderer must be someone from within the Anderson's home."

"But even if that is true, it is only an assumption that her murderer and Hawkins' murderer are one and the same."

"Think it over, Watkins. Two murders within a fortnight. Both victims associated with the same small secret organization. Is it coincidence? That is highly improbable."

I began to see his point, and responded.

"So the murderer is not Miss Ellie?"

"Not if Miss Ellie is a woman."

"Well. I have been deceived before, but in her case I think the evidence is incontrovertible. And it's not Richards either?"

"No."

"Then it must be either Louise-Phillipe or Dr. Anderson."

"Exactly."

"But since Dr. Anderson was in Torquay at the time of his wife's murder, then it must be Louise-Phillipe."

"There is an alternative."

"That Anderson hired the murderer?"

"Yes."

"For both his wife and Hawkins?"

"Yes. And there is still another alternative. Anderson could have committed the murders himself. It is possible that he went to Torquay and also murdered his wife."

You can well imagine that I was completely perplexed by his comment. But before I could pursue it further, he rose from the couch abruptly and began to pace about nervously, lighting another cigarette.

66

"Where's Caldwell? He should be here by now."

I tried to calm him.

"Don't worry. I'm certain he'll arrive shortly."

He continued to pace about, apparently deeply concentrated on some troubling thought.

"Watkins, I would very much appreciate your doing me a favor."

"Yes?"

"Would you wait here for Caldwell and Detective Kemp while I leave."

"Yes. Certainly."

I did not ask for an explanation in the tone of my voice or the look of my eye, nevertheless he explained.

"I am overwhelmed by Hawkins' death. I recognize that I do not show it, but I am. I cannot comprehend the murder of one human being by another. In fact, I cannot comprehend the death of a human being. It makes human existence altogether absurd."

He walked to the edge of the couch and for the first time looked directly at Hawkin's lifeless body. He was very intense and gritted his teeth in obvious agony.

"His murder, his death, makes his existence absurd. Damn! Watkins! You and I are absurd too. Our existence will shortly terminate arbitrarily in non-existence. Our extraordinary individual consciousness that partakes of the divine, that has the capacity for love and beauty, for truth, for goodness, for reason, for joy, and for a thousand other things, will cease shortly in non-being, will transform to nothing, nothing at all!"

He started for the door, but paused just before stepping into the hall. He looked directly at me.

"Watkins. Nature has made fools of us all. Gracing us with the gift of conscious life, then abandoning us to death."

And then he was gone.

CHAPTER VII

CASSANDRA

There was a lull in the investigation in the few days following Hawkins' untimely death. Sherlock left for Torquay on the following afternoon after a brief conference with Kemp. Kemp had arrived almost simultaneously with Caldwell as I awaited them both at Hawkins' flat. Caldwell fell completely apart. The full impact of the danger to the members of the Templar Guild and to himself, the new threat to the mission to which they were all committed, along with the tragic fact of Hawkins' death itself, wore obviously too much for him to injest all at once. He wept uncontrollably, and eventually had to be sedated. Kemp, on the other hand, was very efficient. A photographer was present, a fingerprint expert, and a sergeant of the police who, along with Kemp, meticulously searched every square foot of the flat, including the bedroom. I left while the search was still in progress, after briefly recounting my experience of the evening's events to Kemp.

On the afternoon of the following day, I was surprised to receive a call from Cassandra. It seems that just before taking the train for Torquay, Sherlock had telephoned Sylvester to report to his client, that this new murder had now altogether cleared him as a suspect, even in the eyes of Kemp. Kemp accepted Sherlock's testimony that the person with whom he scuffled could not be Sylvester, who was neither physically strong nor physically fit. Apparently Kemp, like Sherlock, believed that both murders were committed by the same person. Sherlock had concluded his conversation with Sylvester by asserting rather definitely that when he returned from his trip, probably within 48 hours, the case would be resolved.

As Sylvester passed this information along to Cassandra, it obviously whetted her appetite, for she wanted to meet with Sherlock and with me as soon as he returned. She made no mention of Sylvester's accompanying her, and I assumed at the time that it was because of his pending examinations, although I still thought that it was odd. During the conversation she put me on the spot by asking whether we now believed Louise-Phillipe to be the murderer. I, of course, hesitated to reply that Dr. Anderson was equally suspect, since she might pass that information along to Sylvester, whose relationship to Anderson was so intimate. If Anderson were the murderer then he was an extremely dangerous man. Not knowing exactly what to say, I responded to her question by asking whether she thought Louise-Phillipe was guilty. She insisted, quite adamantly, that he was not. She added that the suspicion now directed towards him was partly what prompted her to call. She also claimed to have some information, some important information, that she had to impart. I assured her that I would contact her immediately upon Sherlock's return, and then did something quite silly, I suppose to impress her with my role in the case. I said that we had new information which I could pass on to her if only she would promise to keep it in absolute secrecy. Curious as a cat, she, of course, reassured me that she would never breathe a word of it, even to Sylvester. At that moment I felt a great intimacy between the two of us sharing this secret together. I then told her that Louise-Phillipe was an undercover agent for the French government and hung up.

Sherlock returned two mornings later at around 10:30 A.M. I reported Cassandra's call. He said that he had hardly eaten since he left for Torquay, that he was ravished, and that we should get together for lunch. Cassandra lived in Earl's Court. She enjoyed its international flavor and its proximity to the Victoria and Albert Museum, where she spent much of her time in study. Sherlock suggested an Indian restaurant below the street level in a side street near the Earl's Court Tube Station. The food was good, the prices reasonable, and none of us had much money to spare. It was agreed. The three of us would meet there as soon as we could. I took the underground to the Earl's Court Station, and following Sherlock's precise directions quickly found the restaurant. I worried that I was over-dressed for this casual get-together, with a nice suit and tie, but I wanted to look my best for Cassandra, and could pretend that I had some medical meeting or another shortly after our luncheon. I realized, of course, that my aspirations in regard to her were merely fantasy, but the fantasy temporarily satisfied my thirst for a romantic relationship with a woman, which in my busy tenure as an intern, had recently been sadly lacking.

As I approached the entrance to the restaurant, the smell of the Indian food was overwhelming. It was marvelous. I entered the restaurant and realized that there was a room at street level and a room below. I went below where the smell of the food was even more pungent, and saw Cassandra seated at a table waiting. I confess that my heart jumped when I saw her. In the setting of the restaurant, with the waiters shuffling about all dressed in white, she looked absolutely beautiful. I realized that her hair was very dark, and wondered whether she was Welsh. The thought occurred to me that she identified with Louise-Phillipe because he was part Welsh. And then I remembered telling her that he was a French spy, and felt very silly. But I collected myself, pretended to be relaxed, and went over to her table. She rose and kissed me on the cheek as a greeting. As her lips brushed my cheek and I felt her presence close to me, I was thrilled. I did not show it, however, and immediately as I was taking my seat, I asked her not to mention Louise-Phillipe. I explained that in retrospect, I thought I had been indiscreet, and that I didn't know why I had done it. She laughed, bantering with me.

"Perhaps you wanted to shock me."

70

I feigned naivete.

"But why should I want to shock you?"

"Because you enjoy playing the role of detective, and detectives like to shock."

"Yes. I suppose that's the reason."

"And it's attractive to women, being a detective."

I feigned surprise.

"Is that really so? Are women really attracted to detectives?"

"Well. I don't know about all women, but I certainly am."

I can tell you that my heart was beating inside a mile a minute. She was flirting with me. That was obvious. And I was now in a world just with her, with no thoughts of Sylvester or engagements, believing for that moment that the two of us could fall in love. It was exhilarating!

"I certainly do find Sherlock attractive, and he's a detective."

You can imagine my deflation at that point. I was crushed with disappointment, even though I had all along suspected a mutual attraction between her and Sherlock. I'm certain that my rapid descent from heaven to hell was written all over my face for her to read, but she continued right along with her banter.

"You detectives are all attractive, so intense and involved in your crime. Seeking retribution for all wrongdoers. Champions of good over evil, immersed in the fascinating, the bizarre, world of crime. It really is rather romantic."

"Would you like Sylvester to be a detective?"

"Oh! No! Sylvester's not suited for the part. Besides, I would never marry a detective. That would be too nerve-wracking for me."

And then the following words came out of my mouth, I'm not sure why.

"Well, then you can't exclude me as a possibility, because I'm actually in medicine and only pretend to be a detective on the side." I laughed as if I were merely carrying on the banter, but she suddenly turned serious, and looked at me quite intently.

"You don't particularly like my fiancee, Sylvester, do you?"

71

And then more words came out of my mouth, and again, I'm not at all sure why.

"I don't particularly dislike him. It's just that he stands between you and me." I laughed and then added, "But the real triangle is between you and Sylvester and Sherlock. Though I must confess that I still find you tempting."

"That's because you sense that I'm having second thoughts about my engagement to Sylvester — even though I know that I love him."

That took me totally by surprise, but I nodded as if I had sensed that all along. I felt tremendously uplifted, because now there was at least a chance with her that had not existed before. At the very same time I felt like a total fool for allowing myself to become enamoured with her, knowing that almost certainly I would be rejected. My mixed feelings, however, were quickly put aside, because she gestured toward the entrance, I turned, and saw Sherlock coming down the stairs.

He immediately came to the table, smiling, but excited and intense. I judged his trip to be a success from his demeanor. We greeted one another, and each of us ordered a curry for lunch. Sherlock quickly settled down to business. He looked at Cassandra expectantly and she responded to the cue.

"I have some observations about the original Order of the Knights of the Temple, properly viewed in their medieval setting, which I believe may shed light on the motives of the murderer."

"By all means do proceed and tell us your thoughts, and afterwards I'll report fully the results of my trip to Torquay."

"Torquay?"

She was astonished. Evidently Sherlock had not told Sylvester the destination of his journey, and the implications of a trip to Torquay were now racing through her mind. Sherlock had obviously traveled there to verify Anderson's alibi. And since he had told Sylvester he expected to have the case resolved when he returned, Anderson must be the prime suspect, or at least, one of the two prime suspects along with Louise-Phillipe. She grimaced and again said, "Torquay," as if to re-affirm what she had just heard. Sherlock nodded confirmation and we sat quietly for a few moments while she put further pieces and facts together and reasoned to further conclusions.

"Is it possible that Anderson and Louise-Phillipe are in this together?"

"It's possible, but I don't think it's likely."

"So you think it's one or the other."

"Yes."

"And which ever one it is, he did not have an accomplice."

"That's correct. But you were about to convey your thoughts on the motives of the murderer."

"I'm not sure that they're still pertinent." She looked at me as if for support and I said:

"On the other hand, perhaps they are."

Sherlock added:

"Yes. Please proceed."

The dinner was brought at that point, and we settled into our lunch. Finally, Cassandra seemed to have sufficiently collected her thoughts and her self-confidence. She began.

"In my reading of medieval history, the Knights Templars are merely the most extreme example of a widespread medieval phenomenon, namely, the wedding of the European Warrior Ideal with the Middle-Eastern Christian Ideal of sacrifice in this earthly existence for an immortal existence in the life hereafter. The crusades were a variation of pilgrimage. During the medieval period, by undertaking a pilgrimage to some sacred place, one's sins were automatically remitted, and salvation in a heavenly after-life assured. When the leader of the Christian Church in Europe, Pope Urban called for the first crusade, he called for the knight-nobility of Europe to pilgrimage as warriors to re-capture Jerusalem from the Saracens. This first crusade cemented the wedding of the traditional European warrior, who valued prowess and courage in battle, with the Christian ideal of an earthly sacrifice to attain immortality. The Church treated the undertaking of a crusade as a pilgrimage, which counted as penance for all of one's previous sins, and guaranteed a resurrection from the grave after death in an immortal and blissful life."

Cassandra had not eaten one bite of her food while sketching her interpretative model of medieval Europe. Sherlock and I were eating heartily. She took a bite and then continued.

"Now, what does the Templar Guild possess that someone, indeed everyone, would covet? It is obvious. It is the secret of immortality, the dream that has gripped humankind for millenia. To conquer death! Doesn't it seem logical to suppose that the murderer's motive was to

73

gain possession of that knowledge for himself? Most people believe that you are justified in taking another person's life in self-defense, if that other person is attempting to take your life. And a good many people believe that you are justified in taking another person's life where that is a necessary means to preserve one's own, say, where there is a scarcity of food. It is an easy extension of this line of thinking to a position justifying murder to prevent one's natural death from aging."

Sherlock responded.

"We have information that appears to agree with your hypothesis. Either Anderson or Louise-Phillipe was almost certain to be selected by the Guild as a stand-in to replace Laura Anderson in case of her death. Either of the two, therefore could have committed the murder to have an even chance to replace her, and to gain access, at least eventually when it was fully perfected, to the Guild's secret."

Cassandra seemed quite pleased at Sherlock's concurring in her hypothesis. She had not attended to his qualification, "appears," but I had, and as I suspected he followed with a counter-objection.

"But how do we account for Hawkins' murder then on your hypothesis? Why would someone willing to use the means of murder to achieve the end of immortality, proceed ahead to murder the key person who could make achieving that end possible? It doesn't make sense. It is inconsistent."

Cassandra had obviously already considered this objection, for she quickly replied with several alternatives to account for it.

"Well. Perhaps Hawkins, who was so very brilliant, figured out the identity of the murderer and had to be silenced. Or perhaps the murderer thought he could coerce Hawkins into revealing the Guild's secrets, but Hawkins resisted. Or more likely if the murderer is Anderson or Louise-Phillipe, he knew he had an even chance to fill the vacancy left by Laura Anderson. And now, if he murders a member of the Guild, he has a chance of replacing that member and having direct access to its secrets."

This last hypothesis sounded to me far-fetched, so I challenged it.

"But the Guild is a guild of scientists. Why would they select as one of their members a doctor, much less a chef?"

"I agree that Louise-Phillipe is very unlikely, but Anderson does research in medicine, at least in the area of new instrumentation. That's what I've been told by Sylvester."

Sherlock was thinking hard.

74

"I'm not sure about his having a good chance to replace Hawkins. The likelihood that he would both replace Laura Anderson and then also replace Hawkins is marginal. But I do think that one of your hypotheses, or some other hypothesis, could account for the second murder. In any case, if we independently solve Laura Anderson's murder, the solution to Hawkins' murder will follow."

I was very curious and wanted to get to the point.

"Did you prove conclusively on your trip to Torquay that Anderson is the murderer?"

He looked intently at Cassandra and asked:

"If I reply, can you be trusted not to say a word until the case is completely resolved. It is of the greatest importance that the murderer not be aware of what I have discovered."

"Yes. Absolutely. You can trust me."

Then for some odd reason I blurted out:

"How do we know you can be trusted? For all we know, you could be another female agent for the CIA." I addressed myself to Sherlock. "I have already informed her of the fact that Louise-Phillipe is a French spy." I suppose that I was serious, because I now looked directly at Cassandra and added, "I like you very much, but we have only known you for a very brief period of time. And we have already been deceived by Louise-Phillipe, not to mention the murderer."

Sherlock reassured me.

"We needn't worry about Cassandra. I did a thorough check on her long ago."

Cassandra looked surprised and just a little bit offended.

"Did you find any skeletons in my closet?"

"Only a Welsh grandfather who made a healthy fortune in contraband before the war. So I can report to you the results of my trip to Torquay." He smiled, she smiled, and I felt like a third wheel on a bicycle. I also felt like a traitor for calling her integrity into question. Sherlock continued.

"I have determined that Dr. Anderson murdered his wife."

We allowed that declaration to settle for a moment, although by now

75

it was not a great surprise. Cassandra had an immediate question.

"Could he have had an accomplice?"

"Yes."

"Could that accomplice have been Sylvester?"

"Yes. It's possible."

Now, I really was surprised. Cassandra, on her part, was crestfallen. She looked at me.

"That's why I mentioned having second thoughts. Sylvester has a thing about death. He worries about it. He and Anderson are very close. And I know that he is capable of violence."

Sherlock would not let that go by.

"The perfect portrait of a murderer, or of the vast majority of people in the world. Take your pick."

"So you don't agree. But you said that it's possible that he's an accomplice."

"Yes. It's possible."

Cassandra looked deeply troubled.

"I know exactly what you're thinking. She must not love him very much if she suspects him of murder, or even complicity in murder."

"No. You don't know what I'm thinking at all. Just the contrary, it is perfectly obvious to me that you can love someone without trust. Love comes in all shapes and sizes and the same love can wander through many seasons. Frankly, I'm sorry that you feel guilty over your suspicions, but I think you're silly for doing so."

That seemed to me a little harsh. I suspected at the time that Sherlock really did think less of her for her doubts, that he made her feel uncomfortable to punish her, and that his words were just a cover-up. I didn't think it was intentional, but I didn't like it in any case. He continued.

"But let me tell you about Anderson and my trip to Torquay. In my mind, the good Dr. Anderson has always been a suspect. At the very beginning of this case I found it odd that his wife had not bequeathed him a single thing in her will; not a memento, a mutually cherished object,

76

nothing. I suspected that their relationship was not a happy one. Moreover, as the case developed, the precise facts of his trip to Torquay became evident. It seems that he was seen at 8:00 P.M. when he retired, and then not again until 5:30 A.M. the next morning when the fishing party gathered for breakfast."

I interrupted and observed.

"Then he could have secretly departed for London shortly after 8:00 P.M., committed the murder and returned before the breakfast gathering. A perfect alibi."

"No. There is no perfect alibi. But yes. That's exactly what he did...But there has been a problem proving that. The only train departing from Torquay after 8:00 P.M. leaves at 9:30 and doesn't arrive in London until 1:00 A.M. There are also no commercial flights from the local airport."

"Could he have rented a car?"

"That is a good and precise question, attentive to the possibilities. However, my investigation revealed that no Torquay rental agency received a customer that evening. Moreover, no private charter planes departed from the airport."

"Your investigation was quite thorough."

"Of course It would have been useless were it not."

"But then how did you determine Anderson's guilt. If he committed the murder, he had to transport himself to London. But since there was no way he could do that, we must conclude that he didn't commit the murder."

"Your logic is impeccable, Watkins. However, I doubt the truth of one of your assumptions, namely that there was no way he could transport himself to London."

"Well. He certainly didn't flap his wings and fly, or teleport himself by astral projection."

"No. He certainly didn't. And I confess that it was not until I was on the return train to London, disappointed and perplexed, that the solution occurred to me. I realized I had failed to investigate something else implied in the hypothesis that Anderson is the murderer. If he traveled from Torquay to London to commit the murder, and did commit the murder, and then was seen again in Torquay at 5:30 A.M., it follows that..."

"He had to travel the return trip from London back to Torquay, which is obvious."

"Exactly. But neither Kemp nor I thought of it because we could find no evidence of the first leg of the trip to begin with. But it always pays to investigate the consequences of one's hypotheses independently. Which I did. And I discovered that a man fitting Dr. Anderson's description, rented a car at 12:45 P.M. from an all-night travel agency near Trafalgar Square, and that this same man, calling himself 'Robert Shelton,' delivered the car to one of the agency's representatives the following evening at 7:00 P.M."

"After his return from the fishing trip."

"Yes."

"But Holmes. If Robert Shelton is our Dr. Anderson, he first had to travel from Torquay to London!"

"Indeed he did. Think, Watkins. Think hard! Anderson planned this brilliantly. He knew that he would travel by train with members of the fishing party. He was seen until 8:00 P.M. He was at breakfast the next morning at 5:30 A.M. If anyone considered him suspect, they would investigate any of the usual means of public transportation out of Torquay in the evening and come up empty-handed. Even suppose that some persistent investigator like myself inquired about a possible return trip after the murder to Torquay — just some man who happened also to fit his general description." He looked at his watch and exclaimed. "My goodness! I have to rush over to meet with Detective Kemp. His men should by now have confirmed my theory as to how Anderson traveled the distance from Torquay to London in time to commit the murder by midnight." He rose abruptly, fumbled for some cash which he gave to me, and started to leave. Cassandra, however, restrained him by his arm and asked:

"Could an accomplice have picked him up and driven him to London?"

Sherlock gleamed at her with great pleasure.

"That's close. Very close. A good guess. But I don't think there was an accomplice." And with those words he left with a flurry and bounded up the stairs out of the restaurant.

CHAPTER VIII

CATCH HER OFF GUARD

I must confess that I was beside myself with curiosity. But I was at a stalemate with my conjectures, and rather than spin my wheels conjuring hypotheses, I determined to pry the answers out of Sherlock that same evening, or at the latest on the following morning. Cassandra and I left the restaurant shortly after Sherlock, she to walk to her flat, and I, from the manner of my dress, apparently to attend some important event. Of course, I merely returned to the clinic to complete my day's work.

In the very late afternoon I rang up Sherlock from the clinic, but there was no answer. I returned to my flat, the day's work completed, and rang him again, but once more to no avail. I did leave a message for him to ring me up no matter how late the hour. And I resolved to stay at home for the evening to await his call.

The evening wore on and my impatience grew more and more intense. I tried unsuccessfully to read, and then began to straighten up some of the disorder in my flat. I cleaned the kitchen sink and counter-top, and then went into the bathroom to clean that too. I even put all of the clothes in my closet in order. While engaged in this compulsive behaviour, I tried to resolve the puzzle of Anderson's trip from Torquay to London. But my thoughts kept returning to Cassandra. At one point I even wondered whether she was Anderson's accomplice. I realized that if she were using Sylvester to gain proximity to the Templar Guild she undoubtedly did not love him, and this meant that my chances with her were vastly increased. However, I quickly realized that if her relationship with Sylvester was only a means to some devious end, then so, almost certainly, was her relationship to me. Indeed, for all I knew, she had a husband somewhere waiting for her. To be honest, I was uncertain whether I preferred her to be authentic or not. If she were authentic, her engagment to Sylvester was genuine and my chances were slim, if not nil. On the other hand, if she weren't authentic, she probably had no genuine interest in me, but was merely doing her job — whatever that might be. Either way the prospects weren't bright.

I occupied my mind with such useless thoughts until finally, some time around 11:00 P.M., I was surprised by a visit from Sherlock himself. He was obviously weary from a very busy and eventful day, but his mind was fully alert. I was, of course, pleased to see him, particularly when he informed me that all of the details of Anderson's comings and goings had finally been established beyond any doubt. I restrained my curiousity, however, and treated his visit casually. I suppose that I was miffed at him for keeping me in the dark — I thought unnecessarily. I addressed him as follows:

"I am certainly pleased that the case is now closed. I presume that you will shortly be in search of a new client. You should have little difficulty now that your reputation has been established."

"On the contrary, Watkins, you are mistaken on both counts. First of all, I have insisted that all credit in this case be attributed to the official authorities, particularly Detective Kemp. My role for public consumption is simply as a representative of an innocent and beleaguered client. Secondly, the case is not at all closed and Kemp is very distressed. He sees no way of proving any charges against Anderson. Anderson has so brilliantly planned his crimes that even though his guilt has been discovered, the evidence is not sufficient to mount a case against him in a court of law. Where are the witnesses? Where is the murder weapon?"

I was completely taken aback by this turn of events. I was also puzzled that Sherlock betrayed no real disappointment in his voice. He continued.

"Anderson told Louise-Philippe he planned to leave his automobile at the riding stables to be washed while he was in Torquay. There is a small stables at the far end of the riding club now unused, where one of the younger stable boys named 'Billy' washes cars for extra money. Anderson left his car there on Friday. Billy only works at the club after school Monday through Friday, and he said he did wash the car Friday afternoon."

"Then Anderson must have returned to the stables sometime, probably early, on Friday evening, driven the car to Torquay where he left it parked, and then returned to London in time to awaken with the household on Saturday morning."

"Yes. He left that same mid-morning with the fishing party by train for Torquay. And then, after pretending to retire around 8:00 P.M., he drove his own car to London, murdered his wife, returned his car to the old stables, and then rented a car for the return trip to Torquay."

"That man has amazing stamina."

"Indeed. And an amazing mind as well."

"But then, doesn't his auto incriminate him? Can't Kemp build a case upon that?"

"No. Put yourself in Anderson's position. Suppose that you're

80

Anderson and that Kemp charges you with murder, exposing all that we have said. He adds that the knows that you are guilty. How would you respond?"

"I could say, 'It's true, and now you know that it's true, but you can't prove it in a court of law'."

"But at your trial Kemp could testify that you said that, and along with the circumstantial evidence and Kemp's believability, that might be sufficient to convince a jury."

"Well. Then I would profess my innocence."

"Yes?"

"I would deny that I ever returned from Torquay on that fateful Saturday evening, or that I ever drove my auto to Torquay as it is claimed that I did."

"That's one possibility."

"Or I could admit my unusual behavior with my automobile, but explain that I returned to my office to apprehend someone whom I suspected of tampering with my medical files."

"That's possible."

"And I might have confirming evidence within my office that the files had recently been tampered. I might have seen to that beforehand. A corroboration of my alibi."

"Yes. Indeed."

"Or perhaps I could say that I had a secret paramour with whom I had planned a rendezvous that evening."

"What is her name?"

"I would have a name."

"So you see my point. If Detective Kemp simply arrests him, there is a reasonable chance he will get off. He undoubtedly already planned some detailed alibi in case his comings and goings were exposed."

A feeling of great disappointment began to overwhelm me. I was certain that we had failed, that Scotland Yard had failed, and that a ruthless murderer was about to escape scot-free. I said:

"The perfect crime."

81

"Almost, but not quite. You see, when Anderson drove his automobile from the old stable, he did not exit through the main entrance of the riding club. There is a security officer on guard there at night. Instead he left by a country road that leads off the riding club property and eventually joins the highway. Thanks to the careful work of Kemp we have his car tracks! We also have Billy who will testify that he returned to the old stables on Sunday morning to retrieve some rags he had left there, and that he was shocked to discover that the car he had just cleaned was now definitely soiled."

"But is that true?"

"No."

"And yet you want him to testify to that?"

"Not in court, but in Anderson's presence. You see, we must somehow catch Anderson unaware, and cause him to drop his pretence of innocence. In fact, I have proposed a plan to Kemp which he has agreed upon, and it is one in which you play an important role. I will not describe all of the details since I want your participation to be spontaneous and genuine, but it is essential that your part in the drama be enacted precisely."

"Do you mean you expect me to be an actor?"

"Yes. That's exactly what I mean. Tomorrow morning at 9:00 A.M. you will ring up Dr. Anderson at his office and will convey to him the following unfortunate news: Kemp is now finally convinced that Sylvester committed both murders, and intends to arrest him. He is leaving Scotland Yard within the hour for the Berkshire Riding Club where Sylvester and Cassandra are spending the day. This last information will not arouse any suspicion since Anderson and Sylvester are both members of the club and are both fine equestrians. I have been informed that Cassandra is an excellent rider too. Anderson knows that Sylvester has finished his examinations and has been anxious to return to a steady riding schedule.

"I must emphasize that you must be convincing. Anderson is brilliant and brilliantly suspicious. You must convince him that all of this is taking place, and especially that Kemp is finally persuaded of Sylvester's guilt. Say that Kemp now insists Sylvester traveled on an earlier train from Sussex. Also tell Anderson that I am on my way by taxi to Berkshire to be with my client, that you are leaving immediately, and that he should make post-haste in his auto too. I am certain he will follow your directions, since he must pretend concern for his nephew — which I'm convinced he actually does feel."

"May I ask you a question?"

"But, of course, why do you ask?"

"Well. Because it is a different kind of question. You might call it a personal question.

"You may certainly ask. I can always refuse to reply."

"Why did you neglect to tell me at the luncheon yesterday the facts you uncovered proving Anderson's guilt."

"There were two reasons. First. I did not consider them to be facts, because they had not yet been verified. And second: I do not fully trust Cassandra."

"You really distrust her?"

"Well. No. I do not distrust her. I merely think it is possible that her involvement in this case is not what it appears on the surface to be."

"She does manage to become involved."

"Yes. And not only through Sylvester, but also through you."

That caught me off guard, but he continued before I could ask him to explain.

"My questions about Cassandra, I must add, are not limited to her specific actions since we became involved in this case. They begin earlier, and have to do with her relationship to Sylvester."

"You think that they're not suited to one another, that their relation-ship is odd?"

"No. It's not that. It's Anderson himself, and Louise-Phillipe, and the female CIA operative who had Caldwell on a line. Hardly anyone involved in this case is what he or she appears to be. So why should we take Cassandra at face value? I confess I even found myself wondering whether Miss Ellie was a superb actress playing the role of a lively, sexy chamber-maid. Fortunately, I quickly ceased such speculation as idle and inefficient."

"How did Cassandra and Sylvester meet?"

"At the riding club. She was not a member, but was temporarily leasing a horse."

"An apparently natural way for her to meet him if that were her prior intention."

"Or the intention of her employers. And don't forget her involvement with you."

"She has no involvement with me! She is certainly far more interested in you! And that has been true all along."

Sherlock had been pacing back and forth across the carpet, but he now stopped abruptly, and looked at me with genuine surprise.

"You don't mean that. That's certainly not correct."

"Yes I do mean it. Look. She has no serious interest in me. She likes me, but she is genuinely attracted to you. She as much as told me that herself. Besides, she's attractive, you've kept her at a distance, and even given her a difficult time. She's very intelligent and attracted to your intelligence. And I'm just a young doctor starting out and so is Sylvester."

"Well. I must disagree with you. It is perfectly obvious that she is in love with Sylvester, but uncertain about that love, and that she is very definitely attracted to you. You have always been blind when a woman was attracted to you. You still have not accepted the fact that different women like different types of men." He smiled a sly grin. "You can't have them all."

"I don't know what you mean."

"Certainly you do. You may be attracted to a woman who is just not attracted to your type. It could be your looks, your mannerisms, your attitudes, whatever. Being turned down a few times has bruised your ego and caused you to distort your self-image." He laughed. "You forget the other women who have been attracted to you." And now he really began laughing. "In fact, in these matters you're so dimwitted, you forget that in general women are very attracted to men."

"All that you've said about me may be true. Indeed, it is true. Nevertheless, I'm certain that your view of Cassandra is very, very confused!"

Confusion, of course, is the most devastating charge one can level against a logician, but I pressed him even further.

"In fact, your views on Cassandra are patently inconsistent, and I would add, are evidence of a disturbed emotionality on the subject." I now laughed, confident that I would win this game of one-upmanship. I was bluffing, since I had no explicit argument to advance, but my instincts told me I was right. So I started to talk. When in doubt, start to talk, I always say.

84

"First you insist that it's possible Cassandra is not whom she appears to be. You even suggest that she may be employed by someone, that she may not have met Sylvester accidentally. Then you insist it's obvious she's in love with Sylvester and also very much attracted to me. Well! You can't have it both ways! If you can't be sure she's the person she presents herself to be, then you can't be sure of anything about her."

"Not even that she's intelligent, or that she's attractive?"

"No. No. You know very well what I mean. You can't be sure she's in love with Sylvester and not merely using him as a means. And you can't be sure she's attracted to me. Admit it. When it comes to women your logic flies right out the window and you're bloody inconsistent."

"Well. I won't admit to all that. But I suppose you're partly right about Cassandra."

"Partly right?"

"Yes. I think there's something you have overlooked."

"And what could that be?"

"It is my observation that she is attracted to you. You're correct that I can't be certain of that observation if I also hypothesize that she might be a spy. And it does conform to that hypothesis to assume that her behaviour towards you and Sylvester is only pretence. But it only conforms and does not necessarily follow. You believe that if she's some sort of undercover agent she can't possibly be attracted to you, or can't be in love with Sylvester. But that doesn't follow at all. My observation is that she is attracted to you, period, whether she is playing a role or not."

For some reason Sherlock's observation did not encourage me.

"Well. It doesn't really matter. We'll never know whether your observation is correct or not."

"Why not?"

"Well. How can anyone tell — I mean, definitely?"

"I believe that there is a way, at least it has always worked for me."

"What do you mean?"

"If you encounter a person completely by surprise, when their response to you is unprepared, you can tell at once how they feel about you. Their natural feelings about you are spontaneously expressed, in their faces, in their eyes, in their words, but particularly their eyes."

"So I merely have to catch her off guard?"

"Yes."

"And I can tell immediately by her response?"

"Yes."

"Then that's exactly what I will do tomorrow morning at the riding club. I will kill two birds with one stone. I will enact the part in the drama that you and Kemp desire of me, and I will determine the true nature of Cassandra's emotion."

Little did I know at the time that I would succeed magnificently in one of these aims but fail miserably in the other.

CHAPTER IX

THE CLIMAX

As the taxi pulled up the front entrance of the clubroom, I could see the main riding arena off to the left, although it was partially blocked from view by one long wing of stables. Sylvester was standing alongside the arena intently watching a rider who was still hidden from my view. A moment later a magnificent horse emerged moving at a very brisk trot under the relaxed control of Cassandra, whose long dark hair undulated behind her.

I stepped out of the taxi and was drawn towards the scene in the main arena. The feeling of the crisp early morning there in the countryside, mixed with the musty horse smells from the stables, intensified my experience of the event unfolding before me: Cassandra, a true beauty of the human species upon a powerful but graceful stallion, the two moving through space in perfect rhythm together. My breath caught in my throat, an exhilerated emotion overcame me, and I thought, 'How can I help but fall in love with her.'

Cassandra circled the arena once more, as I paid the taxi driver. She then came to a halt, dismounted, walked her horse out of the arena, and began to brush him down. Sylvester said something to make her laugh and then walked away, fortunately not in my direction. I realized that this was my opportunity! She was on the other side of the horse from me and was unaware that I had arrived. I walked briskly but as quietly as I could in her direction. I slowed as I drew near to her, almost creeping on those last few steps.

And then, one of those fateful coincidences occurred, one of those sheer coincidences that sometimes determine our lives, starting us on the road to fortune or on the road to ruin. Just as I stopped very near, almost touching the horse, Cassandra looked up. And in that instant of surprise recognition, as I focused with intent upon her eyes — at just that very instant — I was startled by the sound of the stallion who suddenly began to urinate loudly in the dirt below. My eyes glanced at this, and then back to Cassandra, who had just observed my eyes making that glance. I know that I blushed.

To this very day I wonder whether that horse acted on purpose, and specifically with malice of forethought against me. I personally believe that horses make choices like humans. Those who disagree and who insist that horses are animated by instinct, forget that human beings are animated by instinct too.

In any event, it got worse. The startling sound, along with my desire not to soil my shoes and cuffs, prompted me to step back abruptly, which unfortunately brought me into collision with a bucket, which event startled the horse, who began to neigh nervously. You can imagine my position. There was nothing I could do. So I smiled and said:

"Good morning, Cassandra! I just wanted to say, 'Good morning,' before going to the clubroom." She responded, "Hello," and I turned on my heel and walked away.

To my good fortune, I was diverted from my fiasco by the arrival of Sherlock, who was followed immediately by Detective Kemp in a police automobile with two other officers. They entered the clubhouse together. I decided to wait outside, and soon a voice came over the loudspeaker paging, "Mr. Sylvester Anderson." Kemp, his two officers, and Sherlock, then reappeared from the clubhouse. Almost immediately, Sylvester, with Cassandra on his arm, appeared from the stables walking in the direction of the clubhouse.

The timing of this enactment was fortuitous, for just at this moment Anderson pulled into a parking area to the right of the clubhouse. On impulse I went to meet him. He parked, and as I greeted him, we could already hear the voices of Kemp and Sylvester raised in a heated debate. Sylvester was adamant in protesting his innocence and Kemp was equally adamant in insisting upon his guilt. As Anderson and I hurried towards the encounter, we could see Sylvester angrily reach out for Kemp, but fortunately, Cassandra restrained him, and Sherlock took him by the arm and led him aside. Kemp, exuding confidence and righteous indignation, addressed Anderson as we came up.

"I regret to inform you Dr. Anderson that we have finally determined that your very own nephew is the perpetrator of the two vicious crimes of murder!"

"That is impossible!"

"No! It is not impossible. Moreover, it is true. On the Saturday night of your wife's murder, he did travel by train from Sussex, but he did not travel directly through to Waterloo. Instead, he disembarked at the Berkshire Station and jogged the distance from the station here to the riding club. He knew you intended to leave your auto at the old stables while you were in Torquay. He then drove your auto from here to London. He has a set of keys to your car, does he not?"

"Yes. But..."

Kemp gestured away Anderson's rebuttal before it could be made and called to one of his officers:

"Bring young Billy here from the clubhouse!"

He turned back to Anderson.

"We have a trainer who will testify that while working late on Saturday evening he observed a man of Sylvester's description walking towards the old stables. And our expert here" — He gestured to the remaining officer — "has identified the tracks of your automobile on the country road leading away from the old stables to the highway. To avoid the security guard at the main entrance, he slipped out the back way."

Young Billy now appeared with the first officer, and though obviously embarrassed and confused, he blurted out the following apology to Anderson.

"Dr. Anderson. Excuse me, sir. Your auto — I don't know — I washed it, honestly I did. But on Sunday I came back to find it all soiled again. The wheels were dirty. The whole auto was dirty."

Anderson looked at Billy with total disbelief and while still in this state of shock, Kemp grabbed him by the arm and started towards the old stables. At the same time he called out to Sherlock.

"Bring Sylvester along! Once and for all we'll settle this case!"

I hurried along with Kemp and Anderson, and soon the entire entourage was walking with determination on the path towards the old stables, including Cassandra, whose face was the picture of grief. Kemp would not let up.

"If anyone is still in doubt, and that includes you too Watkins, we will now establish the final damaging piece of evidence that will seal Sylvester's fate."

He called back to Sherlock, who, arm in arm with Sylvester, was now walking immediately behind us.

"The famous powers of deduction of your illustrious grandfather. We can deduce evidence of Sylvester's presence at the stables: If he were there, then his footprints will be there, perfectly obvious for anyone to see!"

Sylvester shouted out at him.

"And I swear that I am innocent. And that you are a bloody fool!"

"Well! We shall see who is the fool!"

As we drew near the old stables, Kemp turned to Sylvester and gestured towards his shoe.

89

"Take one off! And it doesn't in the least matter whether those are the shoes you wore that evening or not!"

Sylvester complied with a defiant look. The expert took his shoe and walked into the old stable, which was open on the side facing the path.

I have retained within my memory, forever indelibly imprinted, a visual picture of that moment: Kemp standing stolid and superior, his arms folded across his chest; Sylvester, his face filled with fury, flanked by Cassandra on one side and his defender, Sherlock, on the other; Anderson, intense and bewildered, no longer the man of total self-control; the uniformed officer standing off to the side of Kemp, a visual symbol of the Law; and the expert, uniformed too, now walking with measured steps, his eyes intently surveying the ground.

A quiet came over the group as each one of us concentrated our attention and expectation upon the expert. We stood poised, as a painting, a still-life, with only the movement of one person walking in deliberate steps, criss-crossing the ground. As I recall the experience now, I remember how time slowed dramatically, almost coming to a halt. Each of us awaited the moment of recognition on the face of the expert as he continued to search. No one moved. This was the climax of the drama.

More time passed and then finally, the expert shook his head, looked up at Kemp and said:

"His footprints, Sir, are nowhere to be found!"

I heard a gasp from Anderson next to me as if he had been struck a hard blow. I looked, as we all looked, at Kemp, whose face was completely crestfallen.

"Are there any footprints?"

"Only young Billy's and Dr. Anderson's."

Kemp tugged at his moustache and kicked his foot in the dirt.

"Are the tire tracks still there?" He pointed to a dirt road leading away from the side of the stables.

"Yes sir. They're definitely there."

"But then who drove the auto on that Saturday night?"

Before he had even finished phrasing his question, the answer dawned upon him, for he turned abruptly to face Anderson, as the rest of us, following the focus of his attention, did too.

90

"It was either young Billy or you!!"

Sherlock now stepped forward to face Anderson.

"And it wasn't young Billy! Watkins, you were right all along! The murderer was from within the household!"

The next events happened in a flurry, one after the other: I was shoved hard by Anderson, who stepped backwards, grabbing Cassandra by the arm, pulling her away from the group. He retreated a short distance and then stopped and produced a revolver, which he directed threateningly at all of us. And then, in the very next moment — I will always be amazed at this — I found myself walking directly towards him, while at almost the same instant, Sherlock began to walk towards him too. I found myself saying:

"It's all over, Anderson. The game is over."

The ugly muzzle of his gun was pointed directly at my stomach. I could feel the threat of massive damage to my midriff. Yet I experienced no sensation of fear. And I said:

"You will have to kill me before I will let you harm Cassandra." I stopped, and Sherlock stopped too, no more than three of four meters from the barrel of his gun. Except for the after-sound of my voice there was total stillness. All reality seemed pinpointed on this one event.

I was close to Anderson now and could see the terror in his eyes. I realized, as I saw him with Cassandra in his grasp, threatening us with a lethal weapon, that he was a coward, and not merely in this moment, but as a person through-and-through. I said to him in a voice full of authority and conviction:

"Hand over the gun!"

And as effect follows cause, his arm holding the gun dropped to his side, the light of terror went out of his eyes, and Cassandra stepped loose from his grip. Sherlock stepped forward, taking the gun from his hand, and Sylvester walked quickly up to Cassandra.

I will not detail Dr. Anderson's arrest and imprisonment. He was taken away immediately, and Sylvester and Cassandra left immediately too — I assumed, to be at his side during his difficulties. Within a few short minutes of the climax of the drama, the riding club had returned to normal. It was as if the events that had transpired there had not transpired at all. They did not leave even the faintest imprint upon the site where they had occurred. I expected Sherlock to leave momentarily as well, but instead he took me by the arm and led me to the lounge of the clubhouse. To my surprise, a pleasant surprise, Louise-Phillipe was there seated at a table waiting for us. Everyone in the world, it seemed, had been in on the plot. We greeted one another, and I asked Sherlock what was on my mind.

"Were Sylvester and Cassandra, like everybody else in the world, in on the drama too?" (He smiled and nodded affirmatively). "I must confess that I was so engaged in the reality of the enactment, that I was surprised when the expert did not find Sylvester's footprint." (I laughed at myself, and then turned to Louise-Phillipe) "So the case is completed and you have joined us to celebrate another round in the triumph of good over evil?"

"Well. I have come to confess my sins."

"And to think that you were lying to us all along."

"Not about everything, just about some things."

"And pray tell us, when were you telling the truth?"

"I testified I did not murder Laura Anderson."

"And?"

"I declared myself a believer in justice and equality."

"And what else?"

"Well..." He laughed heartily. "I suppose the rest is lies."

Sherlock laughed too and said:

"Your distant ancester De Molay?"

"It's true. He's no ancester of mine."

I added:

"You certainly had me fooled, with your convincing words and ways. To think you've been an undercover agent all along, while I thought you were a chef who could tell me why my souffles won't rise."

"Oh! No! Watkins. I am a chef and my profession is the culinary arts, not espionage. I am only on a temporary assignment, and it is all because of a friend. I do not have good taste in friends. As they say, "Le mauvais goût mene au crime." 'Bad taste leads to crime.' My friend, who is in intelligence, conscripted me, a humble chef. I resisted, but with both the French and the British governments pleading and entreating, what could I do? I had to give in."

Sherlock was quick to ask:

"The British government too?"

"Why yes! The French government took the first steps, but then the British were allowed in. The action was on their own turf."

"And I suppose you will be returning to France?"

"Oh! No! Monsieur Holmes. I will remain at the Anderson's home as chef. I will be needed. Sylvester will be residing there, along with the remaining members of the Guild. It has already tentatively been arranged."

He read the looks of disbelief on our faces and explained:

"Last night we convinced the professors our governments mean them no harm. They are fearful since Hawkins' murder, and welcome the protection."

I felt compelled to ask:

"And how do we know, Louise-Phillipe, that you're telling us the truth now?"

"I suppose you don't know."

"No. We don't. The French and British intelligence are probably biding their time until it is opportune to step in and take control."

"I personally would resist that."

"But you may only be a pawn in their game."

"Yes. That's true." He smiled. "But at the moment I am an indispensable pawn. The Guild has confdence in me. They trust that my loyalties are first to humanity, and only second to my government."

Sherlock intervened.

"And do you trust the Guild?"

That caused him to pause. His look changed and became intense.

"Sherlock, you do not trust them?"

93

"No. I do not."

"I do not fully trust them either."

"Do you believe they really trust you?"

"They say they do."

"Do you think the French and British intelligence trust you?"

That question he liked, for he rolled his head back and laughed.

"Sherlock, I like so much your humour. A young man with so much wit. But you are too suspicious — which, don't tell me, I know, is the pot calling the kettle black. But, of course, you are right? Those spies don't trust me. They don't trust anyone. That is their job."

I reminded him.

"And now you're a spy too, so whom can you trust?"

"I can trust you, and Sherlock."

"And Sylvester?"

"Yes, of course, Sylvester."

"And Cassandra?"

"Ah! Somehow I knew you would ask."

He looked at Sherlock and then back to me.

"What a rivalry!"

I know I blushed, and Sherlock cringed and said:

"You misunderstand."

Louise-Phillipe seemed to take pleasure in our discomfort, for he laughed and continued.

"Perhaps it is you who misunderstands. Don't you see that she is a great power, perhaps for good, but perhaps also for evil? I do not trust her, but she does have a magnificent potential!"

Sherlock seemed to take offense at Louise-Phillipe's comments, for he countered defensively.

"She seems rather harmless to me — that is, unless she's a spy too."

Louise-Phillipe disagreed.

"No. I think she is dangerous whether a spy or not. It makes no difference. She is a danger to the heart and the soul."

"That seems like a lot of poppycock to me! Why do you insist on attributing to this woman so much more power than she has or could possibly deserve?"

"Ah! Sherlock, you do not comprehend because you have logic and a strong will. If you were a mere mortal, such as Watkins or me, ruled by passion, then you would know that what I am saying is true."

I had to add my own thoughts on the subject.

"You seem to think that she's quite ordinary, whereas I see her as quite unusual, with unusual intelligence and unusual depth."

Louise-Phillipe was smiling broadly at me, so I quickly added:

"I realize that I view her through romantic eyes, but in certain respects she is superior." Sherlock was staring at me, so I asked him point blank. "Don't you agree? Tell me the truth. Do you agree or not?"

"I certainly do not agree! But not for the reasons you think. You — and Louise-Phillipe too — value persons who in your eyes have superior power or superior beauty. You contrast these superior beings with the rest of ordinary humanity. You can't resist! You always judge! You always compare and contrast! For you, there must always be the first; there must always be the last! Compare and contrast! It's size! It's all in your attitude towards size!"

To my total amazement, Sherlock struck his fist on the table, bolted upright, and with a slightly crazed look in his eye, continued his oration.

"Smaller and larger! In this I am larger. In that you are smaller. It's size! It's size! It's all in the size. Compare and contrast! There's always the first. There's always the last!"

He concluded his diatribe, and without even a gesture of farewell, walked away from our table and exited the lounge. But just as abruptly, he re-entered, walked back to the table and seated himself, his eyes boring intently into Louise-Phillipe and me. I turned towards Louise-Phillipe.

"He thinks he's so intelligent. He assured me I could determine

Cassandra's true feelings towards me if I could catch her off guard unaware of my presence. At the exact moment of surprise recognition, he said, I could see it in her eyes. And I believed him. I tested his theory, just a while ago, here at the stables. Cassandra did not see me approach. In fact, I was standing almost on top of her and her horse before she realized my presence. And just at that moment —" I leaned over the table, looking at Sherlock again — "Just at that moment her damn stallion burst forth with a torrent of urine into the dirt below!!"

Sherlock looked at me in total amazement. I did not for a moment change my dead-pan look. But then Louise-Phillipe burst into uncontrollable laughter, and almost immediately thereafter Sherlock did too. As you can well imagine, the three of us merely sat there and laughed until we almost cried.

EPILOGUE

I feel obliged to conclude my account of Sherlock's entrance into a career of criminal investigation with a report of our last discussion of "The Anderson Murders," as they came to be known in the press. The conversation was educational to me becuase it revealed further insights into the nooks and crannies of Sherlock's mind. We met at the World's End Pub only a few days after the extraordinary events at the Riding Club. Sherlock was quick to inform me of the good news.

"Anderson's conviction is assured."

"Excellent! That's excellent!"

"Yes. The drama was a success — which is a great relief to me."

"Well! It was a conviction that we were after."

"But we needed a confession most of all. I'm sure you're aware that I designed the drama with that one aim in mind."

"Yes. I did think of that. The pressure upon Anderson believing that his beloved nephew, poor Sylvester, might be punished in his place."

"That too. But most of all it was the shock of becoming the focus of so many human consciousnesses at once."

"What do you mean?"

"Well. He first had to deal with one piece of incriminating evidence after another — even though it was directed against Sylvester: The trainer who saw him, Billy finding the car soiled, the tracks proving the car had been taken. All of that was designed to unsettle him, to put him on edge. But at the moment the prints expert came up empty handed, and Kemp turned towards him with his mock realization, and I did too, everyone there, that entire motley crowd, including you, all at once focused, each like a beam of light on Anderson in stage center. That was the critical moment of the drama intended to flush him out from behind his mask of innocence." Sherlock breathed the sigh of relief of a director whose dramatic production has not fallen flat on its face. "You see, I have observed that small children who are otherwise behaving quite normally, abruptly behave abnormally when they are thrust into the center stage of attention without prior warning. Their consciousness becomes embarrassed and befuddled. They begin to squirm and jerk

97

with their bodies, and sometimes even to kick. Their behaviour often angers their parents who are completely unaware of what has occurred. As adults we become accustomed to certain rapid changes in stimuli to our consciousness, and sometimes even train ourselves to be properly composed in the limelight, say to give a public lecture. But this primitive childlike response to a sudden thrust into the spotlight of several human consciousnesses at once often occurs to adults as well. Thank goodness it worked with Anderson." He smiled as if laughing at himself. "You know I was suspect of Anderson from the beginning, literally from our very first encounter with Kemp. And your argument — as we see now a very good argument — that it was someone from within the household, only re-inforced my suspicions. Naturally, I was uncertain, but I once asked myself the question, 'If I eliminate all consideration of alibis, who within the household would have a motive, a sufficiently strong motive, to willfully terminate the life of Laura Anderson?' The obvious answer was Dr. Anderson himself, particularly in light of the details of Laura Anderson's will. From the very beginning it struck me as odd that nowhere in her will was anything bequested to her husband — not a fond memento, a contribution to one of his favorite charities, nothing! From this fact I drew the obvious conclusion that the relationship between the two of them was almost certainly empty and estranged, that their marriage was almost certainly a marriage of form and not of substance."

"This is a revelation to me!"

"It is simply attending to details, particularly to details that have implications, and in this instance, details that stand out as odd or incongruous. Of course, I could make nothing of this detail in the first stages of the investigation, but it gnawed, as the Germans say, like a hintergedanke — thought in the back of my head — keeping alive the hypothesis that Anderson himself was the culprit."

"Well! You were certainly correct in doing that. But I must confess that the most surprising feature of this case to me is its ultimate outcome; Sylvester moving into the Anderson home, Louise-Phillipe remaining there, and most of all, the Templar Guild moving in there too. Isn't that a risk for Sylvester?"

"Yes it is. I advised him against the move, but he wouldn't listen. By the way, he sends his regards and thanks you for your courageous behaviour."

"You mean foolhardy behaviour."

"Yes, perhaps that too."

"Not just perhaps, for I must confess that I did not experience the slightest sensation of fear when I started walking — and you started walking too — towards Anderson. That's certainly not courage."

"Why not? Don't you think that courage can be fearless?"

That took me aback.

"I'm not sure."

"Courage comes in all varieties."

"I suppose you're right."

"Yes I am. And I must tell you what I found most surprising about this case."

"My infatuation with Cassandra?"

"No. Your romantic fantasies are nothing novel to me."

"I didn't overstep my bounds, did I?"

"No. I don't think so. Besides, she has been uncertain about her relationship with Sylvester. I don't believe you violated her rights, or his rights for that matter."

"Good." I felt extremely relieved. I wasn't sure whether I had exposed some of my private fantasies inadvertently to public view. "But I digressed. You were about to say what you found most surprising. May I take a guess?"

"Of course."

"It was the Templar Guild."

"Yes. Your instincts are good and you are absolutely right. Naturally, I had no reason to be surprised, since I have often reflected upon the technological revolution that threatens to overthrow humanity." He looked very troubled. "Perhaps I thought it was further off."

"You fear that humanity is unprepared for this revolution."

"Yes. But I also fear the changes in themselves, even if we do accommodate to them."

"I thought nuclear annihilation was your greatest fear."

"It is, because of its priority. But suppose that we survive, and that because we have attained de facto immortality, we cease altogehter to reproduce ourselves with new offspring? Don't forget the significant role of death to life."

"Perhaps given sufficient time, we'll mature; very wise persons in very young bodies. Can you imagine being 2000 years old in a 20 year old's body?"

"But without new generations, who will rejuvenate the race? I fear we may be entering a period of the waning of human life, at least as far as it can be creative. Perhaps Nature has grown weary."

"What do you mean?"

"The human species is Nature's species, don't you agree?"

"Yes."

"The human species is Nature's creative endeavour here on the skin of this planet. And what does that mean?"

Sherlock now looked at me intently, the passion of his thought projecting through his eyes. He proceeded immediately to answer his own question.

"The human species is Nature, in this space-time portion of it, having become self-conscious and rational. You and I — Yes. You and I — are part of Nature's Mind. Don't you understand? Life reproduces itself in offspring and then dies, passes away: that is the origin of variety and creativity! Can you imagine ten billion uncreative and bored human beings living indefinitely into the future? Is this what it is all about? Are stupor and self-satisfaction the destiny of humanity, of Nature's Mind?" Sherlock's look now turned to agony. "I once believed that humanity was one of Nature's great creative forces, perhaps even its greatest, but now I'm not so certain. And what's worse, annihilation by nuclear weapons, or a monotonous and uncreative future?"

"Certainly not annihilation! Your trouble is that you're a pessimist. What about love? Why can't love thrive when humanity has no offspring? Don't forget that we're imagining mature personalities housed in twenty year old bodies. Why can't we retain the physical and mental excitement of youth? It's not all anxiety, you know."

"I suppose you're right. Perhaps I believe that everything withers with age, that everything decays with time, that time renders everything meaningless."

He had conceded me a point, but did not sound convinced. He now abruptly interrupted our dialogue by glancing at his watch and blurting out:

"She should be here by now."

"Who?"

"Who do you imagine? Cassandra. But only for a moment to say goodbye."

"What?" I was stunned. I knew that she had planned a several month sojourn at the Bibliotheque Nationale in Paris researching the Knights Templars, but I thought she had already departed. I'm certain my jaw dropped to my chin. I had not been forewarned. Sherlock had set me up, and was now eyeing me with a wisp of a sly grin in the corner of his mouth. He continued with me in his trap.

"I didn't want you to feel constrained to dress for the occasion, which you always seem to do when Cassandra is present. She probably thinks you're a fashion model."

I restrained my temptation to strangle him on the spot, and instead struck back with words.

"Birds do it. And humans do it too. It's a biological instinct. And you make it sound like the behaviour of a fool. But let me tell you this. The drab are left behind in the lurch and you yourself could learn a lesson or two from the Birds."

He broke out laughing at me, and I'm sure was ready to counter-attack, when at that very moment Cassandra came up, startling us with a greeting:

"And here we have two of England's most renowned criminal investigators!"

Sherlock smiled and my heart stopped beating and leaped into my throat.

"And Watkins, you saved my life." Her voice seemed sincere. "How can I thank you? You risked your life for me."

"It was nothing."

"You're far too modest."

"But I would have done it for anyone."

"And I all along thought that you did it because of me."

"I did, of course, I did. I could not stand to see an innocent young historian in the clutches of a dastardly villain."

"I must have made a pretty picture." She laughed and turned to Sherlock. "And I must thank you. You risked your life too."

"It was nothing."

"You are also too modest. And don't tell me you would have done if for anyone."

"Alright. I won't."

She smiled and with her focus still concentrated on Sherlock, continued in a more serious vein.

"I hope that you will talk to Sylvester as I asked. It's been done. I have broken off the engagement!"

She reached out and took his hand, and I was crestfallen in the realization that her heart was drawn to him. She then drew back and announced:

"I have only come for a moment to say good-bye and to personally thank you from my heart. I must be going immediately! I leave for Paris early in the morning, and I still have very much to do. But I must confess that I have one serious regret over leaving London at this time."

Sherlock looked at her inquiringly.

"And what is that?"

She abruptly leaned toward me, kissing the side of my cheek, and said:

"You!"

And with that she whirled and walked away.

INTRODUCTION

The goals of this study are:

(i)   To improve the clarity and preciseness of our thought,

(ii) To make explicit and to extend our natural intuitive
      capacity for deductive reasoning,

(iii) To identify and to perfect our skill in using various
      forms of inductive reasoning,

(iv) To develop our critical awareness of fallacious forms
      of reasoning and erroneous grounds for belief.

I will proceed in a step-by-step analysis of the detective story, and will advance towards the four goals stated above simultaneously. Since deductive reasoning is fundamental to our reasoning processes, it will be highlighted in the beginning of our endeavour.

Our use of our intelligence is a perfectible skill capable of dramatic improvement. We all know that cooking and mechanics are perfectible skills, and that with some determination and attention to detail, we can become a good cook or a good mechanic. We also know that with devotion, along with attention to detail, we might even become a connoisseur chef or a master mechanic. Some of us forget, however, that in a similar way our use of our intelligence is a perfectible skill too. With some determination and attention to detail, we can improve that skill and make very good use of our intelligence. Of course, not everyone wishes to become a good cook or a good mechanic, but almost everyone wishes to make the best use of his or her intelligence. It is the assumption of this work that the reader is committed to that goal.

CHAPTER I: ANALYSIS

In this analysis of the first chapter of the story, I will introduce four of the most fundamental and common operations of human thought. These four familiar operations are critical to our capacity as rational agents. Each is a deductive pattern of reasoning in which a concluding thought follows necessarily from one or more prior thoughts.

Deductive reasoning, in general, always involves the form or pattern or structure of thoughts linked together. From "All Chimpanzees are mammals," and "All mammals are animals," we can deduce, "All chimpanzees are animals," because the first thought has the structure, "All A's are B's," the second thought has the structure, "All B's are C's," the third thought has the structure, "All A's are C's," and the following is a valid deductive pattern of thinking:

"All A's are B's"	(premise)
"All B's are C's"	(premise)
"All A's are C's"	(conclusion)

The specific content of these thoughts; that they have to do with chimpanzees, mammals, and animals is irrelevant to the logical relation between them. Thus, the following argument, which has an identically similar pattern, is a valid deductive argument too:

"All conservatives are marsupials."	(premise)
"All marsupials are animals"	(premise)
"All conservatives are animals."	(conclusion)

Basic deductive reasoning is intuitive and obvious. It is acquired with our acquisition of the language; particularly with such words as: "and," "or," "not," "if...then," "all," "some," and "is." Of course, we sometimes use our reasoning bluntly and crudely rather than precisely and artfully, and we sometimes cannot resist the temptation to subtle forms of fallacious reasoning. Nevertheless, you and I correctly employ basic deductive operations of thought over and over again each day.

Besides treating deductive reasoning in the analysis of this first chapter, we will also analyze a fallacy, the fallacy of inconsistency. And we will learn a method of argument called "reductio ad absurdum," a technique for exposing inconsistency — whether someone else's or our own.

In the pursuit of clarity, we will distinguish, in terms of their structure, five basic different kinds of thoughts; namely, negated thoughts *(negations)*, thoughts conjoined and asserted together *(conjunctions)*, Conditional thoughts *(conditionals)*, either/or thoughts *(disjunctions)*, and general thoughts *(generalizations)*. We will also point out certain thoughts that are equivalent to one another, and note the distinction between contradictions, i.e. thoughts that are necessarily false, and tautologies, i.e. thoughts that are necessarily true.

1. MODUS TOLLENS: A Deductive Operation of Thought
THE DISCONFIRMATION OF AN HYPOTHESIS

"And Sylvester's fiancee, who accompanied him during most of that Saturday evening?"

"At most an accomplice, but almost surely not even that."

"Because she has no motive?"

"Correct."

Kemp wishes to rule out Sylvester's fiancee as a suspect because she has no apparent motive for murdering Laura Anderson. His reasoning can be represented as beginning with two thoughts as premises from which a third thought is deduced as a conclusion:

"If Sylvester's fiancee deserves to be a suspect, she must have an apparent motive."   premise)

"She does not have an apparent motive."   (premise)
"She does not deserve to be a suspect."   (conclusion)

The concluding thought, that she does not deserve to be a suspect, follows deductively and necessarily from the two assumed thoughts by one of the most fundamental and common operations of human thought, an operation labeled by logicians, *"Modus Tollens."* We repeatedly employ modus tollens every day: "If Mary is home by now from her date with Byron, then her bedroom light will be on; but her bedroom light isn't on, so I guess she's not home." "If Jim were really falling in love with me, then he would have asked me to the dance. He didn't ask me to the dance, so I know he's not really falling in love with me."

The structure or logical form of modus tollens is the following:

IF P, THEN Q   (premise)
NOT Q   (premise)
NOT P   (conclusion)

106

Modus tollens is an extremely important deductive operation of thought, and we shall return to it again and again. But let us already observe that it is an essential component of scientific and hypothetical reasoning.

When we advance an hypothesis, we infer consequences that follow from that hypothesis and then test or observe to determine whether these consequences are true. If one of these consequences proves to be false, then we know — by modus tollens — that the hypothesis is false and needs to be revised, if not rejected altogether. The structure or logical form of the *Disconfirmation (or Refutation) of an Hypothesis* is just the structure or logical form of modus tollens:

IF hypothesis (h1), THEN consequence (c1)

NOT consequence (c1)
NOT hypothesis (h1)

(OR)

On the assumption that the hypothesis is true, it follows that the consequence (c1) is true.

But the consequence (c1) is false.
Therefore, the assumed hypothesis is false.

2. MODUS PONENS: A Deductive Operation of Thought

"Well. Suppose, just hypothetically, that she (the chambermaid) did not have the key;...."

"Yes? So? Suppose that to be true?"

"Would you still consider the chambermaid a prime suspect?"

"No. I would not."

We can represent Kemp's reasoning here as follows:

If the chambermaid did not have a key, then she should not be considered a prime suspect.   (premise)

She did not have a key.   (premise)
She should not be considered a prime suspect.   (conclusion)

107

The concluding thought of this reasoning follows deductively and necessarily from the two assumed thoughts by *Modus Ponens*. The structure or logical form of modus ponens is the following:

$$\frac{\text{IF P, THEN Q} \qquad \text{(premise)}}{\text{Q} \qquad \text{(conclusion)}}$$

IF P, THEN Q   (premise)
P   (premise)
———————————
Q   (conclusion)

Some examples of modus ponens are:

(i)   If Tallin is in Estonia, then Tallin is in the U.S.S.R.   (premise)

     Tallin is in Estonia   (premise)
     Tallin is in the U.S.S.R.   (conclusion)

(ii)   If Watkins is not 42 years old or more, then he cannot be a candidate for the presidency of the United States.   (premise)

     Watkins is not 42 years old or more.   (premise)
     Watkins cannot be a candidate for the presidency of the United States.   (conclusion)

(iii)   If God created this world, then this world is perfect.   (premise)

     God created this world.   (premise)
     This world is perfect.   (conclusion)

Modus ponens, like modus tollens, is one of the most important operations of human thought. Whenever a conditional thought of the form. "If..., then...," is asserted, and the *antecedent* (what comes after the "if" and precedes the "then") is asserted too, the *consequent* (what comes after the "then") follows necessarily by modus ponens. On the assumption that the truth of one thought implies the truth of a second thought, along with the assumption that the first thought is true, we can deduce the truth of the second thought. In other words, modus ponens is one of the more common means by which we extend our knowledge and draw inferences to new truths.

3.   UNIVERSAL INSTANTIATION: A Deductive Operation of Thought

"But then, from your line of thinking, it follows that both Sylvester and the chambermaid must have a motive."

Kemp has already stated that if Sylvester's fiancee committed the murder, then she must have had a motive. Sherlock treats this statement as applying generally:

"Anyone who committed the murder, must have had a motive."

Logicians represent *general thoughts* or *generalizations* such as this in the following way:

(FOR ANY x) (IF x committed the murder, THEN x must have had a motive.)

Sherlock now deduces two instances of this generalization by the deductive operation of thought, *universal instantiation*:

(i) IF <u>Sylvester</u> committed the murder, THEN <u>Sylvester</u> must have had a motive.

(ii) IF <u>the chambermaid</u> committed the murder, THEN <u>the chambermaid</u> must have had a motive.

It is also possible to correctly deduce many other instances of this generalization by universal instantiation, for example:

(iii) IF <u>Sherlock</u> committed the murder, THEN <u>Sherlock</u> must have had a motive.

(iv) IF <u>the prime minister of England</u> committed the murder, THEN <u>the prime minister of England</u> must have had a motive.

Etc., etc.

Universal instantiation is the Deductive Operation by which instances of general thoughts are deduced from those general thoughts.

4. DISJUNCTIVE SYLLOGISM: A Deductive Operation of Thought

"And is it your opinion that Sylvester is innocent?"

"Yes."

"Which leaves us with the chambermaid."

"Only if we accept your oringinal assumption that the murderer was either she or Sylvester, which I do not."

Detective Kemp's reasoning here utilizes another of the most common deductive operations of thought, *disjunctive syllogism.*.

Either the chambermaid committed the murder or
Sylvester committed the murder.   (premise)

Sylvester did not commit the murder.   (premise)
The chambermaid committed the murder.   (conclusion)

The structure or logical form of disjunctive syllogism is:

EITHER P OR Q   (premise)
NOT P   (premise)
Q   (conclusion)

And since it makes no difference whether one negates the thought to the left of the "or" or to the right of the "or," disjunctive syllogism also includes:

EITHER P OR Q   (premise)
NOT Q   (premise)
P   (conclusion)

Some examples of disjunctive syllogism are the following:

(i) London is either in England or in Argentina.   (premise)

London is not in Argentina.   (premise)
London is in England.   (premise)

Either Francoise or Guillame left the bathroom in
a mess.   (premise)

It can't be Guillame because he's not yet home.   (premise)
It must be Francoise — who left the bathroom in
a mess.   (conclusion)

Either demons exist and can 'possess' us or the
Bible is false.   (premise

The Bible is not false.   (premise)
Demons exist and can 'possess' us.   (conclusion)

110

5. VALIDITY AND INVALIDITY

TRUTH AND FALSITY

It is important to underscore the fact that the conclusion of Kemp's argument noted above, "The chambermaid committed the murder," follows validly and necessarily from the two premises; "Either the chambermaid or Sylvester committed the murder," and "Sylvester did not commit the murder," whether these premises are true or not. Indeed, Sherlock accepts the reasoning as valid, but does not accept the conclusion as true, because he does not believe in the truth of the first assumption that either the chambermaid or Sylvester committed the murder.

On the assumptions that either the chambermaid or Sylvester committed the murder and Sylvester is not the murderer, it follows that the chambermaid must be the murderer. If those assumptions are true, since the conclusion follows necessarily by disjunction syllogism, a valid deductive operation of thought, the conclusion must also be true. Obviously, if one or more of the assumptions is false, the conclusion can be false too. Some examples of perfectly valid deductive arguments with at least one false premise and a false conclusion are:

If San Francisco is in California, then San Francisco is in the U.S.S.R.	(premise)
San Francisco is not in the U.S.S.R.	(premise)
San Francisco is not in California.	(conclusion)

London is either in France or in Argentina.	(premise)
London is not in France.	(premise)
London is in Argentina.	(conclusion)

All human beings are immortal.	(premise)
Steve Martin is a human being.	(premise)
If Steve Martin is a human being, then Steve Martin is immortal. (Universal Instantiation)	(conclusion)
Steve Martin is immortal. (Modus Ponens)	(conclusion)

Let us also observe that the relation between validity and truth and falsity does not preclude the possibility of valid deductive arguments with one or more false premises and a true conclusion. Some examples are:

111

All residents of Wichita are residents of Alabama.   (premise)

All residents of Alabama are residents of the U.S.   (premise)
All residents of Wichita are residents of the U.S.   (conclusion)

The structure or logical form:

$3+1 = 5$ (premise) $a = b$

$5 = 2+2$ (premise $b = c$
$3+1 = 2+2$ (conclusion) $a = c$

It is vitally important in understanding the nature of human reasoning and in perfecting our own skills at reasoning, that we distinguish between *validity* and *invalidity* on the one hand, which apply to arguments, and *truth* and *falsity* on the other — which apply to single thoughts or statements. The assumptions or premises of an argument and its conclusion are each independent assertions, and each of these independent assertions is true or false. An argument is a chain of reasoning from one or more independent assertions to some assertion as a conclusion.

The relationship between validity and truth in deductive arguments is the following:

IN A VALID DEDUCTIVE ARGUMENT:

(I)   IF THE PREMISES ARE TRUE, THEN THE
      CONCLUSION MUST BE TRUE,

(II)   IF THE CONCLUSION IS FALSE, THEN AT LEAST
       ONE OF THE PREMISES MUST BE FALSE.

The distinction between valid and invalid reasoning on the one hand, and true and false assertions on the other, cannot be too often underscored. The proper appraisal of any argument must mark the distinction between the appraisal of:

(i)   the truth or credibility of the premises of the argument, and

(ii)   the validity of the argument's reasoning

These are clearly separate matters. An argument can fail either by having

112

false premises or by employing invalid reasoning (or perhaps by both). If the premises, assumptions, or data, with which an argument begins are false, then it must be rejected no matter how cogent its reasoning. For from false premises we can validly deduce all sorts of false conclusions. Consider, for example:

> Washington D.C. is either in France or Nicaragua.
>
> Washington D.C. is not in France.
> Washington D.C. is in Nicaragua.

On the other hand, if the reasoning in an argument is invalid, it must be rejected no matter that the premises or assumptions with which it begins are indubitably true. The following argument, for example, must be rejected even though it contains true premises. It employs a fallacious form of reasoning called, "The Fallacy of Denying the Antecedent":

> If Steve Martin is a candidate for the presidency, then he is a U.S. citizen.
>
> Steve Martin is not a candidate for the presidency.
> Steve Martin is not a U.S. citizen.

With these considerations in mind, let us lay down the following practical guidelines for the critical appraisal of arguments:

(I) We can always appraise an argument from the sole vantage of its reasoning to determine whether or not it is valid, without at the same time troubling over the truth or falsity of its premises.

(II) We can always appraise an argument from the sole vantage of the truth or falsity of its premises, without troubling over the validity or invalidity of its reasoning.

(III) Whenever we do accept the conclusion of an argument as true, we must do both of these things. An argument that has both valid reasoning and true premises, we will call a *"sound"* argument.

6. INCONSISTENCY: A Fallacy

REDUCIO AD ABSURDUM: A Technique For Exposing Inconsistency

In our discussion in (2.) of modus ponens, it was pointed out that Kemp agreed to the following:

"If the chambermaid did not have the key, then she should not be considered a prime suspect."

After extracting this agreement from Kemp, Sherlock adds the following:

"But Sylvester did not have a key either, and by the same reasoning should not be identified as a prime suspect....But you do identify him as a prime suspect. And that, of course is a contradiction."

Sherlock's reference to the "same reasoning" can be represented as follows: Kemp's belief that, "If the chambermaid did not have the key, then she should not be considered a prime suspect," seems naturally to apply in general to anyone:

Anyone who did not have a key, should not be considered a prime suspect.

(FOR ANY x) (IF x did not have a key, THEN x should not be considered a prime suspect.)

By Universal Instantiation, it then follows:

If Sylvester did not have a key, then Sylvester should not be considered a prime suspect.

Given the additional reasonable assumption that Sylvester did not have the key, Sherlock deduces the conclusion, by modus ponens, that Sylvester should not be considered a prime suspect:

If Sylvester did not have a key, then Sylvester should not be
Considered a prime suspect.   (premise)

Sylvester did not have a key.   (premise)
Sylvester should not be considered a prime suspect.   (conclusion)

Sherlock now underscores an inconsistency or strict contradition in Kemp's thinking by the logician's and debator's technique of making that

114

inconsistency or contradiction explicit:

"But you do identify him as a prime suspect...And that, of course, is a contradiction."

An Inconsistency or Strict Contradiction Is Affirming A Thought And At The Same Time Denying That Thought; It Is Asserting A Thought To Be True While At The Same Time Asserting That Thought To Be False.

Some examples of inconsistencies or strict contradictions, explicitly formulated, are:

Sylvester is a prime suspect and Sylvester is not a prime suspect.

Damascus is in Syria and Damascus is not in Syria.

God exists and God does not exist.

Sherlock deduces a contradiction from several of Kemp's assumptions; in other words, he makes a hidden contradiction in those assumptions explicit. The deduction of a strict contradiction from a set of assumptions is called a *Reductio Ad Absurdum*. It is important to distinguish reductio ad absurdum from, "the deduction of a false consequence from a set of assumptions, which then by modus tollens implies that at least one of the assumptions is false." For Reductio ad absurdum is a proof that a set of assumptions are not consistent with one another, that they are incompatible with one another.

7. TAUTOLOGIES

"Is there a special significance to the cloak draped over the victim's body? Since it was worn by the medieval monastic order of the Knights Templars?"

"Perhaps. Perhaps not."

Kemp's response here, strictly interpreted, is a *tautology*.

A Tautology Is A Thought So Structured That It Holds Necessarily, Is True Necessarily, No Matter What The Facts May Be.

115

It is a curious feature of our human mentality that we can construct thoughts whose truth derives from their structure, and not from their relationship to the world. Ordinarily we believe that the truth of a thought such as, "London is in England," depends upon the fact that London is in England: The thought "London is in England" is true and not false because it correctly records a fact or state of affairs in the world. But Kemp's reply, strictly rendered, is:

"Either the cloak has significance or it does not have significance."

This thought is non-committal, to say the least. It is true if the cloak has significance, and it is also true if the cloak has no significance. Indeed many — though not all — logicians insist that since the truth of a tautological thought derives from its structure, it therefore cannot convey any information whatsoever about the world.

The structure or logical form of Kemp's thought can be represented as:

EITHER P or NOT P

"EITHER (P) OR NOT (P)" is one kind of tautological form. Any thought that is an instance of this form is a tautology. Thus, all of the following are tautologies:

"EITHER Pernambuco is in Brazil OR Pernambuco is NOT in Brazil."

"EITHER God exists OR God does NOT exist."

"EITHER there will be a third world war OR there will NOT be a third world war."

It is important to note, as it was observed above, that "EITHER (P) OR NOT (P)" is only one kind of tautological form. For there are numerous other kinds of tautological forms, and indeed, as we shall see later, their number is strictly infinite. (Note: For convenience hereafter, tautological forms will be referred to as "tautologies.")

It is also important to note that strict contradictions, whose logical structure we characterized earlier as, "(P) AND NOT (P)" are not the only kind of contradiction, that is, are not the only kind of thought that is necessarily false. For there are numerous other kinds of contradictions, and in fact, the number of kinds of contradictions, like the number of kinds of tautologies, is strictly infinite.

116

8. EQUIVALENT THOUGHTS

There are thoughts that are equivalent to one another even though their structure or logical form is different. For example, the conditional thought:

(i) "If the chambermaid is the murderer, then she had the key." is equivalent to the thought:

(ii) "If the chambermaid did not have the key, then the chambermaid is not the murderer."

Observe that if we let "A" stand for "the chambermaid is the murderer," and "B" for, "The chambermaid had the key," we can represent the logical form for (i) and (ii) as:

(i) A implies B

(ii) NOT B implies NOT A

Naturally any two propositions that have the logical form of (i) and (ii) are equivalent to one another. For example, the following pairs of conditional thoughts are equivalent to one another as well:

"If Jorge is eligible to vote, then Jorge is at least 18 years of age."

"If Jorge is not at least 18 years of age, then Jorge is not eligible to vote."

"If Francesca is on the Dean's list, then Francesca has a 3.0 or better academic average."

"If Francesca does not have a 3.0 or better academic average, then Francesca is not on the Dean's list."

The following generalization is thus obviously true:

P implies Q

is always equivalent to

Not Q implies Not P

It is important to record that there are various other kinds of equivalent thoughts, and that as our study progresses we will enumerate several of them as pertinent to our aim for lucidity of thought. Some further examples of equivalent thoughts are the following:

117

I) "It's not the case that either Boston or Berkeley is in Texas."

"It's not the case that Boston is in Texas and it's not the case that Berkeley is in Texas."

The logical form of these two thoughts can be represented respectively as:

(i) Not (Either A or B)   A: Boston is in Texas
                            B. Berkeley is in Texas

(ii) Not A and Not B

The following generalization is thus obviously true:

Not (Either P or Q)

is always equivalent to

Not P and Not Q

II) "Khartoum is in Sudan and Addis Ababa is in Ethiopia."

"Addis Ababa is in Ethiopia and Khartoum is in Sudan."

The logical form of these two thoughts can be represented as:

(i) (A and B)   A: Khartoum is in Sudan
                   B: Addis Ababa is in Ethopia

(ii) (B and A)

The following generalization is thus obviously true:

(P and Q)

is always equivalent to

(Q and P)

118

SUMMARY

We will build upon the material that has been introduced in the analysis of the first chapter. The most important operation of human thought is probably generalization, which we will engage in considerable detail later. Almost as fundamental are: (i) the three basic logical operations having to do with "not," "or," and "If...then..," namely, Modus Tollens, Modus Ponens, and Disjunctive Syllogism, along with (ii) Universal Instantiation, and (iii) the confirmation/disconfirmation of hypotheses — of which modus tollens is a part.

All deductive reasoning, we have learned, depends upon structure or logical form, that is, upon patterns of reasoning from one or more particular thoughts to some other particular thought as a conclusion, where these thoughts are linked together by their structure and not their specific content.

The concept of structure or logical form thus also applies to particular thoughts themselves, as well as to patterns of reasoning. The thoughts, "If Wagga Wagga is in New South Wales, then Wagga Wagga is in Australia," and "If Juliet is 18, then Juliet is an eligible voter," both have the same logical form, no matter that they differ in their specific content.

We cannot too often re-iterate the point made in Section 5, that an argument can be unacceptable for basically one of two reasons: (1) the reasoning it employs is unacceptable, and (2) one or more of its premises is unacceptable. The distinction between validity/invalidity on the one hand and truth/falsity on the other applies to all forms of reasoning, whether deductive or not. In a valid deductive argument, the conclusion follows necessarily from the premises. Let us call this "deductive validity," and let us employ the term "cogent" to the various other forms of non-deductive, or inductive, arguments whose conclusions follow from their premises but not with deductive necessity. (As we develop the analysis of various forms of inductive reasoning, the difference between these forms of reasoning and deductive reasoning will become clear.)

Now, with these considerations in mind, let us lay down the following practical guidelines for the critical appraisal of arguments:

> We can always appraise a specific argument from the sole vantage of its reasoning to determine whether or not it is valid (or cogent), without at the same time troubling over the truth and falsity of its premises. We can always appraise a specific argument from the sole vantage of the truth and falsity of its premises, without troubling over the validity or

cogency of its reasoning. Whenever we appraise an argument to determine whether we ought to accept it and its conclusion, we must do both of these things. Arguments that have both valid or cogent reasoning and true premises, are sound arguments. Thus an argument fails to be sound, and we ought not to accept its conclusion, if either, (i) the reasoning it employs from premises to conclusion is not acceptable, or (ii) one or more of its premises is false.

STUDY AID

SOME BASIC KINDS OF THOUGHTS

NEGATIONS   Structure: Not (P)

Example: "Peking is not in India."

CONJUNCTIONS   Structure: (P and Q)

Example: "Managua is in Nicaragua and Tegucigalpa is in Honduras."

DISJUNCTIONS   Structure: (P or Q)

Example: "Tangiers is either in Morroco or Algeria."

CONDITIONALS   Structure: (If P, then Q)

Example: "If Tallin is in Estonia, then Tallin is in the U.S.S.R."

GENERALIZATIONS:*   Structure:

                              (For any X) (If X is F, then X is G)

Example: "All Students are intelligent."

*There are other forms of generalizations which we will treat in later sections.

DEDUCTIVE OPERATIONS OF THOUGHT

MODUS TOLLENS:

If P, then Q

Not Q
_____

Not P

MODUS PONENS:

If P, then Q

P
_____

Q

DISJUNCTIVE SYLLOGISM:

P or Q

Not P
_____

Q

P or Q

Not Q
_____

P

UNIVERSAL INSTANTIATION:

(For any x) (If x is F, then x is G)
_____

If a is F, then a is G

(where "a" is some individual entity)

I.   In the following examples, identify the deductive operations of thought (the deductive rules of inference) that are employed; either Modus Ponens, Modus Tollens, Disjunctive Syllogism, or Universal Instantiation. Note that more than one deductive operation may be employed in one example.

    (a) If the murderer had to have a key, then the chambermaid did it. The murderer did have to have a key. Therefore, the chambermaid did it.

    (b) Either the butler or Sylvester committed the murder. We can prove that Sylvester did not commit the murder. So it must be the butler who did.

    (c) Either the murder was committed after midnight and the butler did it or the murder was committed before midnight and the chambermaid did it. It's not true that the murder was committed after midnight and the butler did it. Therefore, the murder was committed before midnight and the chambermaid did it.

    (d) Anyone who is seriously studying logic will become smarter. If Helen is seriously studying logic, then she will become smarter.

    (e) If the murder was committed after midnight and the murderer had to have a key, then either the butler or the chambermid did it. The murder was committed after midnight and the murderer did have to have a key. Thus, either the chambermaid or the butler did it.

    (f) If either the butler or Sylvester committed the murder, then the murder must have been committed after midnight. The autopsy shows that the murder was not committed after midnight. So neither the butler nor Sylvester committed the murder.

    (g) If Sylvester committed the murder, then he had a strong motive to do so. If he had a strong motive to commit the murder, then that motive must have been greed. Sylvester did commit the murder. Thus, he did have a strong motive to do so. And we can conclude that this motive must have been greed.

(h) If Sylvester did not commit the murder, then either the butler or the chambermaid did it. If Sylvester did commit the murder, then he arrived at the Anderson home by midnight. But he did not arrive at the Anderson home by midnight. Thus, we can conclude that he did not commit the murder. Furthermore, we can conclude that either the butler or the chambermaid did.

(i) We know that Sylvester did not have a key, and we know that anyone who committed the murder had to have a key. It therefore, follows that if Sylvester committed the murder, he had to have a key. And it also follows that Sylvester did not commit the murder.

Extra Credit:

(j) The escape route of the robbers of Caesar's Palace in Las Vegas is either to Moapa or Lathrop Wells in the North or to Henderson or Sloan to the South. If they took the route through Moapa, then they had to proceed either to Alamo or to Santa Clara, (Utah). If they went through Lathrop Wells then they either had to double-back into Death Valley through Death Valley Junction or proceed further north to Beatty. They did not go South. They could not go through Lathrop Wells because the road was washed out. And the Utah State Troopers assure us that they did not enter Utah through Santa Clara. We can conclude, therefore, that they must have proceeded to the town of Alamo.

II. Give two examples each of valid deductive arguments consisting of:

(i) true premises and a true conclusion.

(ii) One false and one true premise, and a false conclusion.

(iii) one false and one true premise and a true conclusion.

(iv) two false premises and a false conclusion.

(v) two false premises and a true conclusion.

III. Identify which of the following contains an inconsistency and is subject to a reductio ad absurdum, and which is the disconfirmation of an hypothesis.

(i) A murder was committed in the Smith household, but the autopsy is not yet in. I suspect that Julio Sanchez did it, although he was identified as being at the cinema until midnight. The autopsy is now in and the coroner reports that the murder was committed near 11:00 P.M. So I conclude that Julio didn't do it after all.

(ii) No super-power should, for any reason, have a 1st Strike Nuclear Capacity, that is, the capacity to destroy another power out-right. Instead they should only have the defensive capacity to heavily damage in return any power that might attack them. The Russians seem to be moving toward a 1st Strike Nuclear Capacity, which, of course, in my view they should never do. If they do achieve a 1st Strike Capacity, the United States would be naive not to respond by doing so as well. In international politics one must be prepared to meet threat with equal threat if one is to survive.

(iii) Either Don Giovanni or Helga Schmidt or Reiko Matsumoto committed the murder. Helga and Reiko are both intelligent and attractive, and Don is intelligent too. We have established that Reiko could not have committed the murder because she was attending an art exhibit of the works of Henri Rousseau. We also know that the murderer must not be intelligent because he or she left the murder weapon at the scene of the crime. We have ruled out Helga because she has never had a weapon in her life. So we conclude that Don Giovanni must have commited the murder.

(iv) The suspects for the robbery of Caesar's Casino in Las Vegas left the robbery scene in a blue Cadillac. Although we put out an all-points bulletin, they were not apprehended anywhere in town. We thus assumed that they left town by one of the four major highways, and within five minutes of the robbery we had Highway Patrolmen in barricades on each of the four highways at points twenty miles outside of town. Several hours have passed and the robbery suspects have not been apprehended or seen. We think now that our first assumption was incorrect, and that the suspects are hiding discretely somewhere within the city of Vegas.

(v) I thought the factory's productivity declined by 3% last month because it was closed one working day for a holiday. I made the mistake of suggesting that explanation to my manager who pointed out to me, in no uncertain terms, that there was a working day holiday in each of the three previous months with no decline in productivity at all.

(vi) We know that either Horace or Brutus committed the murder and that the murderer had to enter through the second floor landing. Horace who is old and infirm only could have committed the murder if he entered through the back door on the first floor. If Brutus committed the murder, he had to have a key to the garage where a ladder that would reach to the second floor was customarily kept. But we have determined that Brutus did not have a key to the garage, and thus could not be the murderer. We conclude, therefore, that it must be Horace, who somehow entered through the back door on the first floor.

IV. Identify the deductive operations of thought employed in each step within the following arguments, along with the line or lines used as premises for each deduction. Employ the abbreviations; "M.T." for Modus Tollens, "M.P." for Modus Ponens, "D.S." for Disjunctive Syllogism, and "U.I." for Universal Instantiation.

(i) 1. Either the butler or the chambermaid committed the murder.

2. If the butler committed the murder, then he entered the mistress' bedroom after midnight.

3. If he entered the mistress' bedroom after midnight, then he had a key to the mistress' bedroom.

4. But the butler did not have a key to the mistress' bedroom.

---

5. The butler did not enter the mistress' bedroom after midnight.   (M.T., 3, 4)

6. The butler did not commit the murder.   (_____)

7. The chambermaid committed the murder.   (_____)

126

(ii) 1. Either there will be an East-West agreement over Europe or there will be a nuclear war.

2. If the Soviet Union continues its military build-up in Europe, then NATO will continue its military build-up too.

3. If NATO continues its military build-up, then France will not participate in that build-up.

4. If there is a successful East-West agreement over Europe, France must participate in NATO's military build-up.

5. Recent information proves that the Soviet Union will continue its military build-up in Europe.

---

6. NATO will continue its military build-up. (_____)

7. France will not participate in this build-up (_____)

8. There will not be a successful East-West agreement over Europe. (_____)

9. There will be a nuclear war. (_____)

(iii) 1. If China and the Soviet Union reach a detente, then the U.S. will cease to be the dominant center of military power.

2. If the U.S. ceases to be the dominant center of military power, then world tensions will cease.

3. And, if world tensions cease, then all of the European Countries will prosper.

4. France is a European country.

5. China and the Soviet Union will certainly reach a detente.

---

6. The U.S. will cease to be the dominant center of military power. (_____)

7. World tensions will cease. (_____)

8. All of the European countries will prosper. (_____)

9. If France is a European country, then France will prosper. (_____)

10. France will prosper. (_____)

(iv) 1. God is omnipotent.

2. God is omniscient.

3. If God is omniscient, then God can conceive anything that can be conceived.

4. If God is omnipotent, then anything God can conceive God can create.

5. If God is omnipotent, then anything God can create, God can destroy.

6. An indestructible entity can be conceived. (It is simply an entity that has the property that it can never be destroyed.)

---

7. God can conceive anything that can be conceived.   (_____)

8. Specifically, if an indestructible entity can be conceived, it can be conceived by God.   (_____)

9. An indestructible entity can be conceived by God.   (_____)

10. Anything God can conceive God can create.   (_____)

11. If God can conceive an indestructible entity, Then God can create an indestructible entity.   (_____)

12. God can create an indestructible entity.   (_____)

13. But anything God can create, God can destroy.   (_____)

14. Specifically, If God can create an indestructible entity, then God can destroy an indestructible entity.   (_____)

15. God can destroy an indestructible entity.   (_____)

(But by definition, God cannot destroy an indestructible entity. (15) is a contradiction. The argument is a reductio ad absurdum proving that the premises 1-6 are inconsistent with one another.)

128

CHAPTER II: ANALYSIS

INTRODUCTION

Logic is sometimes conceived and taught as a critical method for appraising arguments that have already been advanced. But obviously, in practice, we employ our reasoning capacities first and foremost to create arguments and chains of reasoning, that is, to actively pursue a sequence of related thoughts to some conclusion. Naturally, the creative development of a chain of reasoning is a dynamic one in which we also sometimes pause to critique our reasoning in the very midst of advancing it; "Perhaps I jumped too quickly to that conclusion," "There must be an alternative here I have overlooked," "Perhaps the assumptions with which I began were inadequate," etc.

We will call the creation or development of a line of argument or reasoning, "Creative Reasoning." This label is quite appropriate and no one should be intimidated by it. You and I effortlessly create many and various chains of reasoning every day to determine where we have misplaced our car keys, to re-arrange a schedule of activities, to predict the grade we will make in a course, to explain why someone behaved in the way he or she did, etc.

The central emphasis of this section will be the nature and role of hypothetical thinking. Creative reasoning almost always involves the use of hypotheses. Hypotheses are themselves often constituted of conditional thoughts, i.e. thoughts that we assert to be true on the condition that something else is true, or will become true. Moreover, as we have seen, the confirmation and disconfirmation of hypotheses essentially involves conditional thoughts linking hypotheses to their consequences: "If the hypothesis is true, then such-and-such consequence must follow."

The use of hypothetical thinking can, of course, be excessively speculative. We can genuinely believe in all sorts of hypotheses for which there is no rational warrant, sometimes with deleterious effects upon our lives. We can also substitute idle hypothesizing for action. Thus, although it is true that hypothetical thinking is one of our outstanding intellectual capacities, it is also one of our most common sources of intellectual weakness. We will therefore treat it not only from the vantage of its constructive use, under the heading of creative logic, but also from the vantage of its misuse, under the heading of fallacious reasoning.

129

It is important to observe that hypothetical thinking characteristically employs both deductive and non-deductive, or inductive, methods of reasoning. We employ deductive reasoning, for example, in the elimination of alternative hypotheses by disjunctive syllogism. We employ a non-deductive, or inductive, mode of reasoning, on the other hand, when confirming an hypothesis to be true on the grounds that some consequences it predicted have proved to be true. In this section, we will begin the analysis of patterns of inductive reasoning to be followed in succeeding sections with two particularly important forms of inductive reasoning; reasoning by analogy and inductive generalization.

We will also be introduced in this section to the first group of fallacies, among a number of fallacies, that we will treat in this study. This will serve to direct our attention to various ways in which we reason poorly and gullibly accept erroneous beliefs.

1.   A SIMPLE HYPOTHESIS: Creative Reasoning

After observing that Miss Ellie's room is at the rear of the house near the library, Kemp says:

"So that if someone entered through the front door, and proceeded immediately up the stairs in the front hallway, it would be unlikely if you heard him at all."

Kemp's thought has the logical form of a conditional, "If P, then Q," or more precisely, it has the form of a conditional whose antecedent is a conjunction, "If P and Q, then R." Kemp is engaged in hypothetical thinking which we can represent as follows:

(i)   If someone entered through the front door and proceeded immediately up the stairs in the front hallway, it would be unlikely if you heard him at all. (An hypothesis and one of its consequences)

(ii) Someone did enter through the front door and did proceed immediately up the stairs in the front hallway.   (hypothesis)

It would be unlikely if you heard him at all. (The consequence of the hypothesis obtained by modus ponens)

2.   AN HYPOTHESIS TO EXPLAIN AN UNUSUAL EVENT BY AN UNUSUAL CAUSE: Creative Reasoning

"No. I'm sure I didn't hear that sound. I would have suffered a fright if I did. I would have thought somebody was sneaking into the house."

Miss Ellie hypothesizes a cause for the occurrence of such a sound. An unusual event — in the context of the household activities — is explained by an unusual cause — in the context of the household activities. It is assumed that the sound is the effect of the movement of the French doors.

The cause of the movement of the French doors is specifically attributed to human agency, and human agency, "up to no good."

"Then you've never heard that sound late at night before?" Kemp wants to have this thought confirmed. He reasons that it is implicit in Miss Ellie's thinking:

> If there are previous occasions on which Miss Ellie heard that sound late at night — perhaps someone in the household, or even the cat, occasionally entered the house in that fashion — then she would not immediately hypothesize an unusual and threatening cause.
>
> She did hypothesize an unusual and threatening cause.
>
> ---
>
> Therefore, there are no previous occasions on which Miss Ellie heard that sound late at night. (Modus Tollens)

Kemp's reasoning here leads him to the hypothesis that she had not heard that sound late at night before. He then explicitly requests Miss Ellie to confirm that fact. Instead she denies it, observing that it admits of one exception.

3. THE PARTIAL CONFIRMATION OF AN HYPOTHESIS: A FORM OF INDUCTIVE REASONING and THE FALLACY OF AFFIRMING THE CONSEQUENT

There are various forms of arguments in which the conclusion does not follow necessarily from the premises, as in valid deductive reasoning, but instead is inferred as only likely, or very likely. All of these forms of arguments and the reasoning employed within them are called "inductive." Thus, the term "inductive reasoning" is a catch-all category term covering every variety of acceptable reasoning that is not deductive. In a valid deductive argument it is logically impossible for the premises to be true and the conclusion false: having true premises and a false conclusion leads to a strict contradiction. In contrast, in an acceptable inductive argument, it is only improbable that the premises are true and the conclusion false. It is unlikely but not impossible for a sound inductive argument containing true premises and good reasoning to have a false conclusion. Thus, whenever we have in our possession a sound inductive argument, we are warranted in believing that the conclusion is likely, but not warranted in believing that it is certain.

131

It is a curious fact that one and the same pattern of reasoning is both the essential pattern employed in the confirmation of hypotheses and also an identifiable fallacy of deductive reasoning, "The Fallacy of Affirming the Consequent." There is a lesson to be learned here. Let us consider an example:

> "Secondly, you are one of a few obvious suspects for this murder. In carrying through with my duty I have had to pursue you as a suspect! And I might add, that in so doing I have discovered that your alibi isn't worth a straw in the wind."

Kemp insists here that he must genuinely entertain the hypothesis, as a possibility, that Sylvester is the murderer. In pursuing that hypothesis he has discovered that Sylvester's alibi does not stand up. At one level, Kemp's hypothetical thinking can be represented as follows:

If Sylvester is innocent, then his alibi will stand up.

His alibi does not stand up.

Sylvester is not innocent. (Modus Tollens)

However, this representation must be misleading since Kemp does not believe that Sylvester is guilty, but thinks that he is "probably" innocent. His thinking can be more subtly and accurately rendered as follows:

Kemp thinks the hypothesis: 'Sylvester is the murderer.'

He then infers a number of likely consequences that follow from this hypothesis, such as:

(a) Sylvester draped the Templar Cloak over the victim's body.

(b) Sylvester had a compelling motive for the murder.

(c) Sylvester's alibi locating him away from the Anderson home near midnight is false.

Etc.

Specifically, we can represent Kemp's thinking about Sylvester's alibi as follows:

(i) If Sylvester is the murderer (hypothesis), then his alibi is false (consequence).

(ii) His alibi is false.

Conclusion: (ii) is a *partial confirmation of the hypothesis.*

The logical form of the partial confirmation of an hypothesis is therefore the following:

If Hypothesis (H1), then Consequence (c1)

Consequence (c1)

_____

(c1) is a partial confirmation of (H1)

It is extremely important to record the fact that from: (i) If Sylvester is the murderer, then his alibi is false, and (ii) His alibi is false, we cannot validly deduce, as a necessary conclusion, that Sylvester is the murderer. To believe that we can is to commit the _Fallacy of Affirming the Consequent_, which has the following form:

If P, then Q   (premise)

Q   (premise)

_____

P   (conclusion)

Consider the following examples of this fallacy:

If N.Y. City is in Georgia, then N.Y. City is in the U.S.

N.Y. City is in the U.S.

_____

N.Y. City is in Georgia.

If Steve Martin is the President of the U.S., then he is at least 35 years of age.

Steve Martin is at least 35 years of age.

_____

Steve Martin is the President of the U.S.

Since it is impossible for the premises to be true and the conclusion false in a valid form of deductive reasoning, it follows that this form of reasoning is not deductively valid. Thus we can never deduce that an hypothesis is true by showing that some consequence following from it is true, or even that several consequences that follow from it are true. Let us consider one further example: suppose we hypothesize that the butler committed the murder and observe that from this assumption it follows that: (a) the murder was committed after midnight — since the butler only returned to the mansion at that time — and (b) the butler possessed a key to the mistress' bedroom. And suppose that the autopsy reveals that the murder was committed at approximately 1:00 A.M., and that the butler did possess a key to the mistress' bedroom. These facts would constitute corroborating evidence for the hypothesis. But obviously they would not constitute a deductive proof. It is possible that Sylvester also returned at midnight, also possessed a key to the mistress' bedroom door, is as likely a suspect as the butler, and indeed, actually committed the murder.

Since the phrase, "confirm an hypothesis to be true," is sufficiently vague to admit interpretation as, "deductively prove an hypothesis to be true," it is advisable to use some such terminology as "partial" confirmation.[1]

With this consideration in mind, let us now state a practical rule for hypothetical thinking, explicitly contrasting the confirmation of hypotheses on the one hand and the disconfirmation on the other.

IF A CONSEQUENCE OF AN HYPOTHESIS PROVES FALSE, THEN, BY MODUS TOLLENS, THE HYPOTHESIS, AT LEAST IN PART, IS FALSE.

IF A CONSEQUENCE OF AN HYPOTHESIS PROVES TRUE, THEN THIS COUNTS AS ONE PARTIAL CONFIRMATION OF THE HYPOTHESIS (BUT NOT A DEDUCTIVE PROOF OF IT).

4. HYPOTHETICAL SYLLOGISM: A Deductive Operation of Thought (Creative Logic)

"No. Nothing. If the autopsy is correct, the crime was committed very near the hour of midnight, a considerable time before I returned."

Two conditional thoughts, linked logically together, are presupposed here:

(i) If the autopsy was correct, then the crime was committed near midnight.

(ii) If the crime was committed near midnight, then I, Sylvester, am not the murderer (because I had not yet returned).

(i) and (ii) taken together imply, by HYPOTHETICAL SYLLOGISM:

(iii) If the autopsy was correct, then I, Sylvester, am not the murderer.

134

The logical form of HYPOTHETICAL SYLLOGISM is:

IF P, THEN Q

IF Q, THEN R
_____
IF P, THEN R

(If a first thought implies a second thought and that same second thought implies a third thought, then that first thought implies that third thought.)

Obviously, the pattern of reasoning employed in hypothetical syllogism need not be limited to two premises and a conclusion. We could also have, for example, the following:

IF P, THEN Q

IF Q, THEN R

IF R, Then S
_____
IF P, THEN S

We will therefore extend the label, "hypothetical syllogism," beyond its ordinary use by logicians, to apply to any chain of reasoning such as the above, no matter how many premises are involved. Hypothetical syllogism is an extremely important mode of hypothetical-deductive thinking. Our capacity to think conditional thoughts is critical to our rationality, and creating and following through a chain of conditional thoughts linked together logically by hypothetical syllogism is a common use of reasoning. We are probably not fully aware of the prevalence of its use, because it does not always occur explicitly. Consider, for example, the following:

"And no one heard you come in either?"

"No. Unfortunately no. Or I wouldn't be subject to your grilling now."

One natural way to represent the thoughts here expressed by Sylvester treats hypothetical syllogism as presupposed:

If someone had heard me enter, they would have testified that it was after 1:00 A.M.

135

If that someone had testified that I entered after 1:00 A.M., I would not now be subject to your (Kemp's) grilling.

If someone had heard me enter, then I would not now be subject to your (Kemp's) grilling.

Or consider another example:

"If I take the earlier flight, I can meet with George, who might suggest a way out of my present financial difficulties, and perhaps keep me from losing my car."

We can faithfully reconstruct the thoughts expressed here by the following chain of conditionals:

1. If I take the earlier flight, then I can meet with George.

2. If I can (do) meet with George, then George might suggest a way out of my present financial difficulties.

3. If George suggests a way out of my present financial difficulties, then perhaps that will keep me from losing my car.

We can deduce and make fully explicit what is implied in this chain of conditional thoughts by two applications of hypothetical syllogism:

If I take the earlier flight, then George might suggest a way out of my present financial difficulties. (Hypothetical Syllogism, 1,2)

If I take the earlier flight, then perhaps that will keep me from losing my car. (Hypothetical Syllogism, 1,2,3)

Observe also the use of hypothetical syllogism in the following:

"Of course! What sort of detective do you take me to be. If Kemp is intelligent, he has investigated Sylvester's alibi. And if he has investigated Sylvester's alibi, he has known these facts all along. — It is obvious that you underrate my intelligence."

Kemp here links two conditional thoughts together:

1. If Kemp is intelligent, then he has investigated Sylvester's alibi.

2. If Kemp has investigated Sylvester's alibi, then he has known these facts all along.

Kemp then reconstructs Sherlock's thinking as follows:

136

3. Kemp has not known these facts all along. (premise)

4. If Kemp is intelligent, then he has known these facts all along. (Hypothetical Syllogism, 1,2)

5. Kemp is not intelligent. (Modus Tollens, 3,4)

The logical form of this argument, and therefore of any argument similar to it in logical form, is the following:

Let:
"A": Kemp is intelligent.
"B": Kemp has investigated Sylvester's alibi.
"C": Kemp has known these facts all along.

1. If A, then B

2. If B, then C

3. Not C
———————
4. If A, then C (Hypothetical Syllogism 1,2)

5. Not A (Modus Tollens 3,4)

Note that there is an alternative way to deduce, "Not C," from premises 1,2,3; using two applications of modus tollens:

1. If A, then B

2. If B, then C

3. Not C
———————
4. Not B   (Modus Tollens 2,3)

5. Not A   (Modus Tollens 1,4)

5. ALTERNATIVE HYPOTHESES AND DISJUNCTIVE SYLLOGISM: Creative Logic

"Do you have a key to the mistress' bedroom, Monsieur de Molay?"

"No. I do not."

"And do you Mr. Richards?"

"Certainly not."

"And Miss Ellie, what about you? Do you have that key?"

"Yes, you know I do — but I am innocent, and can prove it."

Kemp, for the moment, is proceeding on the hypothesis that either Miss Ellie or Mr. Richards or Monsieur de Molay is the murderer. Or to put this differently, he simultaneously entertains three alternative hypotheses: the hypothesis that Miss Ellie is the murderer, the hypothesis that Mr. Richards is the murderer, and the hypothesis that Monsieur de Molay is the murderer.

He also hypothesizes that the murderer must have the key to the bedroom door:

(For any x) (If x is the murderer, then x has the key.)

Kemp applies universal instantiation to this generalization, and obtains:

If Monsieur de Molay is the murderer (hypothesis), then Monsieur de Molay has the key (consequence).

But de Molay says that he does not have the key, which (if true) implies, by modus tollens, that the hypothesis that he is the murderer is false.

Kemp now applies universal instantiation again to the generalization, obtaining:

If Richards is the murderer (hypothesis), then Richards has the key (consequence).

But Richards also denies having the key, which (if true) implies by modus tollens that the hypothesis that he is the murderer is false. By a process of elimination, using an extended or double application of disjunctive syllogism, only Miss Ellie remains:

Either Miss Ellie or Richards or de Molay committed the murder.

de Molay did not commit the murder and Richards did not commit the murder.
_____
Miss Ellie did commit the murder. (disjunctive syllogism)

Kemp continues further with his line of reasoning, utilizing universal instantiation for a third time:

If Miss Ellie is the murderer (hypothesis), then Miss Ellie has the key. (consequence)

Miss Ellie is off the hook, like de Molay and Richards, if she does not have the key; but she does. The fact that she has the key, of course, does not prove that she is the murderer. To believe that it does is to commit the fallacy of affirming the consequence. Rather, her having the key is only a partial confirmation of the hypothesis that she is the murderer.

Naturally, the earlier deductive argument which employs disjunctive syllogism still holds: On the assumption that either she or de Molay or Richards is the murderer and that de Molay and Richards are not, it logically follows that she is the murderer. She is quite clear about this implication, and for this reason responds, "Yes. I do.   (have the key) You know I do. But I am innocent and can prove it."

6.   BIASED BELIEF:

"You assume that Sylvester was on that train, because he's your client."

Kemp contests Sherlock's belief that Sylvester was on that train by challenging the grounds, or lack of grounds, for that belief.

"Because he's your client," suggests that Sherlock believes Sylvester was on that train, not for any good reason, but solely because of a bias in favor of his client. In Kemp's view, Sherlock has failed to be objective; he believes, but without any rational grounds for his belief.

Let us consider a few examples of biased beliefs in the arena of beliefs about persons. Someone informs us that George, who excels us and whom we dislike, has done something wrong. The action is out of character for George and the rumor is implausible on the face of it, but we believe it nevertheless. In fact, George did not commit the action and because of our bias we have an erroneous belief. In an opposite case, someone whom we very much like is reported to have done something wrong, and the evidence for his or her having done so is very good. Nevertheless, we remain adamant in our belief that the wrong was never committed. In fact the wrong was committed and because of our bias we have an erroneous belief.

There are many varieties of biased belief. Consider only the biased beliefs we have in regard to ourselves. Or consider how bias affects our appraisal of arguments. This last is a subtle matter because bias can enter either: (i) at the point of the premises, or (ii) at the point of the conclusion. Let us reflect upon each of these in order.

(i) <u>Bias in regard to premises</u>.

Sometimes we believe that a premise of an argument is true because of a bias, when it is not, and are led then to accept the conclusion as true, when it is not. For example, suppose that we ourselves are industrious and hard-working, that we frown upon persons who are lazy, and that we believe that persons who can work, but who won't, should not receive welfare. And suppose that someone presents us with the following argument:

"You know that except for the severely handicapped, all of those people on welfare could find work, but are too lazy to do so. I believe, and I think you do too, that persons who can work, but who are too lazy to do so, should not be given welfare out of our hard earned tax dollars. So therefore, I think you'll agree with me that we ought to do away with all welfare except for the severely handicapped."

If we aren't sufficiently cautious our bias might lead us to accept the first premise of this argument and thus also the conclusion. Undoubtedly there are persons on welfare who could find work, but are too lazy to do so. However, even if their numbers constitute a significant minority, or even a majority, the premise is not true, and thus we ought not to accept the conclusion as true.

This argument, it should be observed, can be deceptively persuasive because it is deductively valid. It has the form:

(x) (If x is a person on welfare who is not severely handicapped, then x can find work, but is too lazy to do so.)

(x) (If x can find work but is too lazy to do so, then x should not be on welfare.)

(x) (If x is a person on welfare who is not severely handicapped, then x should not be on welfare.)

(Note: We will analyze this particular deductive operation of thought in a later chapter.)

(ii) <u>Bias in regard to the conclusion</u>.

Let us suppose that Kemp is so biased against Sylvester because of Sylvester's condescending attitude that he wants to believe, and does believe, that he is guilty. He might then accept the following argument:

140

"If Sylvester's alibi does not at first stand up, then that will prove that he is guilty and that the case can be closed. We have just discovered that Sylvester's alibi does not at first stand up, and therefore have proved that Sylvester is guilty and that the case can be closed."

Kemp's bias for the conclusion would have misled him into accepting a bad argument as a good argument. His bias for the conclusion would have led him to accept the poor reasoning couched in the first premise, "If Sylvester's alibi does not a first stand up, then that will prove that he is guilty and that the case can be closed." The fact that Sylvester's alibi does not at first stand up is not by itself sufficient grounds for a conclusive determination of his guilt and for the termination of all further inquiry. Of course, as a reasonable detective who keeps his likes and dislikes under restraint, Kemp would not accept this argument. Indeed, he thinks instead that Sylvester is probably innocent.

7.   THE FALLACY OF DENYING THE ANTECEDENT

"Sylvester is clearly intelligent. If he were guilty of the murder, he would never have proposed an alibi that would fall apart so easily — a train arrival totally at odds with the train schedule. So. He must be innocent."

Sherlock's argument here addressed to Kemp can be represented as follows:

(Given the assumption that Sylvester is intelligent)

If Sylvester is guilty of the murder, then Sylvester will have a good alibi.

Sylvester does not have a good alibi.

_____

Sylvester is not guilty of the murder.

It is important to record that the following is not a valid deductive operation of thought:

If Sylvester has a good alibi, then Sylvester is innocent of the murder.

Sylvester does not have a good alibi.

_____

Sylvester is not innocent (is guilty) of the murder.

The logical form of this pattern of reasoning, which logicians label, the fallacy of denying the antecedent is:

If P, then Q

Not P
_____

Not Q

We can prove that this form of reasoning is not deductively valid by exhibiting a concrete example of it containing true premises and a false conclusion. Here are two such examples:

If Steve Martin, the comedian, is a candidate for the presidency (of the U.S.), then he is a citizen of the United States.

Steve Martin, the comedian, is not a candidate for the presidency (of the U.S.).
_____

Steve Martin, the comedian, is not a citizen of the United States.

If Washington D.C. is in Texas, then Washington D.C. is in the United States.

Washington D.C. is not in Texas.
_____

Washington D.C. is not in the United States.

8. THE LOGICAL FORM OF A COMPLEX THOUGHT

"If no one entered the front door, and Sylvester was not yet home, and only you, Miss Ellie, and Mr. Ricahrds, and Monsieur de Molay, were within the house...Do you realize...that one of you must be the murderer?"

In pursuit of our aim of lucidity, let us analyze the logical form of this complex thought. It is a conditional thought with a complex antecedent and a complex consequent alleged to follow from that antecedent. The antecedent is a conjunction and the consequent is a disjunction.

Let "F" :   "Someone entered the front door."

   "S" :   "Sylvester was at home."

142

"E" :   "Miss Ellie was within the house (at the time of the murder)."

"R" :   Richards was within the house (at the time of the murder)."

"G" :   "Miss Ellie is the murderer."

"H" :   "Mr. Richards is the murderer."

"I" :   "De Molay is the murderer."

Utilizing this scheme of abbreviation, we can render the logical form of Kemp's thought as follows:

IF (Not F and Not S) and (E and R and M) THEN (G or H or I)

I. **BASIC KINDS OF THOUGHTS:**

(i) A <u>conditional</u> thought has the logical form:

"If __A__ , then __B__ ."

A: "Antecedent" In ordinary English the following
B: "Consequent" expressions are often used
equivalently to "if":

"on the assumption that"
"provided that"
"given that"
"on the condition that"

(ii) A <u>disjunction</u> has the following logical form:

"Either__A__ or __B__ ."

A: "Left Disjunct" Note that we extend the term
B: "Right Disjunct" "disjunction" to apply also to
either-or assertions involving
three (3) or more alternatives.

(iii) A <u>conjunction</u> has the following logical form:

" __A__ AND __B__ "

A: "Left Conjunct"
B: "Right Conjunct"

(iv) A <u>negation</u> has the logical form:

Not __A__

Reminder: "Neither A nor B" can be rendered either as the negation
of a disjunction:

"Not (A or B)"

or as the conjunction of two negated thoughts.

"Not A and Not B"

II. THREE FALLACIES:

(i)   The Fallacy of Affirming the Consequent

If P, then Q

$$\frac{Q}{P}$$

(ii)   The Fallacy of Denying the Antecedent

If P, then Q

$$\frac{\text{Not P}}{\text{Not Q}}$$

(iii)   The Fallacy of Inconsistency

Affirming that some assertion P is true

and

Affirming that his assertion P is not true

HYPOTHETICAL REASONING

("H_1": "Hypothesis H_1")

("c_1": "Consequence c_1)

DEDUCTIVE

1) The Disconfirmation of
an Hypothesis (Modus Tollens)

   (i) H_1 implies c_1

   (ii)   Not c_1
_____

      Not H_1

2) Deducing a chain of Consequences from an Hypothesis

   (Hypothetical Syllogism)

   (i) H_1 implies c_1

   (ii) c_1 implies c_2

   (iii) c_2 implies c_3
_____

      H_1 implies c_3

3) Eliminating an Alternative
Hypothesis   (Disjunctive
Syllogism)
   (i)   Either H_1 or H_2

   (ii)   Not H_1
_____

   H_2

INDUCTIVE

1) The Partial Confirmation of
an Hypothesis

   (i) H_1 implies c_1

   (ii) c_1
_____

      c_1 is a partial
      confirmation of H_1

2) Hypothesizing the cause of
some phenomenon or event

   (This will be treated in
   detail in Chapter VIII.)

3) Hypothesizing a Generalization
by Inductive Generalization

   (This will be treated in detail
   in Chapters IV & V.)

4) Hypothesizing a Conclusion
Based on an Analogy

   (This will be treated in
   detail in Chapter V.)

146

STUDY MATERIALS FOR CHAPTER II

I. Identify which of the following is:

a conditional

A disjunction

a conjunction

a negation

Note that more than one kind of thought may occur in any one sentence. For example:

"If either Beulah or Paula fall in love with Mortimer, then Mortimer will be ecstatic."

(This is a conditional thought whose antecedent is a disjunction.)

"If neither the Soviet Union nor the U.S. disarms its nuclear misselry, then China will not disarm and Japan will significantly increase its military budget."

(This is a conditional proposition. Its antecedent is the negation of a disjunction. Its consequent is a conjunction, whose left conjunct is a negation.)

(a) Ashley loves artichokes and Adelaide does too."

(b) "If you do not fall in love, then you will not be happy."

(c) "Either philosophers will become kings and we'll have peace or we'll annihilate ourselves in a nuclear war."

(d) "If each year hundreds of millions of children are born from malnutritioned mothers and yachts are still popular items, then our ethic needs to be revised."

(e) "If Helmudt takes out Greta and Helga does not find out, then Helga won't be angry."

(f) "Reykjavik is not in Greenland."

(g) "If Saskatchewan is either in Canada or Australia, and it's not in Australia, then it must be in Canada."

(h)   "Prudence will marry Narayan if he gives up his religion."

(i)   "If neither Felipe nor Guillermo marry Magdelena, then she will marry Elmer."

(j)   "Either Don Juan will marry Fannie or if he doesn't, he'll marry Flora instead."

II. FALLACIES

Identify which of the following is; (i) The Fallacy of Affirming the Consequent, (ii) The Fallacy of Denying the Antecedent, (iii) The Fallacy of Inconsistency. Note that one example may contain more than one fallacy.

(a)   If my boyfriend Vasily is dating Grushenka on the sly, then Grushenka, feeling guilty, will be particularly nice to me. Grushenka has been particularly nice to me. So I know that Vasily has been dating her on the sly.

(b)   Some wealthy persons are unhappy. But I wouldn't greatly object to being wealthy myself. For anyone who is wealthy has lots of friends. And no one who has lots of friends is really unhappy.

(c)   If the robbery suspects exited the city to the North, then they must have traveled by car. It is certain now that they did not exit to the North. So they must not have traveled by car.

(d)   Some people wonder whether the Russians are really determined to take over the world. I believe that we can prove conclusively that they are. Certainly if they are, we should expect to find them attempting to wield their power in various parts of the world. And we do! They are in control of Eastern Europe. They cause border disputes with the Chinese, whom they would like to control. They side with the Arabs against Israel in the Middle East, and they meddle in South-East Asia every chance they can get. If that's not conclusive proof, I don't know what is.

(e)   If the French are the greatest connoisseurs of fine cuisine, then they must be expert at sauces. However, my friend Gloria, who is a very good cook, pointed out to me that it is the Chinese, not the French, who are the greatest connoisseurs in the world. They were even the originators of spaghetti. So I guess the French aren't expert at sauces after all.

148

(f)   The U.S. is a major national power. If the U.S. does not disarm
        then World War III is inevitable. But unfortunately, no major
        national power, including Russia, will choose to disarm. We
        therefore have only one alternative, namely, to move beyond a
        world divided into separate nation states to world government.
        Fortunately, because this alternative of world government does
        exist, World War III is not strictly inevitable, even if it still
        remains very likely.

(g)   Recife is somewhere in South America. If it's in Uruguay, then
        it must be near or on the East Coast, since no part of Uruguay is
        more than 350 miles from the coast. But after checking a
        friend's map of Uruguay, I have discovered that it's not in
        Uruguay at all. So it follows that it cannot be on or near the
        East Coast.

(h)   Humanity is in deep trouble. We are presently far too negligent
        in our relationship to other living beings. If we continue to be
        negligent in this way, then we will disappear as a species once
        and forever from this planet. Personally, however, I do not
        think that we are that short-sighted and will continue our
        negligence to other life forms. Thus, I conclude that we will not
        disappear as a species, but will continue viably far into the
        distant future.

III. Identify the deductive operations in each step within the following
     arguments.   Employ   the   abbreviation,   "H.S."   for   Hypothetical
     Syllogism.

(a)   (1)   The escape route of the Robbers of Caesar's Palace in Las
                Vegas is either to Moapa or Lathrop Wells in the North or
                to Henderson or Sloan to the South.

        (2)   If they took the route through Moapa, then they had to
                proceed either to Alamo or to Santa Clara (Utah).

        (3)   If they went through Lathrop Wells then they either had to
                double-back into Death Valley through Death Valley
                Junction or proceed further North to Beatty.

        (4)   We have determined that they did not go South.

        (5)   We also know that they could not go through Lathrop
                Wells because the road is washed out.

        (6)   And the Utah State Troopers assure us that they did not
                enter Utah through Santa Clara.

149

(7)   The robbers escape route is either through
Moapa or Lathrop Wells.   (_____)

(8)   The robbers did escape through Moapa.   (_____)

(9)   And thus they either went through
Alamo or Santa Clara.   (_____)

(10) And we can conclude, finally, that they
went through Alamo.   (_____)

(b)   (1)   If a third world war between Russia and the U.S. is to be avoided, then either Russia or the U.S. must disarm its nuclear misselry.

(2)   If a third world war between Russia and the U.S. is not avoided, then if this war is a nuclear war, Russia and the U.S. will be destroyed and China will emerge the dominant world nation.

(3)   And if Russia and the U.S. are destroyed and China emerges as the dominant world nation, there will be world socialism.

(4)   In fact, neither Russia nor the U.S. will disarm its nuclear misselry.

(5)   Moreover, if a third world war between Russia and the U.S. is not avoided, then this world war will be a nuclear war.

---

(6)   A third world war between Russia and the
U.S. will not be avoided.   (_____)

(7)   This third world war will be a nuclear war. (_____)

(8)   If this third world war is a nuclear war,
Russia and the U.S. will be destroyed and
China will emerge the dominant world
nation.   (_____)

(9)   Russia and the U.S. will be destroyed and
China will emerge the dominant world
nation.   (_____)

(10) There will be world socialism.   (_____)

(c) (1) God is perfect.

(2) If God is perfect, then anything God creates is perfect.

(3) If the world is perfect, then evil does not exist in it.

(4) God created the world.

---

(5) Anything God creates is perfect. (＿＿＿＿)

(6) If God created the world, then the
world is perfect. (＿＿＿＿)

(7) If God created the world, then evil
does not exist in it. (＿＿＿＿)

(8) Evil does not exist in the world. (＿＿＿＿)

(d) Consider the following argument intended to prove:

"IF GOD SUFFERS CHANGE, THEN GOD IS NOT PERFECT."

Note that this is equivalent to:

"IF GOD IS PERFECT, THEN GOD DOES NOT SUFFER CHANGE."

This latter proposition is argued in the Second Book of Plato's *Republic*, and reproduced in George Boole's, *An Investigation of Laws of Thought*.

Suppose that God does suffer change. If he does then he must be changed either by himself or by some entity other than himself. But if God changed himself, he would change himself to a worse state, and if God acts willingly, he would not change himself to a worse state. And God does act willingly. So God does not change himself. And therefore God must be changed by some entity other than himself. But this leads to the following difficulty. For if God is changed by some entity other than himself, then he is not perfect. And thus we are forced to conclude that God is not perfect.

State the deductive operations and premises employed in the following argument. Nos. 3, 7, 8, 9, 11.

151

(1) God suffers change.   (premise)

(2) If God suffers change, then God is changed
     either by himself or by some entity other
     than himself.   (premise)

(3) God is changed either by himself or by some
     entity other than himself.   (_____)

(4) If God changed himself, he would change to
     a worse state.   (premise)

(5) If God acts willingly, he would not change
     himself to a worse state.   (premise)

(6) God acts willingly.   (premise)

(7) Thus he would not change himself to
     a worse state   (_____)

(8) And thus God does not change himself.   (_____)

(9) And thus God is changed by some entity other
     than himself.   (_____)

(10) If God is changed by some entity other than
     himself, then God is not perfect.   (premise)

(11) God is not perfect.   (_____)

Plato's argument in *The Republic*, intended to show that god is immutable (that the gods are immutable), is the following:

"Now what of this for a second principle? Do you think of a god as a sort of magician who might, for his own purposes, appear in various shapes, now actually passing into a number of different forms, now deluding us into believing he has done so; or is his nature simple and of all things the least likely to depart from its proper form?

I cannot say offhand.

Well, if a thing passes out of its proper form, must not the change come either from within or from some outside cause?

Yes.

Is it not true, then that things in the most perfect condition are the least affected by changes from outside? Take the effect on the body of food and drink or of exertion, or the effect of sunshine and wind on a plant; the healthiest and strongest suffer the least change. Again, the bravest and wisest spirit is least disturbed by external influence. Even manufactured things — furniture, houses, clothes — suffer least from wear and tear when they are well made and in good condition. So this immunity to change from outside is characteristic of anything which, thanks to art or nature or both, is in a satisfactory state.

That seems true.

But surely the state of the divine nature must be perfect in every way, and would therefore be the last thing to suffer transformations from any outside cause.

Yes.

Well then, would a god change or alter himself?

If he changes at all, it can only be in that way.

Would it be a change for the better or for the worse?

It could only be for the worse; for we cannot admit any imperfection in divine goodness or beauty.

True; and that being so, do you think Adeimantus, that anyone, god or man, would deliberately make himself worse in any respect?

That is impossible.

Then a god cannot desire to change himself. Being as perfect as he can be, every god, it seems, remains simply and for ever in his own form.

That is the necessary conclusion." (2)

IV. Deduce the conclusions in the following arguments, utilizing modus ponens, modus tollens, disjunctive syllogism, universal instantiation, and hypothetical syllogism.

    (a)   (Note: This is an argument that was sometimes advanced in the medieval period. Revelations: Chapter I, Verse 7:
           "Behold he is coming with the clouds
           And every eye will see him...")

        Deduce: There is no person who lives on the underside of the earth.

Premises:

(1) If there is a person who lives on the underside of the earth, then there is a person unable to see Christ descend from heaven at his second coming.

(2) But there is no person unable to see Christ descend from heaven at his second coming.

(b) Deduce: The chambermaid committed the murder.

Premises:

(1) Either the butler or the chambermaid committed the murder.

(2) Whoever committed the murder had to have a key.
(For any x) (If x committed the murder, then x had a key.)

(3) The butler did not have a key.

(c) Deduce: The county will prosper.

Premises:

(1) If Smith is not a candidate, then Harris will certainly win.

(2) Anyone who is a candidate is at least 35 years of age.

(3) Smith is not at least 35 years of age. She is only 29.

(4) If Harris wins, then the county will prosper.

154

V. (a) Deduce: The butler committed the murder.

Premises:

(1) The chambermaid did not see the chauffeur before she retired for the evening.

(2) If the chambermaid did see the butler before retiring for the evening, then the butler must have returned by midnight.

(3) If the butler did return by midnight, then he committed the murder.

(4) The chambermaid saw either the butler or the chauffeur before she retired for the evening.

_____

CHAPTER III: ANALYSIS

INTRODUCTION

The first theme of this chapter is the nature of generalization. Earlier, in the analysis of Chapter I, I stated that I consider generalization to be the most important operation of human thought. I should add that I also consider it to be our greatest source of error, our most prominent intellectual Achilles Heel. Since the discussion of generalization is so important, and must attend to both its positive and negative use, I will divide my analysis of it in two parts. In the first part, here in the analysis of Chapter III, I will elucidate the extent to which it is essential to our basic use of language, to basic thought, and to the sophisticated use of thought. In the second part, presented in the analysis of the next chapter, I will detail some of the various ways in which generalization is misused, thereby resulting in blunted perceptions, vague and blurred thoughts, and fallacious reasoning to false conclusions.

Two other important themes we will engage in this chapter are: (i) the value of entertaining alternative hypotheses and of resisting belief in hypotheses that are insufficiently confirmed, and (ii) the nature of generalizations or *'universal thoughts'*, i.e. thoughts that assert that all entities of a certain kind have a certain property or properties, and *'existential thoughts'*, i.e. thoughts that assert that some entities of a certain kind have a certain property or properties.

1. GENERALIZATION: An Inductive Operation of Thought

"The very first fact that you must affirm about human motives, if you are to excel as a criminal investigator or as a practitioner of medicine, is that they admit of an extraordinary variety."

Sherlock's affirmation here of variety is a caution against hasty generalizations in regard to human motives. Before we treat the fallacious use of generalization, which we will defer to the next chapter, let us review several of the positive, and indeed essential, roles that generalization plays in the use of language and the use of thought.

Let us assume that your name is, "Chris." At some point long before you were able to read, you realized that the sound, Chris, was the sound used as your name. Strictly speaking, of course, the sound Chris does not exist as a unique acoustic event with a certain pitch, volume, timbre, and texture. The expression, "the sound Chris," is itself a generalization

157

covering a wide variety of actual acoustic events. It is an abstraction. When persons with high-pitched voices utter the sound, Chris, they do so at a high pitch, and when persons with deeply pitched voices utter the sound, Chris, they do so at a deeper pitch. Your sweetheart, if you have one, may whisper your name on Valentine's Day, may yell it out loudly when calling you from a distance, may speak it with the tone of anger in it when frustrated by your stubbornness: "Chris! Stop it!"

You hear all of these different acoustic events as your name because they are sufficiently similar to one another to be identified as a certain kind of sound, different from some related sounds, such as, "crisp," "kiss," "caress," etc. This implicit generalization over a wide variety of distinguishably similar acoustic events that permits you to recognize your name, is, of course, a feature of every word you use. It is the basis of our capacity to communicate thought and meaning in a language of vocal sound. Naturally, the same point applies to script, to language in its written form. We generalize over a variety of visual images. For example, we read all of the following similar, but different, pieces of script the same, that is, as the same word: ALL, all, *All*, *all*, *aℓℓ*. I should underscore the fact that I have so far only described a very basic feature of hearing linguistic sound. Indeed, it is a feature of hearing any identifiable sound, for example, hearing a sequence of sounds as a familiar melody.

In an alternative way, and at a different level, generalization is also essential to hearing linguistic sound as conveying meaning. When we hear the sounds; dog, Mother, kiss, we do not hear them as arbitrary sounds, but as words in our language meaning what they mean. And most words do not have their meaning as names — which require only a minimal degree of generalization — but are at least at the level of simple nouns. Let me explain.

There is a dramatic shift from using the sound, Mama, as a name for one's mother and the sound, doggie, as a name for one's dog, to learning the meaning of the corresponding nouns, "mother" and "dog," or to put this differently, to grasping the concept and being able to apply the concept of a mother and the concept of a dog. The word, "mother," applies generally to all mothers and the word, "dog," applies generally to all dogs of all shapes and sizes. The concept of a mother is, of course, especially sophisticated since it involves grasping the idea of a woman who stands in a particular relationship to some other person.

It is important to add that almost all of our words (and concepts) for classifying things as kinds of things, are situated within a hierarchy of varying levels of generalization that at some point must be conceptually grasped. Consider the levels from navel orange, to orange, to citrus fruit, to fruit, to member of the plant kingdom, to living being. Moreover, some of the generalizations we grasp are indeed at a high level of abstractness. Review, for example, what is involved in learning the meaning of the word, "two," or the concept, two. You display two oranges to a very small child and say emphatically, "Two." The child picks up a third orange and says, "Two." You shake your head disapprovingly, say, "No. No.," pick up two pencils in one hand, point to them with the other, and again emphatically say, "Two." The child picks up a third pencil, says, "Two," you respond negatively, and try again with two pieces of chalk. After repeating this process a number of times, perhaps over some considerable period of time, one day the child, smiling, presents you with two diaper pins, and proudly says, "Two," and then presents you with two wet diapers, and repeats the word, "Two." The child has generalized to the very abstract concept that any two similar things are two things. Of course, when you now display one safety pin and one wet diaper, and emphatically say the word, "Two," you throw the poor kid into confusion at once. There is still a further generalization to be grasped in understanding the concept two, namely that it is a concept that applies to any set of two things, whether these two things are similar or not.

The learning description I have given above is undoubtedly artificial, but hopefully it does impress upon us the pivotal role generalization plays in the acquisition and use of language and concepts, sometimes at a very abstract level and even with words that are commonly employed and acquired at an early stage of our mental development long before any formal education.

There are many other ways in which generalization is essentially involved in language and thought at the level of our ordinary practical lives, for example, in the grammatical rules of our sentence (thought) construction, or in the rules of games like soccer or poker, or in rules of conduct, such as codes of etiquette or laws governing the use of automobiles on highways. But let us proceed to a brief sketch of the role of generalization in what I earlier referred to as the "sophisticated use of thought."

We can, indeed, not see the forest because we are lost in attending to the individually different trees. Immersed in the detail and the variety, we sometimes fail to generalize to the main features of the subject or the problem with which we are engaged and with respect to which we desire a greater understanding or happy resolution. And that is not too bright, because it usually means that we have missed altogether the important, over-riding, features of the subject which elucidate the detail and the variety, or the main underlying causes of the problem which must be discerned if the problem is to be resolved.

To understand a period of history — for example, the decade of the 60's in the United States — an unsystematic listing of specific events and specific changes that occurred, though helpful, is woefully inadequate for deepening our understanding of that decade. We must, for instance, see from an overview, that many of the changes which occurred were moral changes, were part of a widespread moral re-appraisal and awakening. This is obvious, but it is important.

As the manager of a complex business office, we might be plagued with a variety of persistent and specific problems in various sectors of the office which we have tackled for the most part unsuccessfully one by one. It is possible that these problems really are isolated and localized, and that they can only be addressed individually. But it is more likely that we have failed to step back to view them in general relief, and have thereby failed to discern the underlying cause or causes from which they originate. Perhaps what first appeared to be a set of varied and petty personnel difficulties has its origin in an apparently haphazard and unjust manner in which persons are advanced. Perhaps pockets of inefficiency in the office can be vastly improved by more expedient common channels of information flow.

It is helpful to observe that an intelligent generalization is also often the recognition of a pattern. We correctly generalize that the sequence: 2,4,6,8,10..., continues with: 12,14..., because we discern, perhaps only intuitively, that the sequence is generated according to the pattern of adding +2 to obtain each succeeding number. When we generalize that someone with whom we are intimately involved always responds to constructive criticism with anger, we have at the same time discerned a pattern of behaviour. Doctors are able to diagnose certain kinds of illnesses in their early stages because their symptoms exhibit a certain pattern, sometimes not only in terms of the type of symptoms, but also the order of their appearance. Indeed, almost all of our determination of causes outside of the realm of human action — and many within that realm — depend upon generalization or pattern, and point either explicitly or implicitly to some regularity. Obviously, the very notion of a scientific law is one in which generalization is essential. (This is a point to which I will return in a later, more detailed, discussion of causes.)

Let us be reminded, finally, that generalization is at the heart of our present study: of both (i) structure of thought, and (ii) patterns of reasoning. All conditional thoughts are similar to one another with respect to their structure, in being conditionals. We generalize over their similarity in structure, and exhibit this general similarity of structure as: "If P, then Q," where 'P' and 'Q' can be any proposition whatsoever. The patterns of valid deductive rules of inference as we have rendered them are high level generalizations that apply to the linkage between all thoughts of a certain kind in terms of their structure. For example, exhibiting disjunctive syllogism as follows:

$$
\begin{array}{cc}
\text{P or Q} \qquad & \text{P or Q} \\
\text{Not P} \qquad & \text{Not Q} \\
\hline
\text{Q} \qquad & \text{P}
\end{array}
$$

is just one way of representing the general fact that in every instance in which an "Either-or" thought is asserted and one of the alternatives denied, the other alternative necessarily follows. The use of the variables 'P' and 'Q' to stand generally for any proposition whatsoever is, of course, the device by which this general fact gets expressed.

Our discussion of the positive role of generalization has only been a sketch of a complex subject of vast importance. But it must suffice, since there is still the task before us of comprehending how generalization is so often the cause of intellectual error. That task, as I mentioned, we will engage in the analysis of the next chapter.

2. ALTERNATIVE HYPOTHESES and THE VIRTUE OF WITHHOLDING BELIEF

"Please tell me. Why do you think this particular crime is so complex?

Sherlock asks this question of Watkins and Watkins advances reasons in each case for not ruling out each of the following hypotheses: that Miss Ellie is the murderer, that Louise-Phillipe is the murderer, that Dr. Anderson hired someone to commit the murder. He insists that there are insufficient grounds for believing that any one of the persons mentioned is innocent.

In other words, Watkins withholds belief as to the identity of the murderer, he keeps his options open. Presumably Sherlock agrees with him at this stage of the investigation, with the one exception of Sylvester, whom he believes to be innocent.

It should be underscored, even though it is obvious, that Watkins does not argue in support of the hypothesis that some person, say Richards, is the murderer. Instead, his argument is that: (i) No hypothesis that any one of the suspects is innocent has been sufficiently confirmed to rule that person out as a suspect, and (ii) partly because this is so, no hypothesis that any one of the suspects is guilty has been sufficiently confirmed to the exclusion of any other.

The fact that Watkins resists the temptation of hasty belief or unwarranted belief, is admirable and rational. Let us make this clear by observing that it would not be incompatible with his position if he also believed that it was likely that Miss Ellie was innocent. Nor would it be incompatible with his position if he also believed it was likely that Sylvester was guilty. For in neither of these two instances is his belief settled or final. The central point here is the following: Withholding belief that something is (or is not) the case, does not preclude believing that it is likely (or unlikely) that something is (or is not) the case. The following distinctions in our ways of believing are therefore extremely important to draw:

Believing With Conviction That x Is The Case
Believing That It Is Likely That x Is The Case

Believing With Conviction That x Is Not The Case
Believing That It Is Unlikely That x Is The Case

An example of each of these pairs of distinctions is the following:

"I Believe, and am convinced, that extra-terrestrial aliens have visited the Earth."

"I believe it is likely that extra-terrestrial aliens have visited the Earth (although I could very well be mistaken)."

"I believe, and am convinced, that no extra-terrestrial aliens have visited the Earth."

"I believe it is unlikely that extra-terrestrial aliens have visited the Earth (although I could very well be mistaken)."

Let us observe that this distinction between *belief with conviction* and *belief with likelihood* is observed by Kemp earlier in Chapter II in his views on Sylvester's innocence:

"No. I think that he is probably innocent. And I have thought that all along. But in my years of experience in the detection of crime, I have more than once been surprised to find someone guilty whom I all along thought to be innocent."

Kemp believes that Sylvester's innocence is likely, but his belief is not settled, it is not a belief with conviction.

A more extreme example of withholding belief is illustrated in the next chapter in Cassandra's refusal to hypothesize a cause for the destruction of the Order of the Temple.

"There are various theories, but I am hardly knowledgeable enough to venture an opinion for one theory rather than another."

Cassandra does not believe with conviction that one theory is true over the others. Moreover, she does not even believe that one theory is more likely than the others. She withholds not only belief with conviction but also belief with likelihood.

3. KNOWLEDGE AND FEELINGS OF CERTAINTY

Some persons believe that feeling certain that something is the case is tantamount to knowing that it is the case. Either they do not distinguish between feelings of certainty and knowledge to begin with, or more likely, if they do mark this distinction, they unreflectingly assume that having a feeling of certainty is alone a sufficient ground upon which to warrant a knowledge claim. Let us critique this latter assumption which promises a shortcut to knowledge that avoids the use of the methods of practical reasoning altogether. Let us analyze first the relation between knowledge and truth, since this relation will constitute one of the premises of our argument.

In our ordinary concept of knowledge, and in one standard use of the word "know," it is presupposed that we can only know true assertions, i.e., that we cannot know false ones. We can know that the city of Moscow with the Kremlin in it is in the U.S.S.R. (because it is), but we cannot know that it is in China (because it isn't). We may think we know that it is in China. We may even publicly claim to know that it is. But if conclusive evidence is submitted to the contrary, we will retract our "false claim to knowledge," and admit that we never did know that Moscow was in China.

Now, given the assumption that, (1) "A person can only know a proposition if that proposition is true" ("If a person knows that p, then p'), along with the assumption which we are concerned to refute, (2) "Having a feeling of certainty is alone sufficient for knowledge" ("If a person feels certain that p, then that person knows that p"), and granting two obvious empirical assumptions (3) + (4), consider the following argument:

The argument is formulated in the present tense, although it can be converted to the past tense to accord with the fact that Martin Buber and Jean Paul Sartre are now deceased.

(1) If a person knows that p, then p.

(2) If a person feels certain that p, then that person knows that p.

(3) Martin Buber feels certain that God exists.

(4) Jean Paul Sartre feels certain that God does not exist.

(From 2 and 3 we can deduce:)
(5)   Martin Buber knows that God exists.

(From 2 and 4 we can deduce:)
(6)   Jean Paul Sartre knows that God does not exist.

(From 1 and 5 we can deduce:)
(7)   God exists.

(From 1 and 6 we can deduce:)
(8)   God does not exist.

Since the assumptions (1)–(4) lead to a strict contradiction, "God exists and God does not exist," anyone who asserts them together is guilty of the fallacy of inconsistency, and ought to reject the assumption most likely to be erroneous, that a feeling of certainty is alone sufficient to warrant a claim to knowledge.

Let us therefore reject the false promise of an easy access to knowledge. And let us re-affirm the importance of the various patterns of practical reasoning, both inductive and deductive, and the importance of gathering evidence that goes beyond the evidence of our own, or someone else's, psychological state of certainty.

4.   ALTERNATIVE HYPOTHESES: FOR AND AGAINST

"I suppose... That the murderer is someone from within the household, who is familiar with its layout, and all of the doors, and all of those bloody keys."

Watkins advances an interesting technique of argument or debate. First a tautological truth is presupposed, namely, "Either the murder was committed by someone from within the household or it was not committed by someone from within the household (but by someone from without)." Watkins argues on two fronts. First he argues for the hypothesis that it was someone from within the household on the grounds that it had to be someone familiar with its complex layout of doors and keys. Then he argues against the opposite hypothesis that it was someone from without the household. His argument against this alternative hypothesis proceeds as follows:

1.   If the murderer is someone from without,
      then the murderer is a true professional –
      "someone who could pick the locks."

2.   But if the murderer is a true professional,
      then he or she would have gathered up some
      jewels before departing.

164

3. The murderer did not gather up any jewels
    before departing.

---

4. Therefore, the murderer is not a true professional.
    (Modus Tollens 2,3)

5. Therefore, the murderer is not someone from without.
    (Modus Tollens 1,4)

Note that Sherlock reminds Watkins that his analysis leaves open two alternative hypothese: (i) that the murderer is not a true professional, but someone who could become so flustered when apprehended during the progress of a burglary, he or she would depart without gathering up any jewels, and (ii) that, "...it was a true professional, but there to murder, not to rob." Watkins counters these alternatives with, "But why would a criminal, either professional or not, drape a Templar's cloak over the body?" And Sherlock admits that a criminal's doing so is improbable.

Let us observe that the logical form of the premises and the conclusions of Watkin's argument, which all together constitute the logical form of the argument, can be represented as follows:

1.)	If A, then B	Given that:
		A. The murderer is someone
2.)	If B, then C	from without.
3.)	Not C	B: The murderer is a true professional.
4.)	Not B	C. The murderer gathered up jewels
		before departing.
5.)	Not A	

The argument form above represents every argument with that logical form. In fact, we have seen it represented before in Section 4 of the previous chapter, and we shall see it again in the section that immediately follows.

5. AN ARGUMENT (Louise-Phillipe)
        and
    AN ALTERNATIVE HYPOTHESIS (Sherlock)

    "But Sherlock if I did commit the crime, for what reason would I wish to throw suspicion on myself?... I would be a fool."

We can represent Louise-Phillipe's argument here, including the implicit assumption that he is not a fool, as follows:

1.) If I committed the crime, then I wanted to cast suspicion upon myself (by placing the cloak on the victim).

2.) If I wanted to cast suspicion on myself (by placing the cloak on the victim), then I am a fool.

3.) I am not a fool.

_____

Therefore, I did not commit the crime.

This is a deductively valid argument which we can reconstruct as utilizing two applicatons of modus tollens, and as identical in logical form to the argument in the preceding section:

1). If A, then B

2.) If B, then C

3.) Not C

4.) Not B   (Modus Tollens 2,3)

5.) Not A   (Modus Tollens 1,4)

Since Louise-Phillipe's reasoning is not given explicitly, it could also be reconstructed utilizing hypothetical syllogism and modus tollens as follows:

1.) If A, then B

2.) If B, then C

3.) Not C

4.) If A, then C   (Hypothetical Syllogism 1,2)

5.) Not A   (Modus Tollens 3,4)

Sherlock responds with an ALTERNATIVE HYPOTHESIS to meet Louise-Phillipe's argument. It is an hypothesis which explains how Louise-Phillipe could have committed the murder, placed the cloak over the victim's body, thereby casting suspicion upon himself, and yet not be a fool for doing so.

"What reason could there be?"

"To make it appear as if someone else committed the murder and placed the cloak there to cast suspicion upon you."

In this alternative explanation, Sherlock accepts as true the first premise of Louise-Phillipe's argument, "If I committed the crime, then I wanted to cast suspicion on myself (by placing the cloak on the victim)." But he rejects as false the second premise, "If I wanted to cast suspicion on myself (by placing the cloak on the victim), then I am a fool." Since the argument is deductively valid, and he is challenging the truth of the conclusion, he must, of course, challenge the truth of at least one of the premises.

6. AN HYPOTHESIS OF AN UNUSUAL CAUSE (UNUSUAL HUMAN AGENT) TO EXPLAIN AN UNUSUAL EVENT (AN UNUSUAL HUMAN ACTION)

"And the second reason?"

"The details of this crime are so extraordinary. I am convinced that the guilty party is so eccentric and so deviously brilliant that we will never succeed in un-masking his — or for that matter her — identity."

Watkins argues that the murder is unusual and therefore that the agent of the murder must be unusual too. Sherlock challenges him on the grounds that in his view all murders are unusual. The implication is that all persons who commit murder are therefore also unusual, and that Laura Anderson's murderer is no different from any other. Sherlock insists that Watkins be precise in indicating in what respects he believes Laura Anderson's murder is unusual as a murder, that is, in comparison to other murders.

The first feature to which Watkins points, that nothing was stolen, Sherlock dismisses on the grounds that many murders are committed from a motive other than theft. Sherlock then admits, however, that the placing of the Templar cloak over the victim's body does mark the murder as unusual. He presumably would therefore agree that this partially confirms Watkins hypothesis that the murderer is unusual (eccentric) as far as murderers go. An unusual event, namely, an unusual murder as far as murders go, is explained by an unusual cause, namely, an unusual murderer as far as murderers go.

7. TWO DEDUCTIVE ARGUMENTS

"I believe in equality for all. I am a true Frenchman."

"And thus could not murder one of your equals."

"Brilliant, Monsieur Holmes, you understand me well...That would be like murdering myself."

"Which a true Frenchman would never do either."

"Of course not."

We can reconstruct the combined thoughts of Louise-Phillipe and Sherlock expressed in the first two sentences above as follows:

1.)   If Louise-Phillipe is a true Frenchman, then he believes in equality for all.

2.)   If he believes in equality for all, then he cannot murder one of his equals.

3.)   Louise-Phillipe is a true Frenchman.
_____

4.)   Therefore, Louise-Phillipe cannot murder one of his equals.

The logical form of this argument is:

1.)   If A, then B

2.)   If B, then C

3.)   A
_____

4.)   C

This form of argument (this argument form) is deductively valid, and therefore every instance of it is deductively valid, for example:

1.   If Caracas is in Venezuela, then Caracas is in South America.

2.   If Caracas is in South America, then Caracas is below the Equator.

3.   Caracas is in Venezuela.
_____

Caracas is below the Equator.

Note that we can deduce the conclusion of this argument either:

168

(i) by using hypothetical syllogism with premises 1. and 2., and then modus ponens with premise 3., or (ii) by using modus ponens with 1. and 3., and then modus ponens again with 2.

The second argument in the above exchange, also intended to prove that Louise-Phillipe could not commit murder, can be represented as follows:

1. If I murdered one of my equals, then that would be (like) murdering myself.

2. If I am a true Frenchman, then I would not murder myself.

3. I am a true Frenchman.

4. I would not murder myself (2,3 Modus Ponens).

5. I would not murder one of my equals (1,4 Modus Tollens).

8. A FALSE CONDITIONAL THOUGHT

"But there is a striking connection between the cloak placed there by the murderer and you. How do you explain that?"

"How do I explain that? I am not the detective..."

Louise-Phillipe interprets Sherlock to be asserting the conditional thought:

"If you, Louise-Phillipe, are innocent, then you, Louise-Phillipe, can explain the striking connection between the cloak and yourself."

But Louise-Phillipe denies that this conditional thought is true. It is not true that, "If he is innocent, then he can explain the connection." If it's true 'that he is innocent', this does not imply that it is true 'that he can explain the connection'. He is not a detective, but a chef.

Note that he nevertheless does offer an hypothesis: "I can only think that the murderer put the cloak over the body to throw suspicion directly upon me." Watkins then draws out a consequence of this hypothesis, namely, that the murderer must be aware of Louise-Phillipe's connection with the Knights Templars.

9. EXISTENTIAL THOUGHTS AND UNIVERSAL THOUGHTS (AGAIN)

"*Some* of these chapters of freemasonry are not strictly Christian."

169

"There are Masonry organizations, and perhaps Templar organizations, all over Europe and America"

"Some are secret, *some* are very powerful."

"It is so wealthy and powerful, however, that its grandmasters *sometimes* act in opposition to the Pope's wishes."

All of the above have a similar basic logical form. Logicians call propositions of this form, "Existential Propositions," and they analyze the quantification words of ordinary language such as: "some," "There are," "There is," "There exists," as meaning, "There Is At Least One." For example:

"Some professors are intelligent."

> is analyzed as

"There is at least one intelligent professor."

> or more explicitly

"There is at least one entity that is a professor and that is intelligent."

> or utilizing "x" as a variable,

"There is at least one x such that (x is a professor and x is intelligent)"

> or, utilizing the standard logical sign, "($\exists$ x)"
> for 'There is at least one x such that'

($\exists$ x) (x is a professor and x is intelligent)

The existential statement, "Some professors are intelligent," is called an *Existential Affirmative*. The existential statement, "Some professors are not intelligent" is called an *Existential Negative*. Existential negatives can be analyzed in one of two equivalent ways:

(i)
"Some professors are not intelligent."

"There is at least one x such that (x is a professor and x is not intelligent)"

"($\exists$ x) (x is a professor and x is not intelligent)"

170

(ii)

"Some professors are not intelligent."

which is equivalent to

"Not all professors are intelligent."

"Not (x) (If x is a professor, then x is intelligent)"

We have already referred to universal thoughts and their analysis, but here we can mark the distinction between a *Universal Affirmative*, such as,

"All students are intelligent."

and a *Universal Negative*, such as,

"No professor is intelligent."

As I indicated above, logicians analyze Universal Affirmatives as follows:

"All students are intelligent."

"(For any x) (If x is a student, then x is intelligent)"

and substituting the standard sign, "(x)" for "(For any x)":

"(x) (if x is a student, then x is intelligent)"

Universal Negatives can be analyzed in one of two equivalent ways:

(i)

"No professor is intelligent."

"Anyone who is a professor is not intelligent."

"(For any x) (If x is a professor, then x is not intelligent)"

(ii)

"No professor is intelligent."

"It is not the case that there is a professor who is intelligent."

"It's not the case that there is at least one x such that (x is a professor and x is intelligent)"

"Not ($\exists$x) ((x) is a professor and x is intelligent)"

171

The four basic kinds of thoughts involving the quantifications "All" and "Some" are represented below by visual diagrams. An "x" indicates a member, a shaded area indicates the absence of members. The circles represent classes. For example, the universal thought, "All students are intelligent," is rendered as, "All members of the class of students are also members of the class of intelligent persons," or:

(x) (If x is a member of the class of students, then x is a member of of the class of intelligent persons)

Universal Affirmative

"All students are intelligent."

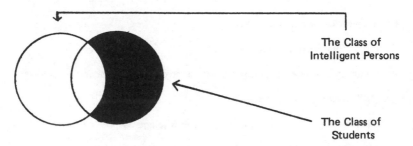

Note: The shaded area, represented as empty, is the class of all students who are not also intelligent persons. The class of students is completely contained within the class of intelligent persons. Every member of the class of students is also a member of the class of intelligent persons. There are no students who are not intelligent.

Universal Negative

"No professor is intelligent."

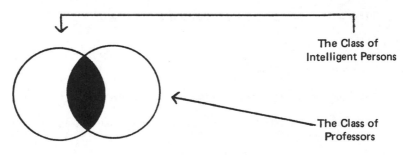

172

Note: The shaded area, represented as empty, is the class of all intelligent
         professors.   We can represent a universal negative, such as the
         one above, in either of two ways: (i) (x)   (If x is a professor,
         then x is not intelligent)   (ii) Not ($\exists$ x) (x is a professor and x is
         intelligent).

Existential Affirmative

"Some professors are intelligent."

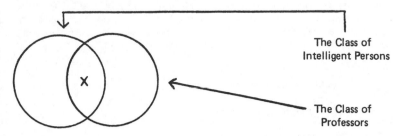

The Class of
Intelligent Persons

The Class of
Professors

Note: There is at least one member of the class of professors who is also
         a member of the class of intelligent persons. "x" denotes that
         member. "x" shows that the over-lap of the two classes is not
         empty.

Existential Negative

"Some professors are not intelligent."

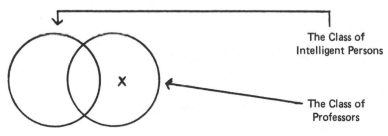

The Class of
Intelligent Persons

The Class of
Professors

Note: There is at least one member of the class of professors who is not
         also a member of the class of intelligent persons. "x" denotes
         that unfortunate member. "x" shows that the class containing
         professors who are not intelligent is not empty.

SUMMARY

Let us pause for a moment in a summary reflection, not only upon the chapter we have just traversed, but upon the entire enterprise in which we are engaged.

The first aim of a student of practical logic is to reflect upon his or her thinking, identifying which intellectual abilities are in need of improvement. The second aim is to make that improvement. To assist in achieving the first aim, rate yourself according to the following, sometimes overlapping, descriptions of intellectual abilities. Use a measure of "1" for "very poor" ascending to "10" for "very good."

I. Ability at Hypothetical Reasoning

    a.) Ability to construct hypotheses   _____

    b.) Ability to revise hypotheses and to construct alternative hypotheses to ones already advanced   _____

    c.) Ability to trace out consequences that follow from an hypothesis   _____

    d.) Ability to enumerate facts relevant to the confirmation or disconfirmation of a hypothesis   _____

II. Ability at Deductive Reasoning   _____

III. Ability in Other Forms of Reasoning

    a.) Ability to form analogies and to develop them   _____

    b.) Ability to form plausible generalizations   _____

    c.) Ability to think of examples   _____

    d.) Ability to critically examine positions and views   _____

IV.   Ability at Rigor in Thinking

    a.)   Ability to advance, in either verbal or written
         form, a rigorous argument   _____

    b.)   Ability to arrange a presentation of ideas
         in a logical and intelligible order   _____

    c.)   Ability to be concise, when necessary   _____

    d.)   Ability to resist the influence of one's
         biases (to be objective)   _____

    e.)   Ability to resist the influence of the
         biases of others (to be objective)   _____

V.   Ability in Preciseness in Thinking

    a.)   Ability to attend to details   _____

    b.)   Ability to note ambiguity and vagueness   _____

    c.)   Ability to uncover, and to make explicit,
         assumptions and presuppositions   _____

    d.)   Ability to present precise concepts and
         thoughts in verbal or written form, i.e.,
         to use words and sentences with a precise
         meaning   _____

VI.   Overall Inventiveness in Thinking

    a.)   Ability to form imaginative hypotheses   _____

    b.)   Ability to think of counter-examples and
         counter-arguments   _____

    c.)   Ability to view subjects from a novel
         perspective   _____

    d.)   Ability to think of alternative courses
         of action   _____

I. Identify which of the following is:

    (i)   A *Universal Affirmative* with the logical form:
        (x) (If x has the property ____, then x has the property ____)

    (ii)   A *Universal Negative* with the logical form:

        (x) (If x has the property ____, then x does not have the property ____)

or

        (Not) ($\exists$ x) (x has the property ____ and x has the property ____)

    (iii) An *Existential Affirmative* with the logical form:

        ($\exists$ x) (x has the property ____ and x has the property ____)

    (iv) An *Existential Negative* with the logical form:

        ($\exists$ x) (x has the property ____ and x does not have the property ____)
or

        Not (x) (If x has the property ____, then x has the property ____)

Note that more than one kind of universal or existential thought may be expressed in one sentence.

    (a)   "Some singers are birds."

    (b)   "Some toilets do not work."

    (c)   "No task is too great for a student."

    (d)   "Everyone I've ever met from Oregon was a nature lover."

    (e)   "Everyone I've ever met from Paris was a lover."

    (f)   "Some New England professors are not pipe smokers, and some pipe smokers are not New Englanders."

    (g)   "Some athletes try harder, but not all athletes who try harder win."

(h)   "Not all Arizonians ride horses; some of them ride burros."

(i)   "Sometimes I like to fall in love and sometimes I don't, because sometimes falling in love is wonderful and sometimes it is not wonderful at all."

(j)   "If all politicians believed in peace, then no country would go to war."

(k)   "If all Parisians are lovers, then no Parisian is a puritan."

II. Distinguish your own degree of belief or disbelief in the following assertions, selecting for each assertion one of (a) — (g).

      (a)   Believe with conviction that the assertion is true.
      (b)   Believe that it is very likely.
      (c)   Believe that is is likely.
      (d)   Believe with conviction that the assertion is false.
      (e)   Believe that it is very unlikely.
      (f)   Believe that it is unlikely.
      (g)   Not sure. Neither believe nor disbelieve.

1)   There is intelligent life elsewhere in the universe.
2)   There have been extra-terrestrial aliens who have visited this planet.
3)   The universe will exist in one form or another ad infinitum into the future.
4)   The universe has existed in one form or another ad infinitum from the past.
5)   There is life after death.
6)   There is transmigration of souls.
7)   Some human beings in the future will be immortal.
8)   The human species will destroy itself.
9)   There exists a supreme God of some form or another.
10) Extra-sensory perception exists.
11) Satan, or the Devil, exists.
12) Moses led the Hebrews out of Egypt.
13) The Egyptian pyramids were tombs of the pharoahs.
14) Dinosaurs existed.
15) There has been an evolution of various animal and plant species over millions of years on this planet.
16) Free-Will exists, i.e. sometimes when we do an act x, we could have chosen either not to do x or to do some alternative act y.
17) Human beings are always motivated to act from self-interest.
18) Horses sometimes make choices, i.e. sometimes when a horse does an act x, he or she could have chosen either not to do x or to do some alternative act y.

19) Some human beings sometimes commit actions motivated from a desire to do good to others.

20) It is impossible to go back in time, i.e. to actually witness or participate in past events.

21) It is impossible to go forward in time, i.e. to actually witness or participate in future events.

III. Deduce the Conclusions of the following arguments.

(i) DEDUCE: The chambermaid committed the murder.

PREMISES:

(1) If the chauffeur did not commit the murder, then either the butler or the chambermaid did.

(2) No one who was at the pub until midnight committed the murder, because the autopsy reveals that it was committed before 11:00 P.M.

(3) The chauffer was at the pub until midnight.

(4) The butler could not have committed the murder, since he was out of town for the weekend.

(ii) DEDUCE: The U.S. will be an enemy of the Vietnamese movement for national independence.

PREMISES:

(1) If Truman is elected, the U.S. will support the French re-colonization of Vietnam.

(2) Any nation which supports the French re-colonization of Vietnam will be an enemy of the Vietnamese movement for national independence.

(3) Either Truman will be elected or Dewey will.

(4) If Dewey is elected, then he must win the majority of the popular vote.

(5) Dewey will not win the majority of the popular vote.

(iii)　DEDUCE:　Russia is a threat to world peace.

PREMISES:

(1)　If the U.S. does not disarm, then not all NATO countries will disarm.

(2)　The U.S. wishes to remain a superpower.

(3)　Any nation that is militarily aggressive is a threat to world peace.

(4)　Any nation that does not disarm is a militarily aggressive nation.

(5)　If Russia disarms, then all NATO countries will disarm.

(6)　No nation that wishes to remain a superpower will disarm.

(iv)　DEDUCE:　Eisenstein will never be a true statesman.

PREMISES:

(1)　Eisenstein is a Massachusetts democrat.

(2)　All intelligent politicians are either conservatives or radicals.

(3)　If Eisenstein is a liberal, then Eisenstein is neither a conservative nor a radical.

(4)　All Massachusetts' democrats are liberals.

(5)　If Eisenstein is not an intelligent politician then he will not accept the Vice-Presidential nomination.

(6)　If Eisenstein does not accept the Vice-Presidential nomination, then he will never be a true statesman.

(iv)　DEDUCE:　God can't both be perfect and suffer change too. Note that this is equivalent to:
"Either God is not perfect or God does not suffer change."

Proceed by deducing a strict logical inconsistency from the following premises.

(1)　God is perfect.

179

(2) God suffers change.

(3) If God suffers change, then God is changed either by himself or by some entity other than himself.

(4) If God is perfect, then if God changed himself, he would change himself to a worse state.

(5) If God acts willingly, he would not change himself to a worse state.

(6) God does act willingly.

(7) If God is changed by some entity other than himself, then God is not perfect.

IV. Distinguish out the premises necessary to deduce the conclusion, numbering them in order. Then deduce the conclusion.

   (i)   We have narrowed the suspects to either Louise-Phillipe or the chambermaid. Since Louise-Phillipe did not have a key to the mistress' bedroom, if he committed the murder, he must have stolen the key from the chambermaid, perhaps during one of their romantic interludes. If he did steal the key from her, then she must now be missing the key. But when we asked her about the key, she responded that it was not missing. Indeed, she produced it from her purse where she ordinarily keeps it. And that's sufficient evidence to incriminate her: we can conclude that she's the murderer.

   (ii) The mistress was murdered in her bedroom in the mansion. We know that one of the following persons, either the chambermaid or the butler or the chef, must have committed the murder, since only they were on the premises at the time. If the chambermaid is the murderer, then the crime must have been committed after midnight, since she did not return from the pub in the village until that time. It also follows that if the chambermaid did not commit the murder, then the murderer could not have entered through the bedroom door. For only the chambermaid besides the mistress had a key to that door. We also know that the murderer had to enter either through the bedroom door or through the window next to the veranda. On the assumption that the butler committed the murder, it follows that he would have had to enter through the window next to the veranda. But the butler was far too elderly to accomplish that feat. It has now been determined that the murder was not committed after midnight, and we can now deduce who committed the murder.

180

CHAPTER IV: ANALYSIS

INTRODUCTION

"Fallacies of Generalization

1. (Character of the Class) The class of Fallacies of which we are now to speak, is the most extensive of all; embracing a greater number and variety of unfounded inferences than any of the other classes."

(John Stuart Mill, *System of Logic*)[3]

I will now fulfill my pledge to treat generalization as one of the most prevalent forms of fallacious reasoning. We previously treated generalization's virtues, and need now to be reminded of its vices.

In this chapter we will also treat a number of other common fallacies. And we will return to the distinction between various degrees of belief, and to the virtue of withholding belief.

1. FALLACIES OF GENERALIZATION OF MEANING

Our propensity to generalize is deeply rooted in our thinking. In the previous chapter we discussed the integral role that generalization plays in our basic understanding of concepts, and of the meaning of words. That discussion now needs to be amended. Utilizing some of the ideas advanced by the influential twentieth-century philosopher, Ludwig Wittgenstein, let us explore how our propensity to generalize leads to an incorrect conception of at least some of the words and sentences we employ every day.[4]

It seems natural to assume that whenever we use words in a sufficiently lucid manner to be understood, it is because we have employed those words in a way that clearly delimits the objects or events that we intend to refer to in the world. And if we are asked to reflect for a moment and to present our view of the nature of language and meaning, and its relationship to the world, we are apt to respond with some such theory as the following:

Language is the primary means by which human beings make statements about the world, and thereby communicate information about the world to one another. For example, I say to you, 'Knossos was in Crete,' and you, understanding the

181

conventions of spoken sound in the English language, and not having known the location of Knossos, the capital of the Minoan Civilization in ancient Greece, now add that piece of geographical and historical information to your store of knowledge. Naturally, we sometimes convey false information to one another, and we sometimes confuse one another because of vagueness or ambiguity. Nevertheless, when words are used properly and we are clear about the objects to which they refer, they do not lead us into semantic error. It is true that we commonly employ one and the same word in different contexts with different shades of meaning, but there is something common to these different uses, the 'core meaning,' which is the same throughout. A proper definition of a word captures this core meaning.

Let us challenge this common-sense theory of language and meaning by first attempting to find a proper definition of a meaning of the word "game," while reviewing in our imagination some of the variety that exists among the kinds of things we commonly call "games." What we quickly discover is that the word "game" has no "core meaning," that there are no properties common and peculiar to all games which constitute the essence of a game — or to put this differently — which taken together make up a proper definition of the word "game."

For example, suppose that we light upon the following, apparently obvious, definition (generalization): "A game (every game) is a structured competition between two or more parties involving a win." A moment's reflection, sensitive to variety and hasty generalization, will expose this definition as unsatisfactory. The card game solitaire is a game, no matter that our definition arbitrarily denies it that classification. Moreover, we cannot defend our definition by insisting that solitaire only "appears" to be a game but is not "really." For solitaire really is a game because that's what we call it.

We could alter our tactics and broaden our definition so that it no longer excludes solitaire and other similar one-party games, simply by deleting the qualifying property, "between two or more parties": "A game (every game) is a structured competition involving a win." But this new definition would force us to deny the status of a game to Ring-Around-The-Rosies. Like many other children's games, Ring-Around-The-Rosies has no win and involves no competition.

We must be wary then of our propensity to generalize and to insist that every word must in every context of its use have the same essential meaning. At least some, if not many, of our words lack such a unique 'core meaning' common throughout the variety of contexts in which they are employed. The variety in the use and meaning of such words is irreducible.

The common sense view of language and meaning that was sketched above errs in another important respect because of our propensity to generalize at the cost of variety. By portraying the sentences of our language as instruments for communicating information about the world, it fixes on only one obvious example, and hastily generalizes the features of that example to apply in every case. The natural paradigm of a sentence used to communicate information is unreflectingly taken as representative of the use of all sentences. And this is patently a mistake. For review only the following uses of language:

(i)	"Please pass the butter."	(Requesting)
(ii)	"Stand at attention!"	(Commanding)
(iii)	"I promise I will do that."	(Promising)
(iv)	"What time is it?"	(Asking a question)
(v)	"Hi. How are you?"	(Greeting)
(vi)	"Help! Help!"	(Calling for help)
(vii)	"Our Father who art...	(Praying)

It is obvious that the uses to which our sentences are put are extraordinarily varied: identified and grouped in kind together, they would constitute an enormous classification. Every activity that is ordinarily, or even sometimes, enacted with the vehicle of language would fall within this classification, for example: praising, warning, consoling, explaining, describing, proposing, announcing, criticizing, joking, begging, inciting, complaining, interrogating, notifying, encouraging, exclaiming, dissenting, counting, agreeing, opposing, forbidding, inviting, protesting, petitioning, contracting, intimidating, counting, swearing, persuading, etc.

2. HASTY GENERALIZATION: AN EXAMPLE

Keeping in mind the variety inherent in our use of sentences, and the temptation to obscure that variety by hastily generalizing from only one kind of example, let us consider an illustration of the error of hasty generalization as it occurs outside of the realm of language and meaning.

Suppose that you are asked to indicate your preference among the three standard moral theories of criminal punishment: (i) *The Retributivist Theory*: "Criminals deserve and ought to be punished as retribution for the wrong things they choose to do, and their punishment should be proportional to the severity of their crime," (ii) *The Deterrent Theory*: "Criminals ought to be punished to deter them, and to deter others, from commiting crimes," and (iii) *The Reformativist Theory*: "Criminals ought to be punished (humanely) in order to reform them."

It is likely that your preference for one of these theories will turn upon your view of criminals and criminal psychology. Review, therefore, the following differing psychologies among those commonly advanced to explain criminal behaviour:

(i)   Criminals are free to choose to do good or to do evil, just like the rest of us. But unlike the rest of us, they willfully and maliciously choose to do evil and to violate the rights of others."

(ii)   Criminals do what they do because they believe they can get away with it. They choose whatever means they need to achieve their ends — as long as those means aren't too costly. Of course, they aren't too different from the rest of us.

(iii)   Unlike the rest of us, criminals are unfortunately born into an environment of injustice, alienation, and violence. They consequently form anti-social attitudes which issue in anti-social behaviour.

Although the matching between these psychological views and the three standard theories of punishment is not a strict one, persons who hold the psychological view (i) are likely also to advocate the retributivist theory; persons who hold the psychological view (ii) are likely to advocate the deterrent theory; and persons who hold the psychological view (iii) are likely to advocate the reformativist theory. Pressing further with the interrogation of your beliefs, which of these psychological views (i), (ii), or (iii), would you be most likely to choose? And does your choice correlate with the matching suggested above?

A wise response to this question recognizes at once that it is loaded, and that it is altogether fitting to refuse to answer it. For each of these psychological theories couches a vast and hasty generalization. We can quickly discern that each is quite false and quite misleading merely by attending to some of the variety that exists in criminal behaviour and motivation. Review only the following very different crimes:

A once-in-a-lifetime white collar crime of embezzlement "to pay off a gambling debt."

A murder committed by a hired professional "for money."

A street gang murder "for revenge" against a member of a rival gang.

184

A physically harmful child-beating "to make the child stop its incessant crying."

A complex train robbery of gold bullion by international professionals "for the money and the glory."

A murder by an escaped mental patient "to rid the world of another Satan."

An arson set by a fired employee "because he was unfairly dismissed by the company after years of loyal work."

An arson set by the owner "to pay his bills or go bankrupt in the recession after twenty-five years in business."

A violation of the selective service act "on grounds of principle."

A father's kidnapping of his own children "because the damn court unfairly awarded custody to the mother."

A strong-arm-man's physically injuring a debtor "to make him pay up and because that's my job."

We naively desire a single, uncomplicated explanation of all criminal behaviour, and indeed, it would be very convenient if the understanding of criminals were so simple and easy. Certainly our disposition to generalize and to find sameness everywhere, encourages us to believe that it is. Nevertheless, when we pause sufficiently to think about it, it is obvious that the kinds of crimes and criminals that there are is extraordinarily varied. The choice, therefore, between the three criminal psychologies described above is a false dilemma of choices. And similarly, the choice of one and only one of the three major theories of punishment — the retributivist, the deterrent, and the reformativist — may be a false dilemma of choices too.

3. TWO DIFFERENT KINDS OF GENERALIZATIONS

For the purposes of clarifying different ways in which we can err in stating and inferring generalizations, let us continue by distinguishing between two kinds of generalization statements: (i) strict generalizations, and (ii) statistical generalizations. Both of these sorts of generalizations are different in kind from, and should be sharply contrasted to, singular statements, that is, statements that refer to a specific individual. Some examples of singular statements are: "Natchez is in Mississippi," "The cup on the table is white," "My piranha fish ate its mate."

185

Statements of generalization, on the other hand, always refer to individuals as members of a class. A strict generalization refers to all members of a class, and as described previously in Chapter II, is either a universal affirmative or a universal negative. The statement, "All students are intelligent," a universal affirmative, is about all students without exception: it is false if there is even one student who is not intelligent. The statement, "No professor is intelligent," a universal negative, is about all professors without exception too. If there exists even one intelligent professor, it is false.

STRICT GENERALIZATIONS

We commonly employ strict generalizations in combination with Modus Ponens in the following form of argument already treated in Chapter II:

"John must have completed 4 years of academic work, because he's a graduate of B.U., and that's what they require of all graduates."

The Logical Form of this argument is the following:

(1) "All graduates of B.U. must complete 4 years of academic work."

(2) "John is a graduate of B.U.

_____

(3) "John has completed 4 years of academic work."

Or:

(1)	(x) (If Fx, then Gx)	Fx: x is a graduate of B.U.
(2)	Fa	Gx: x has completed 4 years of academic work
	_____	a: John
(3)	Ga	

Strictly speaking, Universal Instantiation is employed in this pattern of reasoning, and it has the following form:

(1)	(x)	(If Fx, then Gx)	Premise
(2)		If Fa, then Ga	Universal Instantiation from (1)
(3)		Fa	Premise
(4)		Ga	Modus Ponens (2,3)

The use of strict generalizations in this pattern of reasoning is often only presupposed in common speech and thought. For example:

"Maria must be at least 35, since she has officially filed as a candidate for the presidency."

The logical form of this argument, with the strict generalization exposed, is the following:

(1)   "All official candidates for the presidency are at least 35."

(2)   "If Maria is an official candidate for the presidency, then Maria is at least 35."

(3)   "Maria is an official candidate for the presidency."

---

(4)   "Maria is at least 35."

Let us observe that the strict generalizations in the two examples given, affirm *necessary conditions*. It is not a coincidence that all B.U. graduates have completed four years of academic work, and that all official candidates for the presidency are at least 35. The first is a university requirement and the second is a law. Completing four years of academic work is a necessary condition for graduation from B.U. and having attained at least 35 years of age is a necessary condition for filing as a candidate for president. Neither, we might add is a sufficient condition.

Strict generalizations are often couched in the form of requirements, both legal and non-legal. Scientific Laws, for the most part, also have the logical form of strict generalizations. The empirical law, "All water boils at 212° sea level pressure," is intended to apply without exception. In fact, it is explicitly understood as a causal generalization; that is, heating water to 212° sea level pressure is a *sufficient condition* for, or always causes water to boil.

STATISTICAL GENERALIZATIONS

Statistical generalizations are similar to strict generalizations in referring to a class as well. The generalizations, "80% of the registered voters of Ida County, Idaho are registered as Republicans," ascribes a property to members of the class of registered voters of Ida County. It ascribes that property not to all of them, but only to 80% of them. Of course, a statistical generalization may report a 100% probability, and thus coincide with a strict generalization. In fact, we could classify strict generalizations as one (major) sub-species of statistical generalizations — not an altogether bad idea.

187

Statistical generalizations or probabilities are easily represented as the proportion of one class over another. If there are 1,000 registered voters in Ida County (=y), and 800 registered Republicans (=x), then $(\frac{x}{y})$ or $\frac{800}{1,000}$ or 80% represents the proportional relation between these two classes. If from a class of 6000 persons interviewed (=y), there are 3000 who favor the military budget (=f) and 3000 who do not (=n), the probability of those who do, and those who do not is $\frac{n}{y}$, which in both instances is $\frac{3000}{6000}$ or 50%. Note that the union together of the classes (f) and (n) is just the class y, (all persons interviewed):

$$
\begin{array}{rcl}
(f) & = & 3000 \\
(n) & = & 3000 \\
\hline
(f) + (n) & = & 6000 \qquad (=y)
\end{array}
$$

These facts about probabilities are obvious, but it is important that they be stated and made explicit.

4. DIFFERENT FALLACIES OF GENERALIZATION

Let is now separate out several forms of the fallacy of generalization that are identifiably distinct from one another in order to impress upon ourselves the prevalence and variety of error in this pattern of thinking. The fallacies that we will treat are the following:

(i) The Fallacy of Induction By Simple Enumeration including the sub-fallacies

(a) Too Small A Sample
(b) Too Broad In Scope

(ii) The Fallacy: "Post Hoc, Ergo Propter Hoc."

(iii) The Fallacy of Composition

(i) THE FALLACY: INDUCTION BY SIMPLE ENUMERATION

"it (Induction By Simple Enumeration) consists in ascribing the character of general truths to all propositions which are true in every instance that we happen to know of." (This, that, and the other A is B, I cannot think of any A which is not B, therefore every A is B.")[5]

Induction by Simple Enumeration is perhaps the most simple and uncritical

188

form of inferring generalizations to which we are prone: having observed the coincidence of A and B on one or more particular occasions, and not having observed — or having forgotten or suppressed — occasions where A was present but B absent, we generalize that A and B always accompany one another. Moreover, where A precedes B in time, we identify this generalization as a causal generalization, that is, we identify A as the cause of B. This latter fallacy, to which we will return, is entitled, "Post Hoc, Ergo Propter Hoc."

Induction by Simple Enumeration therefore has the following logical form:

(i)   If Fa, then Ga
(ii)   If Fb, then Gb

$\cdots\cdots\cdots$

$\cdots\cdots\cdots$

_____

(x) (If Fx, then Gx)

The critical point to observe here is the one that we have been insisting upon all along, namely, that generalization is a mode of operation of human thought that is ambiguously sometimes good and sometimes evil. We therefore ought to use generalization in our reasoning, but only where we have placed appropriate limits upon that use. In the case of Induction by Simple Enumeration, this limit can be easily set by observing the following criterion:

Having Observed that "A is Always In The Company of B" Is A Grounds For Hypothesizing The Strict Generalization, "Whenever A, Also B," But It Is Not A Grounds For A Complete Confirmation of That Generalization.

We commit the Fallacy of Induction By Simple Enumeration whenever we unreflectingly confirm some generalization to be true solely on the basis of having observed some particular instances of it. We do not commit this fallacy when by induction solely from observations of particular instances, we hypothesize a generalization whose truth we suspect, but do not confirm.

John Stuart Mill insists that induction by simple enumeration, or "...expecting that which has been found true once or several times, and never yet found false, will be found true again...is the kind of induction which is natural to the mind when unaccustomed to scientific methods." [6] It is also the operation of thought which misleads common-sense to affirm false maxims that fit the universal formula, "Whatsoever has never been, will never be." An example of such a maxim is, "Women, as a class, are supposed not to have hitherto been equal in intellect to men, therefore they are necessarily inferior." [7]   In classical civilizations it seemed altogether natural to generalize from the observation that societies with slavery prosper, to the prediction (into an indefinite future) that all prosperous civilizations will (must) rest upon the institution of slavery.

We can put the moral here differently by reflecting for a moment upon the not-too-uncommon, but all-too-mistaken view that, "Deductive reasoning is reasoning from the general to the particular, and Inductive Reasoning is reasoning from the particular (by simple enumeration) to the general." Having already reviewed several different patterns of deductive reasoning, we know that all deductive reasoning is not limited only to one pattern, Universal Instantiation. There are at least four basic patterns of deductive reasoning, not one of which involves an inference from the general to the particular. Similarly, inductive reasoning is not exhausted in the one operation of thought, induction by simple enumeration. There are different varieties of inductive reasoning, such as, for example, the partial confirmation of an hypothesis.

Let us locate under the heading of the fallacy of induction by simple enumeration, two distinct sub-fallacies; (a) generalizing from *Too Small A Sample*; and (b) hypothesizing or confirming a generalization that is *Too Broad In Scope*.

(a) TOO SMALL A SAMPLE: We are prone, particularly in our reflections upon society, to generalize from only a paucity of data, from only a few observations. We draw generalizations from a few instances or experiences and remain inflexibly prejudiced and mistaken in our under-standing of such diverse subjects as human psychology, the causes of social change, and the nature of politics or religion. We believe to be certainly true, generalizations that are inferred from such little evidence that they are unwarranted even as hypotheses.

It is understandable that we are anxious and hasty in our attempts to comprehend and to explain the world in which we live. But a quick and easy guess is just that and nothing more. And when, on the foundation of too small a sample, we seriously entertain generalizations as likely hypotheses, or more irrationally, immediately place our belief and trust in them, we are only fooling ourselves.

It is important to observe that there is more at stake here than merely "having some mistaken opinions." Our integrity and character is compromised as well. As any genuine inquirer knows very well, integrity is fundamental to inquiry, and the moral and intellectual virtues are in this instance inextricably intertwined.

The fallacy of Too Small A Sample, it should be observed, is committed not only with respect to strict generalizations, but with respect

190

to statistical generalizations too. All too often the evidence for affirming some probability is only a meager sampling of data which does not warrant any extrapolation at all. We may be more acutely aware of this fallacy when it is committed with precise probabilities stated in exact percentages, since we have undoubtedly witnessed instances in which the predicted generalizations of even well-known pollsters have proved to be dramatically incorrect. Indeed, we may be skeptical of precise probabilities of any sort, having found ourselves without an umbrella drenched in a violent thunderstorm, after a so-called "meteorologist's" prediction of 30% probability of light rain.

We may be less critical, however, of statistical generalizations drawn from Too Small A Sample, but qualified with such phrases as: "almost all," "very many," "the vast majority," or at the other extreme, "very few," "a small minority," "not very many," or even between these extremes, "equally divided," or "about half-and-half." Qualifying phrases such as these do have the virtue of avoiding precise generalizations, including strict generalizations, that are not warranted by the evidence. (And this is an important point to which we will shortly return.) But no matter how neatly qualified a generalization may be, if the instances from which it is drawn are insufficient to warrant a belief in it, then we ought not to believe in it. For we ought not to believe that something holds in the vast majority of cases, when it only holds in a few, and we ought not to believe that there are very few of something, when there are very many, or that certain opinions are equally divided when they are not equally divided at all.

(b) TOO BROAD IN SCOPE. It is useful to distinguish out a related, but different, sort of fallacy of induction by simple enumeration. Even where we are warranted on the basis of a sufficiently large sample of instances to 'hypothesize' a generalization, we sometimes conclude with a generalization that is much wider in scope than the instances from which it is drawn will reasonably allow.

For example, on the basis of many observations, and/or a statistical study, and/or a voluminous reading, of urban working women in the United States, we may come to believe in, and to assert to others, general truths about the life and lot of contemporary women. This, of course, is unreasonable. When we generalize about 'contemporary women,' we are at least imprecise if we do not mean all contemporary women, including those in Ghana, China, and Nicaragua. But even if the contexts of our pronouncements makes reasonably apparent to our hearers that we mean contemporary American women, we have still adduced generalizations that are far Too Broad in Scope. For what is generally true of urban women in contemporary America may or may not be true of contemporary American rural women, and what is true of working women in America today may not be true of those who are unemployed.

191

There is a technique that we can employ that is sometimes — though not always — helpful in avoiding the fallacy of Too Broad In Scope. If we self-consciously and with regularity employ some of the qualifying phrases of the sort mentioned above, such as, "almost all," and "very many," we can at least avoid inferring strict and exceptionless generalizations in those contexts where only a statistical generalization is warranted. There are two immediate advantages to this technique. First of all, it operates as a continual reminder of the ease with which we can commit fallacies of generalization in our own thinking. This is certainly an important benefit, since to believe in false generalizations is not only an error in itself, but also characteristically leads to further errors; we utilize the generalizations we believe in as assumptions for thought and action, deducing instances from them (by Universal Instantiation) in particular circumstances. If we have already qualified a generalization in our mind, we will less likely misapply it. If we believe that a generalization holds in most, but not all, cases, we will be cognizant of the possibility that the particular case before us is one in which it does not hold.

The second advantage has to do with our credibility vis-a-vis others. Whenever those persons to whom we address a generalization without qualification are prompted to think of legitimate exceptions and counter-examples, our credibility in their eyes is to that extent undermined. In fact it may be so undermined that they cease altogether to believe in us, even if what we have to say further down the line is informative and intelligent.

It is important to record the fact that even when we are not present along with our words — someone reads them on a page or hears them on a tape — they nevertheless carry with them a persona, a portrait of our person. (Imagine here the personality conveyed in a radio-talk-show person's voice, and remember that all that we hear is the sound from the radio.) We are bright, but sarcastic, or friendly and tolerant, or young and arrogant and rebellious, etc. And we are also believable or not. Of course, there is more than one way in which we can undermine our credibility with others; for example, by being uninformed, or biased, or gullible, or too speculative. But certainly, one of the more common ways is by insisting upon strict generalizations which other persons immediately reject as false because they admit of obvious exceptions.

(ii) THE FALLACY: "POST HOC, ERGO PROPTER HOC"

Having observed that A follows B in every instance we know of, we sometimes employ induction by simple enumeration to infer a causal generalization, that is, to conclude not only that B always follows A, but also that A is the cause of B. To common sense an inference of this sort seems reasonable enough. If adding fluoride to the water is always followed by a decline in the instance of dental decay, it seems only reasonable to generalize that fluoride always causes that beneficial effect. Indeed, we would feel silly if, without offering any further explanation, we insisted that adding fluoride was always followed by a decline in dental decay, but was in no way causally related to that decline.

However, it might not be causally related to that decline, and the qualifying phrase, "without offering any further explanation," is essential to our feeling silly. We would not feel that way if there were a plausible alternative explanation, for example, if a chemical additive used with the fluoride had been proved to be decay preventative in independent studies. Moreover, we would not feel silly observing to a child that although the Night always follows the Day, it is not caused by the Day, or in correcting the child who believed that you must be very strong to be allowed to christen and launch a ship by striking it with a bottle. For the child has committed the fallacy, "Post Hoc, Ergo Propter Hoc," which translated means:

AFTER THIS, THEREFORE BECAUSE OF THIS"

or

"B FOLLOWED AFTER A, THEREFORE A IS THE CAUSE OF B"

I may believe that my headache this morning is caused by the glass of burgundy wine I drank last night, and it may be true, as a limited causal generalization, that any time I presently drink burgundy wine, it will cause me to have a headache. On the other hand, it may be false, and I may have fallaciously reasoned that since my headache followed drinking burgundy wine, the wine must be its cause.

Let us also observe, having this example before us, that were I to decide never to drink burgundy wine again, I would thereby over-extend my generalization beyond the present, committing the fallacy 'Too Broad In Scope.' For even if it is true that my headache was caused by burgundy wine, this physical response may only be temporary, and at some future date I might not suffer this ill effect at all. One might humorously think that it is just for this reason, to avoid this particular fallacy, that the traditional adage ought to be revised to read, "I'll always try anything at least twice."

"Post Hoc, Ergo Propter Hoc" is obviously a very common fallacy. It should also be pointed out that it is often committed even where a generalization is not obviously, or at least explicitly, involved: Upon witnessing two relateable events, one following the other in succession, we can hardly resist seeing the latter as caused by the former:

(i)   "He gave up his job and shifted careers, and nine months later they were divorced. It's a sad fact that a career change so adversely affected their marriage."

193

(ii) "They completely changed their method of advertising exactly one week after their major competitor did. They sure learn their lessons fast."

(iii) "One Year after Watergate and Nixon's resignation the incidence of white collar crime had increased by 18%. It's obvious that the public thinks, 'If the leaders of our country can do it, why can't we?'"

But, of course, the divorce might have been unrelated to the career change, and indeed could have been agreed upon a year or more before. And the advertising change may have been planned well in advance. It may even be the case that their major competitor stole their ideas and 'beat them to the punch.' Finally, Watergate might not at all be contributory to the increase in white collar crime. Perhaps such crime had been increasing at a similar rate for several years prior to Watergate.

(iii) THE FALLACY OF COMPOSITION

Sometimes we erroneously assume that properties of the parts transfer automatically to the whole; that properties of all of the individual members of a group automatically transfer to the group itself. However, this form of reasoning is at times in error, and is thus identified by logicians as "The Fallacy of Composition." If each and every individual member of the graduating class of Theatre Arts majors has exhibited considerable acting talent, then it is just summarizing that fact to say that the present graduating class of Theatre Arts majors is a talented one. On the other hand, if four persons who have hitherto exhibited excellent management skills are brought together to form a management group, it does not strictly and necessarily follow that as a group they will manage excellently. To assume that they will is to commit the fallacy of composition. A particular form of transaction may be forbidden by law in each of the 50 states of the United States, but it does not follow that this transaction is forbidden by the federal law of the United States.

5. SEVERAL OTHER FALLACIES: THE FALLACY "STRAW MAN"

Whenever a position is attributed to some person or group, which position that person or group does not hold, and the position is criticized as if it were a genuine one, we have an instance of the fallacy, Straw Man. A straw man is not a real man, but one made of straw. A scarecrow may appear to be a man — at least to the crows — but it is an imposter. A position attributed to someone may be sufficiently similar to his or her real position to appear to be genuine, even though it is only an imposter. And wherever an imposter position is attacked as if it were someone's real position, we have an instance of the fallacy, Straw Man.

194

For example, suppose someone argues that we ought to register and to vote Democratic on the grounds that the Republican Party is opposed to all welfare, and that any party opposed to all welfare is heartless and undeserving of political leadership. It would be an error to accept this argument since it does not hold. Indeed, it is not an uncommon practice in politics to represent one's opponents in a bad light by fabricating what one knows is a gross distortion of their view, while insisting that it is their view nevertheless.

6. FALSE DILEMMA

But he did not trust them. When I asked what alternative course to theirs he would pursue, however, he had nothing to offer. I chided him with a look which said, 'If you can't recommend an alternative course of action, then your objections are worthless,' and he responded to my look by saying:

"Watkins. There are genuine dilemmas where every course of action that can be pursued is unfortunate. Theirs is perhaps the least unfortunate, but it is unfortunate nevertheless."

Sometimes a person will argue that there are two and only two alternatives (in regard to some subject), that both alternatives are unfortunate, and that therefore the alternative that is the least unfortunate ought to be accepted. The argument has the form:

(i)   Either A or B

(ii)   Both A and B are unfortunate

(iii) A is the least unfortunate of the two alternatives

Therefore: A

Now, if there really are two and only two, unfortunate alternatives, then it may indeed be wise to choose the least painful horn of the dilemma. On the other hand, if there exists an additional (third) alternative that is not so unfortunate, then the dilemma is a *false dilemma*, and the argument ought to be rejected as unreasonable.

Sometimes, using a slightly different technique of argument, a dilemma is advanced in the following way. Someone proposes a position A and admits that although A has undesirable features, the only alternative available to A, B, is even less desirable, and for that reason A ought certainly to be accepted. This technique of argument exhibits the following pattern:

(i)   Tentative proposal of position A

(ii)   The admission that A has undesirable features

(iii)   The assertion that the only alternative to A is B

(iv)   The further assertion that B is far more undesirable than A

Therefore: Certainly A

Here again the dilemma could be a genuine one and the argument not altogether unreasonable. However, if there exists an additional (third) alternative that is not as undesirable as A, and perhaps is not undesirable at all, then the argument turns upon a false dilemma and ought to be rejected as unreasonable.

For example, suppose I argue that the United States ought to unilaterally disarm all of its nuclear weaponry, while admitting that this action would render the United States vulnerable to aggressors. I insist, however, that the only alternative to such disarmament by the United States is a devastating nuclear war that will result in the annihilation of the human race. Now, if we can imagine a plausible third alternative, such as the United States willingness to yield major concessions to the U.S.S.R. in strategic arms reduction, then the argument must be judged as turning upon a dilemma of alternatives that is not a genuine one.

Note that the criticism here is a criticism of the specific argument at hand, judging it to turn upon a false dilemma. Other and different arguments for unilateral disarmament might be advanced, which arguments would have to be judged independently on their own merits.

7. AD HOMINEM

"I see. The conclusion is far too immodest." (Cassandra)

"Indeed it is. Only someone first gullible enough to believe in the existence of God will be gullible enought to believe that the argument proves the existence of God." Hawkins laughed good-naturedly to give a proper tone to the jibe he had cast in Cassandra's direction, and she responded in the same spirit.

"My goodness! That's double-gullibility. Can they try you twice for that? And if you're guilty, do they send you immediately to hell?"

Hawkins may be correct here in pointing out a possible bias on Cassandra's part. However, in attacking her as gullible, he is strictly speaking committing a logical error. Not uncommonly, when criticizing a position or an argument, negative criticism is advanced, not of the position or the argument itself, but of the person advocating the position or argument. The attack here against the person is called an "Ad Hominem." It may be instructive in some exceptional circumstances to criticize persons in a way that bears upon the positions they advocate, e.g. in a court of law to discredit an unreliable witness. But ordinarily it is mispointed to do so. The criticism misses the point, which is the position itself. In the fallacy, Straw Man, the criticism is not directed to the position in question, it is misdirected to an imposter position. Similarly, in the fallacy, Ad Hominem, the criticism is not directed against the position itself, it is misdirected to the person advocating the position.

Thus, for example, if I challenge your position on the grounds that you are too immature to see the consequences of it, I commit the fallacy Ad Hominem. If there are overlooked consequences of your position that are pertinent to its appraisal, then, indeed, these consequences ought to be pointed out and debated. For that is treating the position, as it deserves, on its own merits. But when I attack you as immature, and pass off my criticism of you as if it were a criticism of your position, I commit a serious error in critical reasoning.

8. AD VERECUNDIAM (ILLEGITIMATE APPEAL TO AUTHORITY)

"It employs reasoning so convincing it even bewitched the brilliant medieval churchman, Saint Thomas Aquinas...in the opinion of many, the greatest Christian Theologian of all time." (Sherlock)

"The brilliant St. Thomas was obviously lacking in analytical talent...Even a half-witted logician would refuse to accept the argument and its conclusion." (Hawkins)

Hawkins is on firm ground here challenging Sherlock's appeal to authority in the person of Saint Thomas Aquinas. He can be criticized for committing the fallacy Ad Verecundiam, or illegitimate appeal to authority. This fallacy is usually committed in the following way: someone argues that a position on a particular subject ought to be accepted on the grounds that an authority advocates that position, were the alleged authority appealed to is not a recognized or legitimate authority on the subject in question at all. This description of the fallacy should be qualified in two respects: on the one hand, it is wise to be cautious of even recognized "authorities" and "experts." For even recognized authorities commit errors. Moreover, as we are well aware, many fields of inquiry are in transition, and must confront new discoveries that overthrow previously "well-established facts." A healthy skepticism of experts is therefore not at all unwarranted. On the other hand, it is important to observe that not every appeal to authority is a logical mistake. Quite to the contrary, it is often legitimate to appeal to an authority as a grounds for accepting some belief. It is eminently reasonable, for example, to appeal to the *National Geographic Atlas of the World* to confirm the claim that the city of Belem is in Brazil at the mouth of the Amazon river. An appeal to authority may therefore be either legitimate or illegitimate. The best advice seems to be to exercise caution in accepting or advancing arguments which appeal to authorities as their grounds.

9. TWO WRONGS MAKE A RIGHT

Louise-Phillipe had been growing more and more uncomfortable with Cassandra's dissertation, and he now broke into the conversation with a huff:

"They kill for Christ! They pervert the morals of the Christian Faith, the true teachings of Jesus!"

Cassandra looked up expecting more, but Louise-Phillipe seemed satisfied that he had made his point. She then responded:

"In our era, all of the nobility are knights, and all good knights are willing to take up arms for Christ...The Knights Templars are no different."

Although he does not respond in this manner in the story, Louise-Phillipe could challenge Cassandra on the grounds that if the Templars' killing for Christ is wrong, the fact that other nobility behave in the same manner, does not thereby alter the wrongness of the Templars' action. No. The other nobility behave wrongly too. And two wrongs do not make a right.

Whenever someone argues that an admittedly wrong action is nevertheless not wrong, and gives as grounds that actions of this kind are committed elsewhere, we have an instance of the fallacy, "Two Wrongs Make a Right." In its paradigm form, this fallacy is a species of the fallacy of Inconsistency. For it is an inconsistency to first admit that an action is "wrong," and then shortly thereafter to insist that it is "not wrong" after all.

More commonly, occurrences of the fallacy, "Two Wrongs Make A Right," are not also explicit inconsistencies. For example, suppose I argue:

"It is not so terribly wrong for the National Enquirer to slander public figures, since our leading politicians and government officials slander one another all of the time."

What I am insisting upon in this argument is not fully clear. On the one hand, if I admit that I do judge slander to be wrong, then I have committed the fallacy, and the fallacy of inconsistency too. However, suppose I insist that I genuinely meant to deny that the Enquirer is acting wrongly. And I add that I do not, finally, judge politicians who slander one another as having acted wrongly either. My position, I explain, is that certain wrong actions cease altogether to be wrong when they are commonly committed. Although my position is a controversial one that can be challenged on a variety of grounds, it is not strictly inconsistent, and it does not commit the error of arguing that two wrongs—that are really wrong—make a right. Of course, most studies of critical reaoning would unhesitantly identify my argument, as first stated above, as guilty of the fallacy, Two Wrongs Make A Right. And for practical purposes, we will too.

STUDY AID

SOME COMMON FALLACIES

1. THE FALLACY OF DENYING THE ANTECEDENT:

If P, then Q
Not P
─────
Not Q

2. THE FALLACY OF AFFIRMING THE CONSEQUENT

If P, then Q
Q
─────
P

3. BIASED BELIEF

Believing that an assertion is true or that the conclusion of an argument ought to be accepted as true not for any good reason, but because of a prior bias.

4. INCONSISTENCY

Affirming a set of assumptions which either explicitly or implicitly contain within them a strict contradiction.

5. HASTY GENERALIZATION

Asserting an unwarranted generalization.
Reasoning to a generalization that is too broad in scope or grounded upon too small a sample.

6. POST HOC, ERGO PROPTER HOC

(i)   Reasoning from the fact that B followed A in some particular instance, to the conclusion that A is the cause of B in that particular instance. (A Particular Cause)
(ii) Reasoning from the fact that B has followed A on one or several occasions, to the conclusion that A is always the cause of B. (A Causal Generalization)

7. THE FALLACY OF COMPOSITON

Inferring that a property of the parts must also be a property of the whole.

8. STRAW MAN

Attributing a position to some person or group which position that person or group does not hold, and criticizing the imposter position as if it were a genuine one.

9. FALSE DILEMMA

Arguing in regard to some subject that there are only two alternatives A and B, both undesirable, and that therefore the least undesirable alternative must be accepted — where there nevertheless exists an additional alternative C that is not nearly as undesirable as either A or B.

10. AD HOMINEM

Arguing that a position ought to be rejected because of undesirable qualities of the person or group who advocates it, and not because of undesirable qualities of the position itself.

11. AD VERECUNDIAM (ILLEGITIMATE APPEAL TO AUTHORITY)

Arguing for a position on the grounds that some authority advocates it, where the "authority" appealed to is not a legitimate authority on the subject matter of the position at all.

12. TWO WRONGS MAKE A RIGHT

Arguing that an action committed by one person or group that is ordinarily judged to be wrong is nevertheless not wrong because it is committed by other persons or other groups.

SOME COMMON FORMS OF GENERALIZATION

All persons who work hard succeed.
Everyone who works hard succeeds.
Anyone who works hard succeeds.
Anybody who works hard succeeds.
Whoever works hard succeeds.
A person who works hard succeeds.
People who work hard succeed.
Individuals who work hard succeed.

If you work hard you'll succeed.
Hardworkers succeed.
Every hardworker succeeds.
Hardwork brings success.

The last player dealt at a black jack table always has an advantage.
Advertising agencies are motivated solely for a desire for profit.
Without exception the criminals apprehended are read their rights.
Anything your heart desires I'll give you.
Every time he's late she gets very angry.

No one who hates people will succeed.
No marsupials lay eggs.
There is not a single person on the committee in favor of the motion.
No player on the team wants the coach to quit.
A trainer will never tell you the truth about an upcoming race.

In these exercises identifying fallacies, we will not treat either Biased Belief or the Fallacy of Composition. We will also defer our treatment of Post Hoc, Ergo Propter Hoc until we examine the nature of causal reasoning in more detail in Chapter VIII.

I.   For the purposes of illustration, attempt to identify the fallacies in the following argument. Then turn to the opposite side of this page for the correct identifications.

The liberal democrats do not have an intelligent understanding of the field of international politics. They argue for our withdrawal from Latin America, and indeed, would like us to withdraw our military presence from the remainder of the entire world. But a nation state in the world today must either present a threatening military regard to the rest of the world or be vulnerable to immediate invasion by some other militarily aggressive nation.

If the liberal democrats were intelligent about international politics, then we would be obligated to take their foreign policy views into serious account. But as we pointed out in our opening statement, this unfortunately is not the case. And consequently, we are not in the least obliged to take their foreign policy views seriously. Besides, from our observation of politicians of liberal persuasion in the past, including liberal republicans such as Richard Nixon, no liberal politician can be trusted to keep his word

Hasty
Generalization }

Straw
Man }

False
Dilemma }

(The liberal democrats do not have an intelligent understanding of the field of international politics.)　　(They argue for our withdrawal from Latin America, and indeed, would like us to withdraw our military presence from the remainder of the entire world.)　　(But a nation state in the world today must either present a threatening military regard to the rest of the world or be vulnerable to immediate invasion by some other militarily aggressive nation.)

Denying
the
Antecedent }

Hasty
Generalization }

(If the liberal democrats were intelligent about international politics, then we would be obligated to take their foreign policy views into serious account.　But as we pointed out in our opening statement, this unfortunately is not the case.　And consequently, we are not in the least obliged to take their foreign policy views seriously.)　　(Besides, from our observation of politicians of liberal persuasion in the past, including liberal Republicans such as Richard Nixon, no liberal politician can be trusted to keep his word.)

Identify the fallacies in the following arguments:

(i) If the chauffeur committed the murder, then the murder weapon was a 38 and the murder must have been committed before midday — since he left the premises at that time. Ballistics reports that a 38 bullet killed the victim and the coroner's autopsy reveals that the murder was committed between 10:30 and 11:30 A.M. in the late morning. We can therefore conclude that the chauffeur certainly committed the murder.

(ii) Werner Von Braun, one of the leading experts of the 20th century in the physics and engineering of misselry, has repeatedly and correctly argued for a higher military budget. He points out that the Soviet Union and the Warsaw Pact are willing to attack us, and will immediately attack us, if they believe that our misselry counter-attack will not be too devastating. Of course, there are those who oppose this position, but they are merely selfish citizens unwilling to pay the tax costs necessary to preserve our nation and our way of life.

(iii) The murder was committed either by the mistress or the chauffeur, of that we are certain. We know that if the chauffeur committed the murder, then it had to be committed in the garage. But it has been determined that the murder could not possibly have been committed in the garage. On the other hand, if the murder was committed by the mistress, then it must have been committed in the master bedroom. But there is a difficulty with this hypothesis. We have now determined that the murder could not have been committed anywhere within the mansion. So we are forced to return to our original hypothesis that the murder was indeed committed outside of the mansion in the garage and that the chauffeur certainly did it.

(iv) The student peace protesters want us to immediately disarm no matter the consequences, and to give the Russians our grain, weaponry, nuclear secrets, and everything else. I personally never had the opportunity to be a student with the luxury to protest and it is obvious to me that they ought to love their country and accept their govenment's policies or pack up their bags and become a citizen of another country. I say that we should oppose them and the Europeans who agree with them too. If France and Germany, our so-called allies, won't agree with us, then a few bombs in their backyard should quickly change their minds. The Russians used their bombs with impunity in Afghanistan, and if they can get away with it, then so can we.

205

(v) John: People on welfare, by being on welfare, are encouraged not to work. Certainly you can't motivate persons to be industrious by paying them to be idle. I admit that if the welfare system were handled efficiently, the result would be a healthy economy. But we all know that our welfare system is not just inefficient, it is grossly wasteful. And the consequence is that our economy over-all is unhealthy too — to the disadvantage of the rich and poor alike. So there is no choice but to bite the bullet and decide once and for all either to abolish our wasteful welfare system or continue to suffer its debilitating effects upon our work ethic and the health of our economy.

Mary: Well. I disagree. John can bite all of the bullets he wants. He was never discriminating in taste anyway. Being a poor boy who had the good fortune to marry into money, he no longer has any sympathy for, or any discriminating views about, the unemployed. If our welfare system were the negative contributor to our society that John insists it must be, then our economy would be in total disarray. But is it in disarray? No. Not at all. On the other hand if our system of welfare is in fact a positive contributor to our economy, then the minor setbacks and recessions it suffers can be accounted for on other grounds. And they can be so accounted for: they are the result of a failure to control the money supply, and thus to control inflation. So in direct opposition to John, I conclude that our welfare system positively contributes to a healthy economy and ought to be retained.

(vi) First degree murder should be punished by death. Capital punishment is both morally correct and it is practical as a deterrent too. Intentionally taking the life of another human being, eliminating their earthly existence once and forever, is the most terrible of all acts that a human being can commit. It is always wrong no matter the circumstances, and any individual arrogant enough to commit this terrible act, deserves the ultimate penalty. Of course, the opponents of capital punishment would happily see murderers go scot free. But either you execute them and eliminate the problem or in no time they are back on the streets killing again. Naturally, there are weak-willed liberals and sentimental Christians who insist that capital punishment is cruel and inhumane. They argue that executing murderers is not only wrong, but it doesn't even have a deterrent effect. However, in California in the last few years, since capital punishment was instituted, the incidence of murder has actually decreased. And that must be true of the entire United States, since California sets the pace for the rest of the nation. As a good citizen I therefore

206

conclude that we should forcefully support capital punishment for all cases of murder in the first degree.

II. Deduce The Conclusions of the Following Arguments.

(i) Deduce: The Democrats will certainly lose to the Republicans

Premises:

1.) If Chu Lee wins the Republican nomination, then another Asian American will certainly not be selected as his Lieutenant Governor running mate.

2.) But the convention caucus has already determined that either an Asian-American or an Hispanic will be nominated to run on the republican ticket as Lieutenant Governor.

3.) Of course, if an Hispanic is selected as the republican nominee for Lieutenant Governor, then the Democrats will certainly lose to the republicans.

4.) Chu Lee, it is certain, will win the republican nomination for Governor.

(ii) Deduce: Sanchez will not become a famous American statesman.

Premises:

1.) Anyone who wins the democratic nomination for president must support the reduction of NATO forces.   (premise)

2.) No one who accepts the democratic vice-presidential nomination will be elected vice-president.   (premise)

3.) Sanchez will not accept the position of secretary of state.   (premise)

4.) If Sanchez does not win the democratic nomination for president, then he'll accept either the democratic nomination for vice-president or the position of secretary of state.   (premise)

207

5.) Sanchez does not support the reduction of NATO
forces.   (premise)

6.) Sanchez will become a famous American statesman
only if he is elected Vice-President.   (premise)

CHAPTER V: ANALYSIS

I. ANALOGICAL REASONING AND "THE ARGUMENT FROM DESIGN": A FORM OF INDUCTIVE REASONING

For the purposes of our analysis, let us employ the following succinct characterization of (one rendition of) "The Argument from Design."

(i)   The universe exhibits a structural design.

(ii) A machine exhibits a structural design.

(iii) A machine is made by an intelligent being.

The universe was made by an intelligent being,
namely, that being we call 'God.'

The Argument from Design is not a deductive argument and therefore cannot be deductively valid. Its conclusion does not follow with necessity from its premises, i.e., the logical forms of the thoughts in the premises do not imply the logical form of the thought in the conclusion. Rather, the argument employs an inductive form of reasoning, analogical reasoning, and thus cannot guarantee the truth of its conclusion even if its premises are certainly true and its reasoning is cogent. Nevertheless, there are sound analogical arguments with very likely conclusions which reasonable persons ought to accept, just as there do exist poor analogical arguments which we ought not to accept.

The Argument From Design draws an analogy between the universe and a machine. It seeks to persuade us of the following: Since the universe and a machine are similar in exhibiting structural design, and since a machine was made by an intelligent being, it is likely that the universe was made by an intelligent being too.

We can represent the form of this argument as follows:

Scheme of Abbreviation:

  m: a machine
  u: the universe
  D: the property of exhibiting structural design
  I: the property of being made by an intelligent being

Argument:

  u has the property D

  m has the property D
  m has the property I
  _____

  u has the property I

u and m are similar in having the property D, m has the property I, and the conclusion is drawn that it is likely that u also has the property I. Obviously, an analogical argument may be constituted of more than two properties. For example, suppose that on Tuesday night we were called as detectives to the scene of a murder committed at midnight in the neighbourhood of Hollywood. The murder weapon was a 45, the victim was a derelict alcoholic, and there were a dozen witnesses who saw Jack Smith do it. We send out an all-points bulletin on Jack, but he is not apprehended. Now suppose that on Wednesday night we are called to the scene of another murder, again committed at midnight in the neighbourhood of Hollywood. The victim is a derelict alcoholic, the murder weapon is a 45, but unfortunately there are no witnesses. Drawing an analogy between these two crimes, we would reason that tonight's crime was (probably) committed by Jack too. Of course, we would not at all consider this conclusion to be certain. The murderer could be somone who read a description of Tuesday night's murder, and who patterned his own crime after it to throw us off the scent — knowing that we would reason by analogy.

We can represent the form of this argument as follows:

Scheme of Abbreviation:

  t: Tuesday night's murder
  w: Wednesday night's murder
  M: The property of being committed at midnight
  S: The property of being committed in Hollywood
  F: The property of being committed with a 45
  D: The property of having a derelict alcoholic as a victim
  J: The property of having been committed by Jack Smith

The Argument:

t has the property M
w has the property M

t has the property S
w has the property S

t has the property F
w has the property F

t has the property D
w has the property D

t has the property J
_____

w has the property J

In this argument, because there are four properties in which the two entities compared are similar, the similarity drawn seems a reasonably strong one, rendering the conclusion likely. Indeed, from this example we can extrapolate the following criterion.:

"The more similar the two entities compared, the more likely the conclusion."

We can render this criterion more precisely as follows:

"The greater the number of properties the two entities compared have in common, the more likely the conclusion."

Thus, whenever we advance an analogical argument, it is more cogent and more persuasive to the extent to which we can cite more and more similar properties. Of course, someone can challenge our argument and the similarity on which it rests by producing dissimilarities between the entities compared. "But ballistics reports that the bullets in Tuesday night's crime were fired from a different 45 than the bullets in Wednesday night's crime. Moreover, an informant insists that Jack Smith had a vendetta against the person he murdered on Tuesday night, who refused to pay the money he owed him, whereas he didn't know Wednesday night's victim at all." Let us therefore amend the criterion to read:

"The greater the number of properties the two entities compared have in common, and the fewer the number of properties in which they differ, the more likely the conclusion."

211

This amended criterion is an improvement, but as we will shortly see when we directly engage the Argument from Design as presented within the story, it too is flawed and in need of revision.

Before we do directly engage the argument, for the purposes of clarity it is probably wise to mark the distinction between analogical reasoning on the one hand, and a different sort of reasoning, inductive generalization on the other.

Let us suppose that Jack Smith is a mass murderer, that he has committed and has been witnessed committing six crimes strikingly similar to the crime we have been called to on Wednesday night. Some logicians analyze this sort of case as six analogies each re-inforcing the conclusion that Jack Smith committed Wednesday night's murder. I prefer instead to limit analogical reasoning to two entities (or kinds of entities), and to analyze this case as utilizing either inductive generalization, or the confirmation of an hypothesis, or both.

Analysis I: Utilizing inductive generalization, the form of the argument would be:

1. (i) Murder 1 had the properties; M,S,F,D,H, and was committed by Jack Smith.

    (ii) Murder 2 had the properties; M,S,F,D,H, and was committed by Jack Smith.

    (iii) Murder 3 . . . .

    (iv) Murder 4 . . . .

    (v) Murder 5 . . . .

    (vi) Murder 6 . . . .

---

2. Therefore, all murders — within a certain time period — that have the properties M,S,F,D,H are committed by Jack Smith.
    Inductive Generalization (i)-(vi)

3. Wednesday night's murder has the properties M,S,F,D and H.

4. Therefore, Wednesday night's murder was committed by Jack Smith.   Universal Instantiation and Modus Ponens (2), (3)

212

Analysis II: Utilizing the concept of an hypothesis and its confirmation and disconfirmation, the form of the argument would be:

1. Hypothesis: Jack Smith committed Wednesday night's murder.

2. If Jack Smith committed Wednesday night's murder, then from the evidence of his past six murders, it is likely that:

    (a) Wednesday night's murder has the property M (was committed near midnight).

    (b) Wednesday night's murder has the property S (was committed in Hollywood).

    (c) Wednesday night's murder has the property F

    (d) Wednesday night's murder has the property D

    (e) Wednesday night's murder has the property H

3. (a), (b), (c), (d), (e) are all true. Each count as a partial confirmation of the hypothesis that Jack Smith did it, and taken together render the hypothesis likely.

4. Furthermore, let us explore whether there are other consequences of the hypothesis "that Jack Smith committed the Wednesday night murder" which we can seek to confirm or disconfirm.

We are now prepared to directly engage the critical discussion of the Argument from Design as it occurs within the story. Our analysis will focus in sequence upon the following:

(I)   Some conclusion does (tentatively) follow, but not the conclusion that God exists. (Hawkins)

Related to the above is the criticism that the argument trades on an ambiguity in the use of the word "made." (Stevens)

(II)   The argument is insufficient to ground belief in any conclusion.

It is not a deductive argument. (Perkins)

It is wise to withhold belief. (Stevens)

Do not accept the argument on St. Thomas Aquinas' authority. (Hawkins)

(III)   The argument can be trivialized. (Caldwell)

(IV)   The argument Caldwell advances to trivialize the Argument from Design can be employed to trivialize any and every analogical argument, and therefore must be worthless. (Cassandra)

With this outline before us, let us now begin the analysis

(I)   (Hawkins) "Even if the analogical reasoning the argument employs is worth serious attention, it does not prove the existence of God."

". . . the argument certainly doesn't prove a being that's benevolent or just, or eternal, or perfectly powerful for that matter."

"I see. The conclusion is far too immodest."

". . . Only someone first gullible enough to believe in the existence of God will be gullible enough to believe that the argument proves the existence of God."

First of all, let us observe that in the last segment of this quotation Hawkins charges Cassandra with the Fallacy of Biased Belief. Because of a predisposition to believe in the truth of the conclusion, Cassandra mistakenly presumes that the argument must be a good argument: because it 'proves' what she would like to believe to be true, she is biased in her appraisal of it — or so Hawkins alleges.

214

Hawkin's central criticism is, "that even if the similarity drawn is a strong one warranting some conclusion, this conclusion is something other, and something far less, than what the argument claims to prove." This is an important general point that applies to argumentation in general. An argument may have true premises which, taken together, imply some conclusion, and yet deceive us into accepting a conclusion which its premises in no way warrant. The Argument from Design is a striking example of this error. There may exist a single intelligent maker of the universe, who also has the properties of being benevolent, just, eternal, etc. But the argument doesn't prove any of these latter properties. Thus, the conclusion should be narrowed in scope to, "The universe was made by an intelligent being," and the addition, ". . . namely, that being we call 'God'." should be excised.

The immodesty of the conclusion of the Argument from Design is often overlooked, not only by its proponents, but also by its critics. This oversight has its origin in the failure to clarify beforehand the conception of God the argument alleges to prove. The concept of God is left vague and imprecise. Related to this point is the criticism insisted upon by Stevens, that the argument erroneously trades upon an ambiguity in the use of the word "made." There would be no ambiguity if the conclusion had originally been more precisely rendered as, "The universe was created, ex nihilo (out of nothing)," and if the premise with "made" had been rendered instead as, "fashioned according to some design from pre-existing materials."

Let us be clear that the ambiguous use of the word "made" contributes to the immodesty of the conclusion. There may exist an intelligent being in some way responsible for the design of the universe, and, in addition, this being may have also created ex-nihilo the material of which the universe is (was then) constituted. But the argument doesn't prove the latter, which ought to be excised from the conclusion.

(II)   The Argument from Design is Insufficient to Ground Belief in Any Conclusion, Even the Conclusion That The Universe Was Created by an Intelligent Being

I will treat this criticism briefly, leaving the final determination of its acceptability to the reader.

(i)   "That's not a logical proof and from it nothing whatsoever can be concluded! Not one whit of mathematical or deductive reasoning is employed in it! And one can only prove what logically follows from incontrovertibly true premises — and that's not much." (Perkins)

Perkins' rejection of the argument is an extreme, and probably excessive, instance of withholding belief. As Sherlock indicates, there are cogent forms of reasoning other than strict deductive reasoning.

(ii)   "The inconclusiveness of the debate is its own point."

"And that point?"

"If we place high demands upon the grounds and reasons for our beliefs...the Argument from Design should not alone persuade us of the existence of God."

"Should it more modestly persuade us of the existence of some intelligence as responsible for the design and the creation of the universe?"

"No. It shouldn't even persuade us of that."

Stevens argues for the wisdom of withholding belief in the argument and its conclusion on the grounds that it can be vigorously and inconclusively debated. He advances his own alternative cosmology of a universe existing ad infinitum from the past, and observes the argument's ambiguous use of the word "made."

(III)   (Sherlock) "And I suppose, Dr. Hawkins, that you do not think that the conclusion of the argument shows a single intelligent being as contrasted with a plurality of beings?"

(Hawkins) " . . . . . . In fact, the more complex the machine, the more likely several intelligent beings were involved in its design and fabrication. . . Yes! If you follow through the analogy, the conclusion should be, 'Made by some intelligence, either singular or plural'."
. . . .
(Caldwell) "By the same reasoning, the Argument from Design must conclude that the makers of the universe possessed eyes and fingernails, and were divided in sex between males and females."

Sherlock apparently agrees with Hawkins that the argument's conclusion is immodest. Sherlock observes that the argument does not obviously prove — if it proves anything — the existence of a single intelligent being responsible for the order of the universe. Understood in this way his point belongs above under (I). However, it also sets the stage for Caldwell's criticism that the proper conclusion of the argument is both incredible and totally different from what most of the proponents of the argument ever intended.

Caldwell's criticism here was suggested earlier in the eighteenth century by the famous Scottish Philosopher David Hume in a fascinating and perennially popular treatise entitled, *Dialogues Concerning Natural*

216

Religion. [8] The criticism is subtle, but if we take some care in exposing its logic, it is not difficult to understand.

We begin with the assumption that the similarity drawn between a machine and the universe is sufficiently strong to render the conclusion likely, "that an intelligent God created the universe." That is, we assume that:

> The similarity in properties between a machine and the universe is sufficiently strong to warrant the following: Since a machine has the additional property of being made by an intelligent being, it is likely that the universe is similar to a machine in that respect also, i.e., is made by an intelligent being too.

Caldwell argues that by the same reasoning we can trivialize the argument and show that the universe was made by a being with eyes and fingernails. His argument can be reconstructed as employing two steps: First, generalizing the reasoning employed above to:

> The similarity in properties between a machine and the universe is sufficiently strong to warrant the following: If a machine has an additional property, say the property F, it is likely that the universe is similar to a machine in that respect too, i.e., in having the property F.

Caldwell believes that this general form of reasoning is presupposed in the Argument from Design, that the Argument from Design is just one instance of it. He now deduces a different instance of this general form of reasoning by Universal Instantiation, arriving at the following embarrassing conclusion:

> The similarity in properties between a machine and the universe is sufficiently strong to warrant the following: Since a machine has the additional property of being made by a being with eyes and fingernails, it is likely that the universe is similar to a macchine in that respect also, i.e., is made by a being with eyes and fingernails too.

Note: Caldwell's belief that he has trivialized the Argument from Design by showing that it must affirm the existence of a human-like God or Gods, rests on the assumption that advocates of the argument would altogether reject an anthropomorphic conception of God. It should be observed, however, that this conclusion would not at all be embarrassing to theists who conceive God as human-like, such as believers in the popular Hindu Panetheon, or even orthodox believers in the Hebrew Bible, the Koran, or the Christian New Testament. The latter three, of course, would not accept a polytheistic theology with female deities as well as male.

217

IV: Cassandra's Counter-Arguments:

Cassandra advances two distinguishable, but related, objections to Caldwell's line of argument. Let us consider them in the order in which they occur in the story.

1.)   "By the same reasoning, the Argument from Design must conclude that the makers of the universe possessed eyes and fingernails. (Caldwell)

. . . .

"But intelligence seems relevant to conceiving and making structure, whereas having fingernails does not."   (Cassandra)

Cassandra's objection here points to a critical feature of any rationally acceptable analogical argument, namely, that the properties cited in the premises that constitute the similarity (analogy) must be related to the property cited in the conclusion. She believes that the original argument does exhibit this feature of relatedness (linking design and intelligence), whereas Caldwell's alleged trivialization, which links design with fingernails, does not.

This point is obvious once it is made explicit, but it needs to be made explicit and to be underscored. For purposes of illustration, let us suppose that you believe, and are willing to bet real money, that your team, the Snakes, will win next Saturday's game with the Buzzards, because the Buzzards are a team strikingly similar to the Condors whom your team defeated in a game last Saturday. And suppose further that you rest your belief that the Condors are similar to the Buzzards upon the fact that they both are named after birds, have blue as one of the colors of their jerseys, and require all of their players to wear helmets — a a requirement for all teams in the league. Obviously, you would not be a wise gambler, although you could be a lucky one.

A similar point applies to challenges against analogical arguments. If I sincerely challenge the similarity you have drawn between the Buzzards and the Condors as insubstantial, and proceed to point out that the Buzzards have red as the other color of their jerseys whereas the Condors have black, and that the bird the Condors is named after is an endangered species whereas the bird the Buzzards is named after is not, I would be as foolish and irrational as you.

It is very clear from this commentary that we must revise our criterion to mark a distinction between those properties that are related to the conclusion and those that are not. Let us simply amend the criterion as follows:

218

THE GREATER THE NUMER OF PROPERTIES RELATED TO THE CONCLUSION THE TWO ENTITIES COMPARED HAVE IN COMMON, AND THE FEWER THE NUMBER OF PROPERTIES RELATED TO THE CONCLUSION IN WHICH THE TWO ENTITIES COMPARED DIFFER, THE MORE LIKELY THE CONCLUSION.

2.) "By precisely the same reasoning which concludes that the universe was created by some intelligence, one must conclude that this intelligence also has fingernails — because machines are made by intelligent beings with fingernails." (Caldwell)

"And I suppose the same is true for sex," added Cassandra, thereby prompting a defensive blush from Caldwell; "I mean," she continued, "a division of beings by sex."

"Yes." responded Caldwell, now confused and still blushing.

"And the universe must have been made by a group of persons numbering five to six billion."

"Yes."

"And by a group of persons, one of whose name is Caldwell and is a brilliant young scientist."

"Yes... I admit... It does sound absurd. But that is just the point. The argument reduces to absurdity."

"I don't agree! I can't agree! If you're correct, then every argument that uses an analogy in its reasoning can be reduced to absurdity by your technique."

Cassandra's objection that Caldwell's technique can be applied to any analogical argument, even very sound ones, is well taken.

Suppose that the nature, quality, and performance record of an opponent team, the Ravens, whom your team is scheduled to play this coming Saturday, is very, very similar to that of the Hawks, whom your team played and badly defeated last Saturday, and that on the basis of this similarity you argue that your team is likely to defeat the Ravens too. I would be foolish if I insisted that by "precisely the same reasoning" we can trivialize your argument by concluding that the Ravens, like the Hawks, must wear red and black jerseys and have six brunette cheerleaders, which we know they do not.

219

My error here, and Caldwell's error in the story, is a misuse of generalization. It is logically illegitimate to move from:

(a) Since a machine has the additional property of being made by an intelligent being, it is likely that the universe is similar to a machine in that respect too.

to:

(b) (For any F) (If a machine has an additional property F, it is likely that the universe is similar to a machine in that respect too (i.e., in having the property F)

Caldwell insists that (b) is presupposed by (a), but it is not. (b) is an incorrect generalization from (a) that overlooks the distinction between properties in the premises and the conclusion that are related to one another and those that are not. Moreover, to suppose that (b) is true, is to suppose that it is likely that a machine and the universe are identically similar, that is, similar in every last respect. And this is obviously erroneous. Caldwell's technique applied generally to analogical arguments treats the two entities compared in each argument as identically similar. Cassandra goes directly to this point when she says, "... then every argument that uses an analogy in its reasoning can be reduced to absurdity by your technique."

We can observe this error clearly in our last illustration. We began with:

The similarity between the Hawks and the Ravens is sufficiently strong to warrant the following: Since the Hawks have the additional property of being defeated by my team, it is likely that the Ravens will be similar to the Hawks in that respect too (i.e., will be defeated by my team).

Applying Caldwell's technique, we then illegitimately infer the following generalization:

The similarity between the Hawks and the Ravens is sufficiently strong to warrant the following: (For any F) If the Hawks have the additional property F, it is likely that the Ravens will be similar to the Hawks in having the property F too.

It is from this illegitimately inferred generalization that we can now deduce, by Universal Instantiation, the following false conditional proposition:

220

If the Hawks wear red and black jerseys, then it is likely that the Ravens will wear read and black jerseys too.

We know that the Hawks do wear red and black jerseys and that the Ravens don't. In the original analogical argument in which we projected the Ravens defeat, we never intended to imply that the Ravens were identically similar. Indeed, we knew that they were not. Similarly, those who advance the Argument from Design never intended to imply that God is identically similar to a human being. Indeed, all along they assume quite to the contrary that in many respects God is not.

SUMMARY

Let us summarize the main features of our analysis of analogical reasoning:

(i)   Analogical reasoning is a form of non-deductive reasoning; consequently, even if the premises are true and the similarity drawn between the entities compared is strong, the conclusion is at most extremely likely, and can possibly be false.

(ii)   An analogical argument has the following form:
(For the purpose of illustration let us represent an analogical argument with four properties, although such an argument could have less than four or many more than four properties.)

a has the property F
b has the property F

a has the property G
b has the property G

a has the property H
b has the property H

a has the property I
_____

b has the property I

(iii)   The stronger the simlarity between the entities compared in an analogical argument, the more likely its conclusion, or, more explicitly:

THE GREATER THE NUMBER OF PROPERTIES RELATED TO THE CONCLUSION THE TWO ENTITIES COMPARED HAVE IN COMMON, AND THE FEWER NUMBER OF PROPERTIES RELATED TO THE CONCLUSION IN WHICH THE TWO ENTITIES COMPARED DIFFER, THE MORE LIKELY THE CONCLUSION.

I.   Identify the fallacies in the following arguments:

    (i)   We must blockade Cuba at once or else Cuba will soon control Latin America. Whenever a country is governed by an elite, as is the case in Cuba, it wants to take over the world. Of course, the World Court will insist that a blockade, without a declaration of a state of war is a violation of international treaties, but other countries such as England have not hesitated to use a blockade whenever they thought it was advantageous, whether it was during war time or not.

    (ii)   We must continue to maintain 1st strike misselry based in Europe, and pointed towards Russia. If we do not, Russia will one day invade Western Europe, overcome the NATO forces and subject the remainder of Europe to Communism. They did this before in Latvia, Lithuania, and Estonia; so we know that any time they are given the military opportunity to conquer a country, they will.

    (iii)   Mary: Women should have equal authority in all matters regarding the family.

                  John: But women are not capable of replacing men as the head of the household, and subjecting their husbands to their commands as you feminists so ardently desire.

                  Mary: That's not true. Think of the couples we know. In every one of them, the women are more capable than the men. In character, women are stronger than men — who are just overgrown boys like you.

                  John: Well, I believe that you either retain the man as head of the household or anarchy will reign within the family. Doesn't the Bible agree? If Adam had been taken from Eve's rib then it would follow that a woman should head the household. But, he was not! Eve was taken from his rib instead. And that conclusively proves that a woman should not have the final authority within the home.

                  Mary: And you're just a rude male egotist!

                  John: And it's people like me who made this country great.

    (iv)   Person A: The socialists are determined to win over the entire world for communism. If they succeed, individual freedom will disappear. So we must stop them or plan to live in subjugation to a communist dictatorship. Fortunately, since the U.S. numbers among their determined opponents, they will not succeed, and thus freedom will not disappear. For wherever there are individuals willing to die for liberty, totalitarianism cannot succeed. On the other hand, the supporters of capitalism argue that their form of economy brings perfect justice. But if capitalism brings perfect justice, then there should be no injustice anywhere in the United States — which there obviously is. Unfortunately, the supporters of capitalism are blinded by their greed. And cannot see the miseries of others. . . . And which of these economic systems, socialism or capitalism, will finally win the struggle? There should be more socialist economies now than ever before, if socialism is the economic system destined to win. And indeed there are! Thus whether we approve of it or not, socialism will certainly win the struggle and capitalism will become obsolete.

Person B: I disagree. As the society of concerned physicists points out, neither side will win because political events are moving inexorably towards a catastrophic nuclear war. And although war is an obvious evil, it has been used to resolve disputes before, and might as well be used again. Of course, this resolution will mean the demise of both parties, and perhaps even humanity itself. But if human beings can't live peaceably with one another, then perhaps they don't deserve to survive.

II.   In the arguments below identify the following assertions and forms of reasoning:

    (i)   Reasoning by Analogy: (RA)

a has the property F
a has the property G
a has the property H
. . . .
b has the property F
b has the property G
. . . .
_____

b has the property H

    (ii)   Hypothesizing a Generalization: (HG)

    (iii)   Asserting an Hypothesis: (AH)

(iv) Asserting that some consequence is implied by an hypothesis: (HIC)

(v) Partially confirming an hypothesis: (PCH)

If H, then c

c
_____
c is a partial confirmation of H

(vi) Disconfirming an hypothesis: (DH)

If H, then c
Not c
_____
Not H

(vii) Asserting a chain of consequences following from an hypothesis: (CCH)

If H, then c1	(HIC)
If c1, then c2	(CCH)
. . . .	

(viii) Eliminating Alternative Hypotheses: (EAH)

Either H1 or H2
Not H1
_____
H2

(ix) Reductio Ad Absurdum: (RAA)

Assumption
. . . .
Assumption A
Assumption Not A
_____
This set of assumptions must be rejected as inconsistent

(Reductio ad Absurdum is a form of reasoning in which we reject a set of assumptions as inconsistent by identifying an explicit contradiction or by making an implicit contradiction explicit.

EXERCISES:

Example:
Some persons hypothesize that extra-terrestrial beings in space craft have visited our planet. If this were true, then there ought to be tangible evidence either of these beings themselves or of their space craft. But no tangible evidence of their craft has ever been produced, not even a single remnant. Moreover, the reports of persons who claim to have seen these extra-terrestrials have never been verified, and thus cannot count as tangible evidence either. Consequently, no matter how attractive it may be, we must reject the belief that extra-terrestrial beings in space craft have visited our planet.

AH (Some persons hypothesize that extra-terrestrial beings in space craft have visited our planet.)   (If this were true,
HC then there ought to be tangible evidence either of these beings themselves or of their space craft.)   (But no tangible evidence of their craft has ever been produced, not even a single remnant.   Moreover, the reports of persons who claim
DH to have seen these extra-terrestrials have never been verified, and thus cannot count as tangible evidence either. Consequently, no matter how attractive it may be, we must reject the belief that extra-terrestrial beings in space craft have visited our planet.)

(a) It was a supposition by some medieval theologians that God the Father is identical to God the Son.   These theologians also presumed that God the Father created the universe.   But if God the Father created the universe, and God the Father is identical to God the Son, then it must follow that God the Son created the universe too. Curiously, these theologians denied that God the Son created the universe.   Their view therefore internally conflicts, and must be rejected as unreasonable.

(b) Let us suppose that God is both benevolent and omnipotent. If God is both benevolent and omnipotent, then God will both want to prevent human suffering and be capable of preventing human suffering. But if it were true that God both wants to, and has the capacity to, prevent human suffering, then there would be no human suffering. And as we all know, there is considerable human suffering indeed. Thus it must not be true that God is both benevolent and omnipotent too.

(c) The last time William suddenly became especially attentive to me, surprising me with flowers, and escorting me to the theatre several week-ends in a row, I discovered by chance that he was seeing another woman on the sly. I suspect that he displayed all of that attention for one of two reasons: either because he was feeling guilty or just to cover his tracks. And now, over a year later, after a long lull of luke-warm affection, his romancing me has suddenly heated up. Indeed, he even surprised me with flowers, and invited me to go to a performance of Shakespeare's *A Midsummer Night's Dream*. I suppose he thought I would be pleased, since he knows that I love the theatre.   But his behaviour is too much like a repeat of last year's performance. And I'm convinced that recently his eyes have been roving, and that he's once again chasing after some other woman. And you can be sure that if that's true, I'm not going to be idle. There's a new fellow in our company whom I've had my eye on now for quite some time.

226

(d) The master of the mansion was murdered some time last evening. His body was discovered in the library. We hypothesize that either the chauffeur or the chambermaid committed the murder, since only they were on the premises at the time of the murder — the chambermaid in her room on the first floor, the chauffeur in his apartment above the garage. If the chauffeur committed the murder, then his motive was undoubtedly a passionate love for the mistress. And if his motive was a passionate love for his mistress, then evidence should exist of this love in his quarters. And indeed, a thorough search there revealed a hidden portrait of the mistress, along with love letters that she had written to him. Moreover, we have evidence that the master was murdered outside of the mansion in the garden. And if the chambermaid were the murderer, she would have had to carry or drag his portly body to the library, something we seriously doubt she had sufficient strength to do. So, given our assumptions, we conclude that she did not commit the murder, and therefore, that it must have been the chauffeur who did.

(e) Any nation state that becomes very strong economically always attempts to assert its power aggressively throughout the remainder of the world. This fact of life in a world of nation states is verified by the behaviour of the Soviet Union and by the behaviour of the United States. I believe that within the next two decades either China or Brazil will achieve a very strong economy, surpassing at least Japan, and perhaps the Soviet Union too. I realize that this claim is quite controversial, but after the Second World War, when the former Western European Economic Powers declined, new nation states, the U.S., the U.S.S.R., and Japan moved in to fill the vacuum. We now have a similar situation where the U.S., the U.S.S.R, and some even say Japan, have reached their economic peak, and have already begun a gradual economic decline. And I predict that the most robust of the major developing economies, China and Brazil, will move in to fill a vacuum too. The result, of course, will be that both of these nation states will aggressively attempt to assert their power throughout the world.

(f) One day my friend Dick's car would not start. I told him that if the battery was the cause of the problem, the starter would not turn over properly. "Indeed." He said. "My starter does not turn over at all, so I guess it's my battery." I further pointed out to him that there were two likely possibilities: if the battery really was the problem: either it was low and too weak to turn over the starter, or it was fine, but its electricity was not being successfully transferred to the starter.

If the battery was low, it would probably emit a "tic-a-tic-a-tic" sound when the ignition key was turned on — an awful sound to hear on a cold Monday morning. But Dick said, "When I turned on the key there was no sound at all." Reverting to the other alternative, I observed that if the battery was not transmitting electricity that it possessed to the starter, the culprit was undoubtedly corroded or loose cable couplings on the battery terminals. Dick said that he had not checked that at all, but would do so when he returned home this evening. I recommended that he clean the terminals and cable couplings and tighten the couplings on firmly. The next day I saw Dick, and he smiled broadly and said, "It worked! My terminals were all encrusted. I followed your advice and cleaned them up, and the car started immediately. You're a great friend Jane. I don't know what I'd do without you." As you can imagine I was quite relieved. For as everyone knows, sometimes if your starter won't turn over at all, and there is no "tick-a-tic-a-tic" sound, it means that the battery is completely dead. And sometimes when the battery is dead, this means it is worn out and must be replaced at no mean cost to a poor struggling student.

III.   State and critically discuss <u>The Argument From Design</u>.

CHAPTER VI: ANALYSIS

INTRODUCTION

"Gentlemen . . . The matter of Laura Anderson's murder still lies before us unresolved. You have presented us with general philosophical reasons why no one of you would have a motive to murder anyone. But that is altogether unsatisfactory in elucidating the particular matter at hand. You must be more specific. . . you must tell us first, the exact time Laura Anderson arrived at her meeting with you. Secondly, you must tell us the exact time she departed and her state of mind at the moment. And thirdly, you must tell us the exact nature of the conversation you had with her."

In this chapter, our attention will be focused upon clarity of thought. I will first treat (i) the relation between language and thought, and more specifically, the relation between language and lucid thought. I will then (ii) mark the important distinction between the use or meaning of a sentence and the use or meaning of a word. In section (iii) I will treat the difference between the use of words to refer to entities and to attribute properties. In section (iv) I will elaborate the difference between ambiguity and vagueness, and in (v) I will once again engage the subject of logical form. Finally, in (vi) I will treat examples of alternative hypotheses advanced in Chapter VI of the story.

SECTION I: LANGUAGE AND LUCID THOUGHT

Let me propose by way of introduction to our subject, a general maxim which I believe we ought to diligently follow if we wish to promote clarity in our own thinking. The maxim is the following:

We will never attribute our lack of clarity in regard to some subject as a problem that arises not with our thought, but with the expression of our thoughts in language. We will never insist that though we are vague or confused in our words, we are nevertheless clear in our minds.

Very many of us have deep and persistent problems with language in either its written form or its verbal form (or both). And it is true that the sources of difficulty in language communication are many, and vary in range from our own emotions befuddling our thoughts, to persons so prejudiced they refuse to listen even to facts. However, we would be well

229

advised to proceed on the assumption that the responsibility for communication rests with the communicator, and that the responsibility when we fail in communication is our own.

An important corollary to accepting such responsibility is shattering the general distinction we would very much like to draw between thought and its linguistic expression. For it is easy to believe fervently in a theory of the relation between language and thought that so conveniently lets us off the hook. The maxim which we affirmed above at least sets a mimimum guideline here, since it specifically does not permit us to draw a distinction between clarity in linguistic expression and clarity of thought.

It is not my intention here to deny the existence of "thinking in images" or "flashes of insight," or any other variety of mental activity that in conformity with common usage we would list under the heading of thinking, or of the various meanings or uses, of the word "thinking." Rather, the point is simply that we ought to treat whatever we find already articulated in language as also present in thought. Thus, a creative use of language indicates a creative use of mind; vagueness in the verbal presentation of some subject is weighty evidence for impreciseness of thought on that subject; an articulate and lucid description is evidence of articulate and lucid thought; and confusion in what one has written is evidence of a prior confusion in thought. Indeed, concerning the latter correlation I can report that in over two decades of teaching, I have never once witnessed an instance of confused writing that was preceded by clear thought: "It was clear in my mind, I just put it down in a confused manner."

There is no way to over-emphasize the importance of these observations. It is a nasty fact, but we still ought not to avoid the fact, that whenever we distinguish between linguistic and symbolic skills on the one hand, and intellectual skills on the other, we are on slippery ground. It is easy to fix on the opinion that language is a terrible and an inadequate and a fundamentally misleading medium, when we ought instead to be honest about where our inadequacies have their origin in gaps in our education which we must now overcome, and where we've been just plain lazy or too stubborn to follow intelligent advice. At the very least we ought to be honest with ourselves. We ought to recognize, for example, our dishonesty when we say, "I have a poor handwriting," or "I cannot spell," if we intend these words to constitute an excuse or to point to fixed traits that can never be overcome.

We have already seen how language is put to an extraordinary variety of purposes, or to phrase this differently, that there are an extraordinary number of human actions which are typically enacted in language. These actions, moreover, are not "merely linguistic" in the sense of that phrase that suggests that they are not really important. For we certainly do mean business when we say, "I do," or when we sign our will, or when we say to a dying Catholic friend, "I promise I will care for and raise your children, whose ages are two, three, four, five, six, seven, and eight."

Now two of the most important large categories of language acts in terms of their purposes are, (i) acts whose purpose is communicating information, and (ii) acts whose purpose is persuasion. These two large categories of language acts are especially pertinent to our study. Success in communicating information typically depends upon clarity; imagine here, reporting, describing, explaining, representing, etc. Successful persuasion also often depends upon clarity, although it often depends upon cogency of reasoning too. Clarity and cogency of reasoning, of course, are the twin aims of this study in Practical Logic.

It is important to observe that we affirm these twin aims as ideals, not only in our relationship to others, but also for our own individual fulfillment. We do not want to be confused, vague, and mistaken, but instead prefer our thoughts to be lucid and reasonable — whether we communicate them to others or not. We should not forget that we typically carry on dialogues in language not only with others, but also with ourselves. During any ordinary day, we commonly "talk to ourselves," and not uncommonly in persuasive language employing arguments and counter-arguments for and against certain positions and courses of action. And although we sometimes enjoy being foolish for foolishness' sake, we finally do not want to ground the important decisions of our life upon confused ideas and mistaken beliefs.

SECTION II: USES OF SENTENCES AND USES OF WORDS

It is important to mark a difference between the purposes to which we put our sentences and the purposes to which we put the words that make up our sentences. We have already catalogued some of the many uses of sentences, such as promising, ordering, describing, requesting, etc. It is important now, for the purposes of understanding ambiguity and vagueness, to distinguish out a separate classification for the uses of words (and phrases).

The various components of an automobile engine, such as the carburetor, pistons, spark plugs, and crankshafts, each serve a different purpose, although when functioning harmoniously together, they constitute a working engine used for the purpose of propelling an automobile. Analogously, words (and phrases) that compounded together make up sentences, often serve very different functions from one another, and from the sentence itself viewed as a whole. Let us review a few of the many different uses of words (and phrases) constituting sentences, singling out three major categories or use to attend to in detail.

(i)   To indicate quantity: "several," "all," "a few," "for a long

231

time," "usually," "one, two. . . ." etc.

(ii)   To indicate the communicator's degree of belief in what is asserted: "know," "believe," "feel certain that," "doubt," etc.

(iii)   To indicate in conjunction with other words, time reference: "will," "was," "did," "am," "used to," "plan to," "at some future date," etc.

(iv)   To indicate direction: "down," "to the left," "straight ahead," "beyond," "veer," "Northwest," etc.

(v)   To indicate place: "here," "behind," "there," "in front of," "below," "in," "inside of," etc.

(vi)   To refer (to animate or inanimate entities): "Sylvester," "Nashville," "the desk," "philosophy students," "birds," "rocks," etc.

(vii)   To attribute properties (to animate or inanimate entities): "is brown," "is heavy," "is industrious," "is in Tennessee," "is unhappy," "is rectangular," etc.

(viii)   To indicate logical form: "And," "or," "if," "only if," "all," "is," "any," etc.

Let us immediately observe that we can fail to be precise with respect to any one of these word or phrase uses:

(i)   "You say 'for a long time,' but for how long?

(ii)   "You state that you believe that God exists, but for certain, or probably or what?"

(iii)   "You promise me you will pay me back, but when, tomorrow or next year?"

(iv)   "But how far beyond the grocery store do I go before I turn left?"

(v)   "But where in front of the campus do you want me to meet you?"

(vi)   "When you said, 'philosophy students', did you mean just philosophy majors or all students taking philosophy courses?

(vii)   "But is he really industrious enough to finish his degree while working thirty hours a week?"

(viii) "You say that Gilberto and Katerina plan to visit Hong Kong, but together or independently?"

The three major uses upon which we will focus are (vi), (vii), and (viii). The last, to indicate logical form, we will treat on its own in a final section. In the next section we will concentrate upon (vi) the use of words *to refer to entities and classes of entities*, and (vii), the use of words *to attribute properties*.

SECTION III: REFERENCE AND ATTRIBUTION

For the purposes of illustration, it is instructive for the moment to single out and to attend to the use of sentences "to make statements." We do often employ our sentences to state that something is the case, where what we have stated is either correct or incorrect, or true or false. And as important components of sentences used in this manner, we use words within these sentences to refer to entities and to attribute properties. In the simplest form of sentence used to state that something is the case, one property is attributed to one entity. Thus, in the sentence, "Sylvester is intelligent," the word "Sylvester" is used to refer to one particular person, and the phrase, "is intelligent" is used to attribute one property, the property of intelligence (to Sylvester). Some other examples of statements of this simple form are:

"Nashville is in Tennessee."
"The desk is brown."
"I am industrious."

Utilizing a slightly more complex form, we can, of course, attribute more than one property to the same entity in the same sentence:

A: "Sylvester is intelligent and industrious."
B: "The desk is brown and rectangular."

We can also attribute one property to two entities in the same sentence:

C: "Sylvester and Cassandra are intelligent."
D: "Nashville and Chattanooga are in Tennessee."

We shall shortly see, in our discussion of logical form, that these sentences are properly analyzed as two simple statements constituted together with the conjunction "and":

A: "Sylvester is intelligent and Sylvester is industrious."
B: "The desk is brown and the desk is rectangular."
C: "Sylvester is intelligent and Cassandra is intelligent.'
D: "Nashville is in Tennessee and Chattanooga is in Tennessee."

233

Now, to further imprint the difference between reference and attribution upon our understanding, let us consider some examples first of words commonly used to refer to entities and then of words commonly used to attribute properties:

THE USE OF WORDS TO REFER

(I) To Particular Individuals

Names: "Sylvester," "Nashville," "Donald Duck," "Occidental College."

Individual Descriptions: "the eldest daughter," "the blue pen," "the smallest country in the world," "the winner of the best acting award."

Pronouns: "I," "He," "It."

(II) To Classes of Individuals

Class Nouns: "Students," "Americans," "tomatoes," "books."

Qualified Class Nouns: "Students at Kent State," "Americans living in Mexico," "the tomatoes in the basket," "the books I lent you."

Pronouns: "We," "They," "Everyone"

THE USE OF WORDS TO ATTRIBUTE PROPERTIES

(I) **Property Words For Animate Beings**

	Qualified
"is intelligent"	"is extremely intelligent"
"is industrious"	"Is industrious to a fault"
"is happy"	"is very happy"
"is sleeping"	"is sleeping soundly"

(II) **Property Words For Inanimate Beings**

	Qualified
"is concrete"	"is solid concrete"
"is corrosive"	"is highly corrosive"
"is flammable"	"is highly flammable"
"is two stories tall"	"is almost two stories tall"

234

(III)   Property Words For Both Animate And Inanimate Beings

"is heavy"	"is very heavy"
"is next to the door"	"is right next to the door"
"is brown"	"is dark brown"
"is efficient"	"is extremely efficient"

Now, given these preliminary comments, it should be obvious that two of the more common ways in which we fail to be understood when we use sentences to make statements are:

(a)   Failing to be precise as to whom or what we intend to refer.

(b)   Failing to be precise about the property or properties we wish to attribute.

In other words, the clarity of the sentences we use to make statements depends very much upon the clarity of the words we use within those sentences,   (a) to refer to individuals or classes of individuals, and   (b) to attribute properties.   Some examples of statements that are imprecise in *reference* are the following:

A: "The petition is filed with the Dean."   (... stated in a context where "the Dean" could refer either to the Dean of Students, the Dean of the Faculty, or the Dean of one of the university divisions, such as Letters and Science.)

B: "Freshmen are not as active politically nowadays as they were in the sixties."   (... stated in the context of discussing students at Berkeley and college students in general, where it is unclear whether "freshmen" refers to the class of freshmen at Berkeley, or the class of all college freshmen.)

C: "The liberals are for reform and the radicals are for fundamental change, and they are adamant in their views."   (It is unclear, in this linguistic context, whether the word "they" refers to radicals, or to both liberals and radicals.)

Some examples of statements that are imprecise in the *attribution* of a property are:

D: "Harry is talkative."   (... stated in a context attempting to decide whether Harry ought to be admitted to a club, where it is unclear whether, "is talkative" means 'is too talkative' or 'is a good conversationalist'.)

235

E.   "The tent material has been chemically treated."   (. . . stated in a context concerned to determine whether a tent is flameproof and waterproof, where it is unclear whether "has been chemically treated" means 'has been chemically treated to be flameproof,' or 'has been chemically treated to be waterproof,' or both.)

With these examples before us, let us immediately observe the following important fact about language communication: whether the statements that we made succeed in their intent, and are unambiguous in their reference and their attribution, depends on the context. Allied to this is the further important fact that conforming our sentences to the context in which they are employed is sometimes simply a matter of precision in our reference and attribution. Consider, for the purposes of illustration, the following revisions of the statements above, A–E:

A':   "The petition is filed with the Dean of Students."

B':   "Freshmen at Berkeley are not as active politically nowadays as they were in the sixties.

C':   "The liberals are for reform. The radicals are for fundamental change and are adamant in their views."

D':   "Harry is too talkative."

E':   "The tent material has been chemically treated to be flameproof."

A different side of the point that the extent of detail appropriate for successful communication depends upon the context, is the fact that in numerous contexts detail is not necessary at all. The brief remark, "It was a good party," may be a perfectly adequate reply to the question, "How was the party?" The simple statement, "I am opposed," may be all that is required to satisfy the question, "How do you stand on the measure?" As we have observed, our words and sentences are tools which we employ for a wide variety of functions, and just as the physical tools we employ sometimes do not need to be refined and specialized to efficiently perform the functions we desire of them, so similarly, the linguistic tools we employ sometimes do not need to be refined and specialized either.

SECTION IV: VAGUENESS AND AMBIGUITY

In the proper understanding of the nature of clarity in thought and expression, it is important to mark a difference between two ways in which we can fail in our attempts to be understood. On the one hand, our words and sentences can be ambiguous, and on the other hand they can be vague. As we shall shortly see, these categories sometimes overlap in practice; however, they are decidedly distinct and we will treat them separately, directing our attention first to a brief description of ambiguity.

AMBIGUITY

The word "ambiguous" has two quite distinct uses. In one of these uses it is roughly synonymous with "uncertain," and "undecided." In the statements: "He is ambiguous over which side to take," and "She is ambiguous whether to join our endeavour or not," it is used to attribute a state of mind, and specifically, an uncertain, undecided state of mind, to some person.

In contrast, the use and meaning of "ambiguous" important to us can be roughly defined as, "amenable in a particular context to more than one interpretation." It is in this sense that we label as "ambiguous" the use of the word "they" in the sentence, "The liberals are for reform, and the radicals are for fundamental change, and they are adamant in their views.' It is not clear whether "they" refers to the class of radicals or to the class of liberals and radicals. It is amenable in this particular context to more than one interpretation. And because it is ambiguous in its reference, it renders the entire sentence ambiguous.

It is important to observe that the qualification, "in this particular context" is essential to this example of ambiguity, and to our original definition of "ambiguous." The word "they" is not in itself ambiguous, nor is any other word. The word "bear" has at least two recognizably different meanings, but is not for that reason ambiguous. Indeed, the contexts in which it is used ordinarily renders obvious which meaning is intended. Once again we encounter the importance of context. A word or sentence is clear or it is ambiguous in a particular context, or to put this differently, the context ordinarily makes clear what a word or sentence means, although sometimes, the context fails to do this, and the result is ambiguity.

VAGUENESS

The property of vagueness is not only attributed to words and thoughts, but also to pictorial scenes, whether real or imagined. We say, for example, that a scene or view is "only vaguely outlined," or that some object within a scene or view can "only be perceived in vague outline." This use of "vague" in visual contexts is quite similar to its use when applied to meanings and thoughts: our meanings and thoughts may be "only vaguely outlined" too. It is this use of "vague" that is close in meaning to "imprecise," "ill-defined," and "inexact," and that is different in meaning from "ambiguous."

237

We may discern an automobile vaguely outlined in a fog, knowing quite well that it is an automobile — even though we do not know its make. And someone may describe their thesis for an essay only in vague outline, but sufficiently for us to understand, if only vaguely, what their thesis is. There is an important point to be observed here: when we are vague in our thoughts on some matter, and know that we are vague — we have not thought about the matter sufficiently and are aware of that fact — we need not experience difficulties in communicating our thoughts to others. This is particularly true if we make our vagueness explicit to those whom we address: "I am just beginning to formulate my thoughts on the matter and they are still ill-defined," "I have a rough idea, but only a rough idea, of how to proceed," "I can describe it to you but only in outline."

On the other hand, the consequences of vagueness can be unfortunate in three very different ways. First of all, (i) when the context calls for precision and detail, and we fail to produce it, those whom we address are justifiably disappointed, even if they have understood, vaguely, what we have had to say. We have employed our words as blunt instruments when precise instruments ought to have been applied. (ii) A second and unfortunate consequence of vagueness in communication is perplexity and confusion. Sometimes when we attempt to convey our vague thoughts in vague language, we are unsuccessful even in doing that. Our lack of success in these instances often turns upon the simple fact that we are not aware that we are vague. We assume that our thoughts are sufficiently precise and lucid when they are not. In various ways, perhaps in tone of voice, we convey this assumption to those whom we addressed, who are thereby put off-balance. They think they should understand our meaning far more exactly than they do. And because our words are vague they are amenable to differing interpretations: at one moment they seem to mean one thing, at the next moment another. Our vagueness has led to ambiguity, and the result is confusion. (iii) Sometimes when we are vague and also unaware of it, those whom we address are unaware of it too. Together we join in the deception of having cooperated in an exchange of ideas that are specific and well-defined, when they are not specific or well-defined at all. This is, indeed, an unfortunate circumstance. But what can we do when we are unaware that we are vague and also not called to count for that vagueness by others? This is a stubborn problem, but let us attempt to engage it in the broader context of a set of guidelines to deal with the problem of vagueness and ambiguity in general.

First. Let us re-affirm, and continue to re-affirm, our commitment to the maxim above that, "...we will never insist that though we are vague and confused in our words, we are nevertheless clear in our minds."

Second. Let us proceed on the assumption, an assumption that we stated earlier, that the responsibility for communication rests with the communicator. Specifically, when those whom we address, whether in speech or the written word, are confused over our meaning, we will take this as a signal that what we have communicated is vague and/or ambiguous. And we will attempt to restate, and if necessary to re-think, what we wish to convey more precisely.

Third. We will encourage those whom we address to be demanding of us in regard to clarity and precision. And we will strive to be demanding of ourselves in a similar way. In our writing we will do our best to employ the maxim for a scrupulous writer proposed by the famous English author George Orwell.

"A scrupulous writer, in every sentence that he writes, will ask himself at least four questions, thus:

> What am I trying to say?
> What words will express it?
> What image or idiom will make it clearer?
> Is this image fresh enough to have an effect?

And he will probably ask himself two more:

> Could I put it more shortly?
> Have I said anything that is avoidably ugly?"

Orwell continues, tongue-in-cheek, "But you are not obliged to go to all this trouble. You can shirk it by simply throwing your mind open and letting the ready-made phrases come crowding in. They will construct your sentences for you — even think your thoughts for you, to a certain extent — and at need they will perform the important service of partially concealing your meaning even from yourself." [9]

SECTION V: LOGICAL FORM

Let us consider once again the subject of logical form, continuing beyond our treatment of the subject in earlier chapters. In this section we will treat the basic structure of negations, conjunctions, disjunctions, and conditionals, but now representing their form more explicitly by the use of four symbols. We will thereby be capable of translating many more sentences into their counterpart logical form than we were able to before. In the next chapter we will proceed even further with our study of logical form.

NEGATION

Let the symbol "~" stand for negation, with the understanding that it represents "not," and also, in some instances, the prefixes: "un," "in," and "im."

The sentence:	"Nashville is not in Tennessee."
Given:	N: "Nashville is in Tennessee."
Is translated:	~(N) or simply~N

The sentence:	"Sylvester is unhappy."
Given:	S: "Sylvester is happy"
Is translated:	~ (S) or simply ~S

| The sentence: | "Sylvester is not unhappy." |
| Is translated: | ~ (~ (S)) or simply~~ S |

CONJUNCTION

The symbol " • " will stand for the use of "and" as a conjunction.

The sentence:	"Nashville is in Tennessee and Chattanooga is in Tennessee."
Given:	N: "Nashville is in Tennessee."
	C: "Chattanooga is in Tennessee."
Is translated:	(N • C)

Let us recall that the abbreviated sentence, "Nashville and Chattanooga are in Tennessee," is synomymous in meaning with the sentence above, and is indeed a conjunction of⁴ two separable thoughts. It is thus also properly translated as:

$$(N • C)$$

It is important to observe that the word "and" is not always employed as a conjunction between two separable thoughts. Occasionally we form a complex subject with "and," and attribute a property to this complex subject. The sentence:

"Jamal and Diana were students together."

does not contain two distinct assertions, but only one. It is not synonymous in meaning with:

"Jamal was a student together and Diana was a student together."

The sentence:

"The combination Spain and Morocco is a good holiday package." is not synonymous in meaning with:

"The combination Spain is a good holiday package and the combination Morocco is a good holiday package."

240

The proper translation, then, for the word "and," when it is not employed as the "and" of conjunction is the following:

The sentence: "Jamal and Diana were students together."
Given: A: "Jamal and Diana were students together."
Is translated: A

The sentence: "Jamal and Diana were not students together."
Is Translated: A

In contrast:
The sentence: "Nashville and Chattanooga are not in Tennessee."
Is translated: $(\sim N \cdot \sim C)$

This schema, let us recall, also represents the logical form of "Neither... nor...":

The sentence: "Neither Nashville nor Chattanooga is in Tennessee."
Is also translated: $(\sim N \cdot \sim C)$

Let is also note that, "Neither...nor..." sentences are equivalent to sentences of the form:

                  "It's not the case that either...or..."

The sentence: "It's not the case the either Nashville or Chattanooga
                  is in Tennessee."
Is translated: $\sim (N \vee C)$

Indeed, $(\sim p \cdot \sim q)$ and $\sim (p \vee q)$
                  are equivalent to one another.

Let us summarize our comments by observing that the following four sentences are all equivalent in what they assert to be the case:

   (i)   "Nashville and Chattanooga are not in Tennessee."
   (ii)   "Nashville is not in Tennessee and Chattanooga is not in Tennessee."
   (iii)   It's not the case that either Nashville or Chattanooga is in Tennessee."
   (iv)   "Neither Nashville nor Chattanooga is in Tennessee."

The sentences (i) and (ii) are naturally rendered in their logical form as $(\sim N \cdot \sim C)$, (iii) is naturally rendered as $\sim (N \vee C)$, and (iv) can be rendered as either $(\sim N \cdot \sim C)$ or $\sim (N \vee C)$.

241

It is important to distinguish out one further use of "and" together with "not" within the same sentence. Sometimes our sentences have the logical form:

> "It's not the case that both p and q."
> "Both p and q together can't be true."

The sentence: "John did not go both to Nashville and to Chattanooga."
Given: N: "John did go to Nashville."
                 C: "John did go to Chattanooga."
Is translated: $\sim$ (N • C)

We must be careful to observe that the proper translation here is not "($\sim$ N • $\sim$ C)." The sentence, "John did not go both to Nashville and to Chattanooga," states only that he did not do both of those things. Perhaps he did go to Nashville, but not to Chattanooga. The translation, ($\sim$ N • $\sim$ C) is different from, and stronger than, $\sim$ (N • C), since, as we learned above, ($\sim$ N • $\sim$ C) asserts both that John did not go to Nashville and that he did not go to Chattanooga.

There are several other words and phrases in addition to the word "and" that are used to conjoin two asserted thoughts together in one sentence. Some of these words, like the word "however," mark a meaning difference between the two thoughts asserted, but each of the two thoughts is asserted nevertheless. For example, in the sentence:

> "San Francisco is in California, however, the weather in
> San Francisco is cool."

it is asserted both that San Francisco is in California and that the weather in San Francisco is cool. Thus:

Given: A: "San Francisco is in California."
                B: "The weather in San Francisco is cool."

The proper translation for this sentence is:

(A • B)

Some other typical words besides "and" and "however" that are used as conjunctions are:

"but"	"nevertheless"
"though"	"on the other hand"
"still"	"even though"
"while"	"and so it is also true that"

Sometimes sentences contain *iterated conjunctions* in which more than two thoughts are asserted in conjunction together. An example is the following:

"Tangier, Casablanca, and Marrakech are in Morocco."

Utilizing a standard convention among logicians, we will limit the use of parentheses to surround at most two thoughts conjoined together. Thus:

Given: T: "Tangier is in Morocco."
        C: "Casablanca is in Morocco."
        M: "Marrakech is in Morocco."

The sentence above is translated as:

$$((T \cdot C) \cdot M) \text{ or simply } (T \cdot C) \cdot M$$

Since the position of the parentheses in an iterated conjunction is irrelevant, this sentence may also be translated as:

$$(T \cdot (C \cdot M)) \text{ or imply } T \cdot (C \cdot M)$$

DISJUNCTION

The symbol we will employ for "or" and for "Either...or..." is " $\vee$ ".

The sentence: "Managua is either in Honduras or Nicaragua."
Given: H: "Managua is in Honduras."
               N: "Managua is in Nicaragua."
Is translated: $(H \vee N)$

We will again limit the use of parentheses to surround at most two thoughts. Iterated disjunctions containing more than two alternatives are therefore rendered as follows:

The sentence: "Managua is either in Guatemala, Honduras, or Nicaragua."
Given: G: "Managua is in Guatemala."
Is translated: $((G \vee H) \vee N) \text{ or simply } (G \vee H) \vee N$

or

$$(G \vee (H \vee N) \text{ or simply } G \vee (H \vee N)$$

We have already analyzed the relation of "or" and "not" in the logical form, $\sim(p \vee q)$. Sometimes, though not very often, we also assert statements of the form:

$$(\sim p \vee \sim q)$$

243

For Example, although you recommend John to me as both intelligent and efficient, after witnessing his poor performance, I may be prompted to say:

"Either John is not intelligent or he's not efficient."

Given: I: "John is intelligent."
              E: "John is efficient."

This sentence is translated:

$$(\sim I \lor \sim E)$$

This sentence is also equivalent to:

"It's not true that John is both intelligent and efficient."

Which is translated: $\sim (I \cdot E)$

Indeed: $(\sim p \lor \sim q)$ and $\sim (p \cdot q)$
                     are equivalent to one another

CONDITIONALS

Let the symbol "$\supset$" stand for the implication between the truth of one sentence and the truth of another:

"If A is true, then B is true."

"A is true implies B is true."

or simply

"A implies B"

"If A, then B"

Sentences with this structure are represented by the schema:

$$(A \supset B)$$

As in earlier chapters, we will call "A" the "antecedent" — it comes before the "$\supset$". — and "B" the "consequent" — it comes after the "$\supset$."

Let us immediately observe that there are numerous words and phrases besides "if" that signal the condition (the antecedent) of a conditional sentence. All of the following are properly translated as:

$$(A \supset B)$$

244

Given A, then B
On the condition that A, then B
Provided that A, then B
On the assumption that A, then B
Assuming A, then B

There are also words and phrases in addition to "then" that are used to introduce the consequent of a conditional proposition, such as:

"thus"	"as a consequence"
"therefore"	"it follows that"
"consequently"	"it must be the case that."

The sentence: "If it is true that the chambermaid returned after midnight, then it follows that she could have committed the murder."

Given: C: "The chambermaid returned after midnight."

                  M: "The chambermaid could have committed the murder."

Is translated: (C ⊃ M)

Now, in all of the examples of conditional sentences we have so far considered, the condition has preceded the consequent within the sentence. However, it is not uncommon for the reverse to be the case. Consider the following examples and note their proper translation:

The sentence: "Sylvester will be unhappy if Cassandra does not marry him."

Given: H: "Sylvester will be happy."

                  M: "Cassandra will marry him."

Is translated   (∼M ⊃ ∼H)

The sentence: "Senator Smith will be re-elected provided that he wins Cook County."

Given: R: "Senator Smith will be re-elected."

                  W: "He (Smith) wins Cook County."

Is translated: (W ⊃ R)

It should be clear from these examples that we can affirm the following practical rule of thumb for translation:

The word "if" and all other similar words and phrases such as "given that" and "provided that" always precede the condition (the antecedent), no matter where they occur in a sentence.

There are two further phrases employed to express conditional thoughts that are important to consider, namely, the phrases, "only if" and "unless." Let us consider them in order.

"ONLY IF"

Suppose we believe that in order for Senator Smith to be re-elected, he must win labor's support, and we assert that, "Smith will be re-elected only if he wins labor's support." Suppose we also believe that to be re-elected, Smith must advocate nuclear disarmament, and we assert that, "Smith will be re-elected only if he advocates nuclear disarmament."

Given: R: "Smith will be re-elected"
               L: "Smith wins labor's support."
The sentence: "Smith will be re-elected only if he wins labor's support."
Is INCORRECTLY translated as:
$$(L \supset R)$$

For we do not believe that Smith's winning labor's support is *sufficient* for him to be re-elected, that is, we do not believe that if he wins labor's support, it will certainly follow that he will be re-elected. He must at least advocate nuclear disarmament too. What we believe is that if Smith is to succeed in his re-election, than he must succeed in having labor's support, that if he is re-elected, it will have had to be true that he won labor's support. In other words, "A only if B" in the present context is properly translated as "$(A \supset B)$".

The sentence: "Smith will be re-elected only if he wins labor's support."
Is translated: $(R \supset L)$.

This translation with "L" in the consequent represents the fact that Smith's winning labor's support is a *necessary* condition for his re-election.

Now, to many beginning students of logic it at first seems counter-intuitive to interpret "only if" in this way. But it probably only seems counter-intuitive because "only if" is also employed in other contexts in a logically different way to assert both a necessary condition and a sufficient condition too. For example, in the sentence,

> "John will lend George the money only if George is willing to pay him back by Friday"

"only if" is used not only to state that George's willingness to pay him back by Friday is a necessary condition for John's lending him money, but also that it is a sufficient condition; that is, it is also used to state that if George is willing to pay him back by Friday, John will certainly lend him the money. Thus:

The sentence: "John will lend George the money only if George is willing to pay him back by Friday."

Given: L: "John will lend George the money."

               W: "George is willing to pay him back by Friday."

Is translate not only as: $(L \supset W)$

But also as: $(W \supset L)$

That is, as: $(L \supset W) \cdot (W \supset L)$

Logicians, like mathematics, use the expression "If, and only if," for sentences that mutually imply one another, and often employ the symbol " $\equiv$ " to represent this expression. The logical schema:

$$(L \equiv W)$$

Is therefore a shorthand way of representing the schema:

$$(L \supset W) \cdot (W \supset L)$$

"UNLESS"

"Unless" is a difficult logical word to decipher because its use varies from context to context. Consequently, we will leave the determination of its proper analysis in differing contexts to the discretion of the reader. We will, however, indicate two of the standard contexts in which it occurs and its proper analysis within these contexts. Consider sentences of the form:

$$\sim p \text{ unless } q$$
$$\text{Unless } q, \text{ then } \sim p$$

For example:

(i)   "I will not contribute to the charity unless it is tax deductible."

(ii)   "Unless it is tax deductible, I will not contribute to the charity."

Given: C: "I will contribute to the charity."

              D: "It is tax deductible."

Both (i) and (ii) are translated as:

$$(\sim D \supset \sim C)$$

This schema is also the translation of the equivalent sentence:

"If it is not tax deductible, then I will not contribute to the charity."

Note that the sentence: "If it is not tax deductible, then I will not contribute to the charity." is equivalent to the sentence, "I will contribute to the charity only if it is tax deductible."

And this sentence is translated as:

(C ⊃ D)

This is not coincidental since:

(∼D ⊃ ∼C) and (C ⊃ D)

are equivalent to one another

It is an open question whether the sentence, "I will not contribute to the charity unless it is tax deductible" also means "I will contribute to the charity, if it is tax deductible," that is, if being tax deductible is intended not only as a necessary but also a sufficient condition, and properly also translated as "(D ⊃ C)." We must ask the author of the sentence whether this is also intended. It is safe, for the practical purposes of this study, to therefore limit our translation to (C ⊃ D), or if one prefers, to (∼D ⊃ ∼C).

A similar observation is pertinent with respect to the use of "only if." Sometimes the context makes clear that "A only if B" is used to assert merely that B is a necessary condition (and is therefore properly translated, "A ⊃ B"), and in other contexts it is clear that "A only if B" is used to assert both that B is a necessary condition and a sufficient condition too (and is therefore properly translated, "A ≡ B"). But there is a third possibility that the context does not make clear whether a sufficient condition in addition to a necessary condition is intended. It is safe, for the practical purposes of this study, to limit our translation of "A only if B" in these contexts to (A ⊃ B).

Now, there is at least one standard context in which "unless" is pretty clearly employed to assert both a necessary and a sufficient condition, and thus is properly translated by " ≡ ." Consider sentences of the form:

p unless q

or

Unless q, p

For example: (i)   "Garbedian will be elected unless Takemoto runs."

            (ii)   "Unless Takemoto runs, Garabedian will be elected."

Here it appears as if Garabedian has the election in the bag if Takemoto fails to run, that is, Takemoto's failing to run is a sufficient condition, and, "If Takemoto fails to run, then Garabedian will certainly be elected."

Thus the sentences (i) and (ii),

Given: T: "Takemoto does run."

             G: "Garabedian will be elected."

Are translated: (∼T ⊃ G)

248

The sentences (i) and (ii) also seem to imply that,

"If Garabedian is elected, then it must be true that Takemoto did not run."

If they do imply this — the reader may disagree — that is, if they also assert that Takemoto's not running is a necessary condition for Garabedian's election, then they are also properly translated as:

$$(G \supset \sim T)$$

in other words, they can be translated as:

$$(\sim T \supset G) \bullet (G \supset \sim T)$$

or

$$(\sim T \equiv G)$$

Since being positioned on the left or the right of the equivalence sign " $\equiv$ " is irrelevant to what an equivalence proposition asserts, if $(\sim T \equiv G)$ is acceptable, then so is:

$$(G \equiv \sim T)$$

ALTERNATIVE HYPOTHESES

Let us return once again, for a brief reminder, to the subject of alternative hypotheses, and their confirmation and disconfirmation. Let us review some examples, from Chapter VI of the story, of the creative construction of alternative hypotheses, underscoring the intelligent practice of keeping one's options open (when it is not yet timely to consider them closed), while at the same time producing new alternative options that could possibly be true. Let us immediately observe the inter-relation between the two sides of this sort of mental activity: on the one hand, as we persist in keeping our options open, we are more likely to produce alternative ones; on the other hand, as we actively construct alternative possibilities, we are thereby keeping our options open.

"Then any one of you could have followed Laura Anderson to her home and arrived before midnight."

Sherlock observes that it is possible that any one of the four members of the Guild could have committed the murder, i.e. he observes that there are four genuine possibilities: that either (i) Hawkins, or (ii) Stevens, or (iii) Perkins, or (iv) Caldwell, committed the murder. It is

249

also implicit in these assumptions, given the context, that two or more members may have committed the murder in complicity together although Sherlock does not state this explicitly.

> "In fact, I took a taxi with Professor Stevens, and Perkins went home with Caldwell in Caldwell's car."

> "Did you and Professor Stevens arrive at home by midnight?"

Not to be put off, Sherlock asks Hawkins whether he and Stevens arrived at home in sufficient time, nevertheless, to proceed to Laura Anderson's home to commit the murder.

> "Yes. But we live in the same apartment complex, and we remained talking until at least 1:00 A.M. in the morning."

> "So you are each other's alibi?"

> "Yes."

> "Or possibly you are lying."

Sherlock insists that the hypothesis of their guilt has not yet been definitively disconfirmed. It remains possible, assuming, of course, a complicity on their part to fabricate an alibi.

> "And Professor Caldwell. At what time did you drop off Professor Perkins?"

> "Some time before midnight."

> "Making it possible for you to drive to the Anderson home in time to commit the murder, and even conceivably, for Perkins to take a taxi there too."

Sherlock keeps the hypothesis alive that there was sufficient time not only for Caldwell, but even for Perkins, to have committed the murder. In summary, he persists in not ruling out the possibility that any one of the Templar members may be the murderer.

> "Laura Anderson was our one, and our only one, trusted contact to the outside world. Among other things it was she who was entrusted with the contingency plans in the event that we all suddenly met an untimely death."

> "So. According to this account, her death is a great loss to you, and puts you in a terrible predicament, at least for the

250

moment, unless somehow or other you and she disagreed, or you came to believe that you could no longer trust her."

In a quick rebuttal to the seemingly obvious lack of a motive to murder Laura Anderson, Sherlock argues that nevertheless one cannot rule out the possibility that a Templar member did have such a motive.

It is vitally important to be clear about Sherlock's process of thought here, which may at first appear to be artificial and mispointed. His intent is not to show that the hypothesis "that one or more of the Templar members is guilty" is certainly true, but rather that this hypothesis has not been proved to be certainly false, and therefore, ought not to be ruled out as a possibility.

In fact, it is perfectly consistent with his thinking here to think that it is unlikely that one or more of the members is guilty. It is also perfectly consistent with his thinking not to have formed any particular opinion at all.

We should be reminded here of our earlier discussions concerning the virtue of withholding belief. Sherlock withholds believing with certainty and conviction that each and every one of the Templar members is innocent. Or, as we have so far stated it, he withholds believing with certainty and conviction that the hypothesis "that one or more of the Templar members is guilty" is false. He will not close out his options when it is premature to do so.

There is an important lesson to be learned here concerning alternative hypotheses and their disconfirmation which we ought to state explicitly:

IF AN HYPOTHESIS HAS NOT BEEN DEFINITIVELY DISCONFIRMED, THEN THERE IS NO GOOD INTELLECTUAL REASON FOR RULING OUT THAT HYPOTHESIS AS A POSSIBILITY. (Unless, or course, there exists some competing hypothesis that has been definitively confirmed.)

STUDY AIDS

DISTINCTIONS:

    (i) *The use of a sentence*: i.e to state that something is the case, to order someone to do something, to ask a question, etc.

    (ii) *The use of a word(s)*: i.e. to indicate quantity, to indicate place, to indicate logical form, etc.

    (i) *The use of a word(s) to refer to individual entities or classes of individual entities.*

    (ii) *The use of a word(s) to attribute properties.*

    (i) *Ambiguity*: A word or sentence is ambiguous in a particular context when it is amenable in that context to more than one interpretation.

    (ii) *Vagueness*: A word or sentence is vague in a particular context when it is inexact, ill-defined, or imprecise in that context.

LOGICAL FORM:

Brief rules of thumb for translating sentences into their counterpart logical form:

Not A:	$\sim A$
A and B:	$A \cdot B$
A or B:	$A \vee B$
Neither A nor B:	$\sim (A \vee B)$ or $(\sim A \cdot \sim B)$
Not both A and B:	$\sim (A \cdot B)$
If A, then B:	$A \supset B$
B, if A:	$A \supset B$
A only if B:	$A \supset B$ or sometimes $A \equiv B$
Not A unless B:	$\sim B \supset \sim A$ or $A \supset B$
A unless B:	$\sim B \supset A$ or sometimes $\sim B \equiv A$

(1)   George Orwell, "Politics and the English Languages," *The Collected Essays, Journalism, and Letters of George Orwell*, Volume IV, p. 135.

I.   Translate each of the following sentences to its counterpart logical form:

1.) If Senator Smith is not re-elected, then Representative Brown will not be re-elected either.

2.) If neither Smith nor Brown run for re-election, then Harris will.

3.) Gregory and Hilary both attended Southern Methodist University.

4.) If Harris does not run for re-election, then Smith and Brown will enter the race.

5.) If Smith does not run and Harris does, then the opposition party will be elected and remain in control for the next four years.

6.) Smith will be re-elected only if Harris does not run and the economy remains stable.

7.) If the economy remains stable, Smith will be re-elected, and if Smith is re-elected, he'll either quit during his term of office, or be impeached by the electorate.

8.) If Smith runs, then Brown will run, but if Smith does not run, then Brown will not run either.

9.) Either Brown will run or he will campaign actively against Smith.

10.) Smith will run, if either Harris or Brown resign before their term is up.

1.) Either the murderer slipped through the window and unlatched the door from inside, or someone left the back door unlocked by mistake.

2.) If you don't fall in love, then you will not be happy; but if you do fall in love, then you'll be unhappy anyway.

3.) Unless Smith puts his campaign in order, he will never be elected.

4.) Smith can't run for both the Senate and the House of Representatives.

5.) I will loan you the money and you can fly to Las Vegas, provided, of course, that you give me 50% of your winnings.

6.) If you stay with me forever, then I will love you forever, but if you don't stay with me forever, then I will take you for every cent you've got.

7.) If neither Russia nor the U.S. reduce military spending, the recession will worsen; and if the recession worsens, I will be out of a job.

8.) If there are millions of children who suffer malnutrition, and if the technologically advanced countries have the capacity to eliminate this problem, but do not eliminate it, then they are guilty of a terrible sin. (Note that "have the capacity to eliminate" is different from "do eliminate.")

9.) Although John and Mary both voted for Smith, they both now regret their decision.

10.) China will surpass Russia and the United States if she modernizes her industry and does not increase her military budget.

1.) If Mary promises not to sue John, then the dissolution of their partnership will be good for both of them.

2.) John will marry Helen if she gets a divorce, but if she doesn't get a divorce, he'll either join the Navy or the Marines.

3.) Students get smarter if they study harder, provided, of course, they don't think of themselves as dumb.

4.) If Smith and Brown run and both are supported by labor, then the opposition party will not have a chance.

5.) Smith will win the election unless Brown enters the race and exposes Smith's ties with the underworld.

6.) If you don't study hard then you won't get smarter, but you will get smarter, if you do study harder.

7.) If neither Smith nor Brown is supported by labor, but Harris is, then Harris will win; provided, of course, that Harris continues to take a moderate stand on the major issues.

8.) I will marry you if you give me a jaguar and if you promise not to be unfaithful.

9.) A third world war and a nuclear armageddon are inevitable unless peace assumes greater significance to humankind than property and we do not permit machines to take over our lives.

10.) It's not true that we'll always have death, if genetic engineering continues to be practiced.

II. Give examples of sentences having the following logical form. Translate at least one sentence with "only if," and at least one sentence with "unless."

1.) $p \vee (q \vee r)$

2.) $(p \vee q) \cdot r$

3.) $\sim(p \cdot q)$

4.) $(p \supset q) \cdot (q \supset r)$

5.) $(p \cdot q) \vee (r \vee s)$

6.) $\sim(p \supset q)$

7.) $p \supset (q \cdot r)$

8.) $\sim p \equiv q$

9.) $(p \supset q) \cdot (\sim p \supset r)$

10.) $\sim p \supset (\sim q \cdot r)$

III. Identify which of the following sentences are similar to one another in logical form. Note that a difference in negation counts in this exercise as a difference in logical form.

1.) If Harriet marries either Homer or Herbert, then she will not inherit a fortune.

2.) If Harriet doesn't marry either Homer or Herbert, then she will marry George.

3.) If Irene dates Ike and Irving too, then Ike will be terribly jealous.

4.) Either Lester dates Lillian now and later marries her, or he will run off with Lolita.

255

5.) Marcel will marry Jean Marie only if she gives up Pierre and Paul.

6.) If either Russia or China increase their military spending, then peace will not prevail.

7.) Ir Russia does not increase its military spending, then the U.S. will not increase its military spending and peace will prevail.

8.) If Maria kisses Luigi on their wedding day, then Luigi will be pleased and will smile for the photographers.

9.) Either Russia reduces its military spending and the U.S. does too, or nuclear war is inevitable.

10.) If peace does not prevail, then China will not trade with Japan, but with the U.S.

11.) If Mary marries John, but later divorces him, then she will inherit a fortune.

12.) Russia will increase its military spending if neither the U.S. nor China reduces theirs.

CHAPTER VII: LOGICAL FORM

INTRODUCTION

We will continue with our analysis of the logical form of sentences (and thoughts), but now presupposing an understanding of the operation of negation, and of the compounding of separate thoughts together into conjunctions, disjunctions, conditionals, and bi-conditionals. Our attention will henceforth be focused upon the internal structure of statements as they are constituted of subjects and properties. We have already treated the subject of internal structure in a preliminary way in our discussion of universal and existential statements, and in our description of the distinction between words that denote individuals and words that attribute properties. In Section I we will begin with the internal analysis of quite simple statements. This will be followed by a brief review of the logical form of universal and existential statements, along with some new material covering variations in the structure of such sentences. In Section II we will proceed to an analysis of the nature of relations, including as we find them embedded within universal and existential statements. In III we will categorize relations as transitive, symmetrical, etc., and in IV we will analyze how relations are employed in patterns of deductive reasoning.

SECTION I: SIMPLE STATEMENTS AND UNIVERSAL AND EXISTENTIAL STATEMENTS

We will employ small letters of the alphabet to denote individual entities such as persons, objects, cities, etc. Thus, in the examples below we will use:

> c: Cassandra
> s: Sylvester

In our scheme of abbreviation, we will represent properties with capital letters followed by parentheses enclosing an "x," where "x" is understood as a variable ranging over individual entities and thus replaceable by small letters of the alphabet that denote individual entities. For example, in our scheme of abbreviation for sentences to be translated below, we will use:

> I (x): "x is intelligent"
> H(x): "x is hardworking"
> S (x): "x is a student"
> P (x): "x is a professor"

257

An illustration of a sentence having the simple logical form of one property attributed to one individual is the following:

The sentence: "Cassandra is intelligent."
Is translated: I(c)

Listed below are typical translations employing the basic logical operations:

The sentence: "Cassandra is not intelligent."
Is translated: $\sim$ I(c)

The sentence: "Cassandra and Sylvester are intelligent."
Is translated   I(c) $\bullet$ I(s)

The sentence: "Cassandra is intelligent and hardworking."
Is translated   I(c) $\bullet$ H(c)

The sentence: "Sylvester is either intelligent or hardworking."
Is translated: I(s) $\vee$ H(s)

The sentence: "If Cassandra is intelligent, then she is hardworking."
Is translated: I(c) $\supset$ H(c)

Let us now recall the proper representation of the logical form of universal and existential statements as we treated them earlier in Chapter III.

    (i)   **Existential Affirmatives:**

The sentence: "Some professors are intelligent."
Is translated: ($\exists$ x) (P(x) $\bullet$ I(x))

    (ii)   **Universal Affirmatives:**

The sentence: "All students are intelligent."
Is translated: (x) (S(x) $\supset$ I(x))

    (iii)   **Existential Negatives:**

The sentence: "Some professors are not intelligent."
Is translated: ($\exists$ x) (P(x) $\bullet$ $\sim$ I(x))

The sentence: "Not all professors are intelligent."
Is translated: $\sim$ (x) (P(x) $\supset$ I(x))

The above two sentences are equivalent to one another, and so are their counterpart logical forms:

$$\sim (x) (S(x) \supset I(x)) \qquad (\exists x) (S(x) \cdot \sim I(x))$$

Note also that: $\sim (p \supset q) \equiv (p \cdot \sim q)$

(iv) **Universal Negatives:**

The sentence: "No professor is intelligent."
Is translated: $(x) (P(x) \supset \sim I(x))$

The sentence: "There are no intelligent professors."
Is translated: $\sim (\exists x)(P(x) \cdot I(x))$

These two sentences are equivalent, and so are their counterpart logical forms:

$$(x)(P(x) \supset \sim I(x)) \equiv \sim (\exists x)(P(x) \cdot I(x))$$

Note also that: $(p \supset \sim q) \equiv \sim (p \cdot q)$

Let us now follow up this recapitulation of the basic structure of simple existential and universal statements by sampling some of the more complex forms of such statements. Many of these statements, let us observe, are complex only in terms of the basic logical operations of conjunction, disjunction, etc. and thus are not at all difficult to represent in their counterpart logical form.

Consider, for example, the sentence:

"If Cassandra is a professor, then Cassandra is both intelligent and hardworking."

This sentence is a conditional, whose consequent is a conjunction. It thus has the logical form:

$$p \supset (q \cdot r)$$

Or, more explicitly:

$$P(c) \supset (I(c) \cdot H(c))$$

Observe that the following universal statement has a similar internal structure:
"All professors are both intelligent and hardworking."

This sentence is translated: $(x)[H(x) \supset (I(x) \cdot H(x))]$

259

Or consider the sentence:

"Sylvester is a student who is intelligent but not hardworking."

This sentence has the logical for: $p \bullet (q \bullet \sim r)$

Or more explicitly $\qquad\qquad\qquad S(s) \bullet (I(s) \bullet \sim H(s))$

An existential statement with a similar internal structure is the following:

"Some students are intelligent but not hardworking."

This sentence has the logical form: $(\exists x)[S(x) \bullet (I(x) \bullet \sim H(x))]$

Let us also observe that we can combine existential and universal statements into conjunctions, conditionals, etc., with logical operations between them. For example:

The sentence: "If all students are intelligent, then some professors must be intelligent too."

Is translated: $(x)(S(x) \supset I(x)) \supset (\exists x)(B(x) \bullet I(x))$

Some further examples of existential and universal statements with differing logical forms are the following:

The sentence: "Not all students are both intelligent and hardworking."

Is translated: $\sim (x)[S(x) \supset (I(x) \bullet H(x))]$

$$\text{or}$$

$$(\exists x)[S(x) \bullet \sim (I(x) \bullet H(x))]$$

The sentence: "Anyone who is either a professor or a student is intelligent and hardworking."-

Is translated $(x)[(P(x) \vee S(x)) \supset (I(x) \bullet H(x))]$

SECTION II: RELATIONS

A common use of sentences to make statements, besides attributing properties to subjects, is to state that certain subjects stand in certain relations to one another. Where the relation asserted is between two individuals, we will speak of "two-place relations," where it is between three individuals, we will speak of "three-place relations," etc. Let us review, to begin with, a sampling of some two-place relations.

260

TWO–PLACE RELATIONS:

" ___ is the brother of ___ "   "Julio is the brother of Carlos."
                                       ("Julio is Carlos' brother.")
                                       ("Carlos is Julio's brother.")
                                       ("Julio and Carlos are brothers.")

" ___ is on top of ___ "   "the book is on top of the desk."

" ___ is older than ___ "   "Michelle is older than Jean
                                       Pierre."

" ___ is more talented than ___"   "Hamad is more talented than
                                       Nabil."

" ___ is a student at ___ "   "Herbert is a student at the
                                       Sorbonne."

" ___ is to the left of ___ "   "The garage is to the left of the
                                       store."

" ___ is under the command of ___ "   "The Third Army is under the
                                       command of General Sherman."

" ___ is twenty miles beyond ___ "   "Tijuana is twenty miles beyond
                                       San Diego."

We will represent the logical form of two–place relations with a capital letter denoting the relation, followed by a parenthesis enclosing "x,y," where "x" is a variable ranging over one entity of the relation and "y" is a variable ranging over the other entity of the relation. For example:

$$M(x,y): \quad x \text{ is the Mother of } y$$

Some examples of sentences stating two–place relations, along with their counterpart logical forms, are:

The sentence:	"John is the brother of Mary."	
Given:	$B(x,y):$	"x is the brother of y"
	j :	John
	m :	Mary
Is translated:	$B(j,m)$	

261

The sentence:	"The book is on the top of the desk."
Given:	T(x,y): "x is on top of y"
	d : "the desk"
	b : "the book"

Is translated:	T(b,d)

THREE-PLACE RELATIONS

The logical form of three-place relations is represented in a similar way. For example:

The sentence:	"Tunis is between Cairo and Tangiers."
Given:	B(x,y,z): "x is between y and z"
	a : "Tunis"
	b : "Cairo"
	c : "Tangiers"

Is translated:	T(a,b,c)

The sentence:	"Harry told Mary to call Jane."
Given:	C(x,y,z): "x told y to call z"
	h : Harry
	m : Mary
	j : Jane

Is translated:	C(h,m,j)

The sentence:	"Victor returned the book to Catherine."
Given:	R(x,y,z): "x returned y to z"
	v : Victor
	b : the book
	c : Catherine

Is translated:	R(v,b,c)

The sentence:	"John is going with Carl to Montreal."
Given:	G(x,y,z): "x is going with y to z"
	j : John
	c : Carl
	m : Montreal

Is translated:	G(j,c,m)

262

Let us now examine, and exhibit the logical form of, two and three-place relations, as we find them embedded within universal and existential statements.

The Sentence: (i) "All cities of South America are East of Tampa, Florida."

Given: $S(x)$:   "x is a city of South America"
             $E(x,y)$:   "x is East of y"
               t :   "Tampa"

Is translated: $(x)(S(x) \supset E(x,t))$

Note that (i) above can be equivalently translated as:

$$\sim(\exists x)(S(x) \cdot \sim E(x,t))$$

Literally: "There is no South American city that is not East of Tampa, Florida."

Note also that the sentence:

      (ii) "Not all cities of South America are East of Tampa, Florida."

is translated: $\sim(x)(Sx \supset E(x,t))$

or

$$(\exists x)(S(x) \cdot \sim E(x,t))$$

The sentence: (I) "Some cities of Spain are North of Boston, Massachusetts."

Given: $S(x)$:   "x is a city of Spain"
             $N(x,y)$:   "x is North of y"
               b :   "Boston"

Is translated: $(\exists x)(S(x) \cdot N(x,b))$

Note that the negation of (i):

      "There isn't a Spanish city North of Boston, Mass."

Is translated: $\sim(\exists x)(S(x) \cdot N(x,b))$

or

$$(x)(S(x) \supset \sim N(x,b))$$

263

The sentence:	"Every city of England is North of every city in the United States."

Given:	E(x) :	"x is a city in England"
	U(x) :	"x is a city in the United States"
	N(x,y) :	"x is North of y"

Is translated:	$(x)(y)[(E(x) \bullet U(y)) \supset N(x,y)]$

Note that the negation of the above sentence:

"Not every city of England is North of every city in the United States."

Is translated:	$\sim(x)(y)[(E(x) \bullet U(y)) \supset N(x,y)]$

or

$$(\exists x)(\exists y)[(E(x) \bullet U(y)) \bullet \sim N(x,y)]$$

Literally:	"There is some city of England that is not North of some city of the United States."

The sentence:	"Some city of France is North of every city in the United States."

Given:	F(x): "x is a city of France"

Is translated:	$(\exists x)(y)[(F(x) \bullet U(y)) \bullet N(x,y)]$

SECTION III: DIFFERENT TYPES OF RELATIONS

In this section we will treat six important types of relations. The understanding of the type of a relation is a simple matter, a part of common knowledge, and not at all a matter of special education. The terms that logicians employ to name these different types, such as: "transitive," "symmetrical," etc., are not themselves part of the average person's vocabulary, however, once their meaning is explained, anyone can immediately determine a relation's type. For example, anyone who is explained the meaning of "transitive" and who knows that if a is taller than b, and b is taller than c, then a must be taller than c, can immediately identify the relation of "taller than" as a transitive relation.

SYMMETRICAL RELATIONS:

A RELATION R(x,y) IS A SYMMETRICAL RELATION JUST IN CASE:

If x has the relation R to y, then y has the relation R to x, i.e.,

$$(x)(y)[R(x,y) \supset R(y,x)]$$

An example of a symmetrical relation is: 'x is the sibling of y"

$$(x)(y)[(x \text{ is the sibling of } y) \supset (y \text{ is the sibling of } x)]$$

For instance:

If Desmond is the sibling of Daphne, then Daphne is the sibling of Desmond.

Some examples of symmetrical relations are:

"x is the spouse of y"
"x is a teammate of y"
"x is a colleague of y"
"x is at the same time as y"
"x is similar in color to y"
"x is the same height as y"
"x is the same _____ as y"
"x is the first cousin of y"

Note that a relation may fail to be a symmetrical relation in two different ways:

(i)   A NON-SYMMETRICAL RELATION R(x,y), in which x stands in the relation R to y, is one in which y does not always stand in that relation to x, i.e.:

$$\sim (x)(y)[R(x,y) \supset R(y,x)]$$

or

$$(\exists x)(\exists y)[R(x,y) \cdot \sim R(y,x)]$$

"x is the brother of y" is a non symmetrical relation: If Ulysses is the brother of Iphigenia, it does not follow that Iphigenia is the brother of Ulysses.

265

(ii)   AN ASYMMETRICAL RELATION R(x,y) in which x stands in the relation R to y, is one in which y never also stands in that relation R to x, i.e.:

$$\sim (\exists x)(\exists y)[R(x,y) \bullet R(y,x)]$$

or

$$(x)(y)[R(x,y) \supset \sim R(y,x)]$$

"x is the father of y" is an assymetrical relation: If x is the father of y, it can never be the case that y is the father of x. (Note that this is not true of the relation, "x is the father-in-law of y."   It is possible for a person to be his father-in-law's father-in-law.)

TRANSITIVE RELATIONS:

A RELATION R(x,y) IS A TRANSITIVE RELATION JUST IN CASE:

"If x has that relation to y, and y has that relation to z, then x has that relation to z."   That is:

$$(x)(y)(z)[R(x,y) \bullet R(y,z)) \supset R(x,z)]$$

"x is taller than y" is a transitive relation: if Esmeralda is taller than Beulah, and Beulah is taller than Clementine, then Esmeralda is taller than Clementine.

Some examples of transitive relations are:

"x is the sibling of y"
"x precedes y in time"
"x is East of y"
"x is inside of y"
"x is in front of y"
"x is less than or equal to y"
"x is more industrious than y"
"x is more _____ than y"
"x is less mobile than y"
"x is less _____ than y"

Note that many, although not all, symmetrical relations are also transitive relations:

"x is similar in _____ to y"
"x is identical to y"
"x is the same _____ as y"
"x is the sibling of y"

266

Note that a relation may fail to be a transitive relation in two different ways:

(i)   A NON-TRANSITIVE RELATION is one in which transitivity sometimes does not hold, i.e.:

$$(\exists x)(\exists y) [(R(x,y) \cdot (Ry,z)) \cdot \sim R(x,z)]$$

"x" is the brother of y" is a non transitive relation: Given that Antoine is the brother of Emile and Emile is the brother of Antoine, it does not follow that Antoine is the brother of Antoine, i.e. that he is his own brother.

(ii)   AN INTRANSITIVE RELATION is one in which transitivity never holds, i.e.:

$$\sim (\exists x)(\exists y) [(R(x,y) \cdot R(y,z)) \cdot R(x,z)]$$

or

$$(x)(y) [(R(x,y) \cdot (R(y,z)) \supset \sim R(x,z)]$$

"x is the father of y" is an intransitive relation: If Alphonso is the father of Alonzo, and Alonzo is the father of Bartholomew, Alphonso cannot be Bartholomew's father (for he must be his grandfather).

I. Classify the following relations: (i) as either transitive, non-transitive, or intransitive, and (ii) as either symmetrical, non-symmetrical, or asymmetrical.

1) "x is the husband of y"

2) "x is above y"

3) "x is less than or equal to y"

4) "x is the captain of team y"

5) "x is more resilient than y"

6) "x is North East of y"

7) "x is a descendant of y"

8) "x is a citizen of y"

9) "x is an ancestor of y"

10) "x is at right angles to y"

11) "x is greater in area than y"

12) "x is the sister of y"

13) "x is different in size from y"

14) "x is to the right politically of y"

15) "x is lower in elevation than y"

II. TRANSLATE THE FOLLOWING SENTENCES INTO THEIR
COUNTERPART LOGICAL FORM:

1) All intelligent Americans are Republicans.

2) All Republicans are intelligent Americans.

3) Some Republicans are intelligent, but not all of them are.

4) No city of Spain is South of Richmond, Virginia.

5) Someone told Harry to be pleasant to Mary.

6) Someone is in love with Harry.

7) If Harry is kind to Maria, then Maria will be kind to him.

8) Chicago is West of N.Y. City only if N.Y. City is East of Chicago.

9) Everyone loves someone.

10) All the cities of Russia are North of all of the cities of the U.S.

11) Not every Republican is smarter than every Libertarian.

12) All Democrats are intelligent and resourceful.

13) No Democrat is both intelligent and resourceful.

14) None of the Democratic candidates will be elected unless the President resigns.

15) If all of the Republican legislators speak out against Senator Smith, then Smith will be defeated.

16) Some politicians can fool some of their constituents, but no politician can fool all of their constituents.

CHAPTER VIII: REASONING TO CAUSES

"Moreover, I had already pursued with Sherlock the idea of a diagnostic logic, a method inquiry by which to traverse with rigor from symptoms to disease, and Sherlock had agreed that there was something to it. Indeed, he was convinced that there was an investigative logic proper to detective work, but similar in kind to doctors identifying the cause of an illness. When we had discussed these matters we had quickly moved to the conjecture that all inquiries intelligently engaged have common patterns of logical thinking. And if that were true, we further conjectured, these common patterns could in principle be displayed. (Chapter II)

INTRODUCTION

In this chapter we will concentrate upon patterns of thinking which select from a group of possible causes for some phenomenon or event, one cause which is the more likely. In Section I we will make the important distinction between three very different meanings of "cause," namely: (i) a *necessary cause* or condition for an effect, (ii) a *sufficient cause* or condition for an effect, and (iii) a *unique cause* — both necessary and sufficient — for an effect. In Section II we will catalogue a number of the more important patterns of reasoning confirming or disconfirming the existence of a cause. In the remaining sections we will treat several of these patterns of reasoning in greater detail.

Since the understanding of causal reasoning is critical to the goal of good reasoning, our treatment of the subject here is important. The reader should be forewarned, however, that we will engage this subject in only a preliminary way. A more sophisticated understanding of the nature of causal reasoning would quickly take us into quite subtle and complex areas of the methodology of contemporary science.

SECTION I

NECESSARY CAUSE, SUFFICIENT CAUSE,
AND
UNIQUE CAUSE

Let us begin our analysis of patterns of causal reasoning by distinguishing between three different concepts of cause: (i) Necessary Cause, (ii) Sufficient Cause, and (iii) Unique Cause.

(i) NECESSARY CAUSE (CONDITION)

Sherlock: "Is it important in your mind in identifying the chambermaid as a prime suspect, that she had a key to the mistress' bedroom?

Kemp: "Absolutely."

Sherlock: "But you would not go so far as to claim that she could have been the murderer only if she had that key?"

Sherlock's question here is simply, "Is the chambermaid's possessing the key a necessary condition for her to be the murderer?" Wherever a phenomenon (E) can occur only if a particular cause or condition (C) is present, that cause or condition is a "necessary cause" or "necessary condition" for E. Whenever a person asserts a sentence having the form:

"E can occur only if C occurs"

we will interpret this person as affirming the existence of a necessary cause or condition:

"C is a necessary cause (or condition) for E"

and we will translate, "C is a necessary cause or condition for E" by the schema:

$$(E \supset C)$$

Kemp: "I do not understand."

Sherlock: "Well. Suppose just hypothetically, that she did not have the key, that she lost it or that Mrs. Anderson had lost hers and had temporarily borrowed the chambermaid's key until her own could be replaced?"

Kemp: "Yes. So? Suppose that to be true."

Sherlock: "Would you still consider the chambermaid a prime suspect?"

Kemp: "No. I would not."

Kemp's position here, expressed succinctly, is the following: "If the chambermaid did not have the key, then she did not commit the murder." This conditional thought is another way of asserting a necessary condition.

272

Let us therefore record the fact that we can schematically represent a necessary cause C for an effect E not only as:

(i) $(E \supset C)$

But also as: (ii) $(\sim C \supset \sim E)$

(If C does not occur, then E will not occur either)
(Without C, E cannot occur)

Of course, this is just as we would expect since $(E \supset C)$ and $(\sim E \supset \sim C)$ are equivalent.

Watkins: "If he committed the murder, he had to transport himself to London."

Here we have another example of the affirmation of a necessary cause or condition: Anderson's transporting himself to London (from Torquay on the night of the murder), is a necessary condition for his having committed the murder.

Given: M: Anderson committed the murder.
          T: Anderson transported himself to London (from Torquay on the night of the murder).

Watkins' statement can be translated as:

$(M \supset T)$

Watkins continues:

Watkins: "But since there was no way he could do that, we must conclude that he didn't commit the murder."

By denying the possibility of the necessary condition, Watkins now deduces the conclusion, by Modus Tollens, that Anderson did not commit the murder.

(1) $(M \supset T)$ premise

(2) $\sim T$ premise

_____

$\sim M$ conclusion

The use of Modus Tollens here, to deduce a particular statement to be false, by denying that a necessary condition of that statement is true,

273

is not at all uncommon. Consider the following examples: "If John is a candidate, then he must be at least 32. But he is not yet 32, so he must not be a candidate." Or, "If the problem is in the electrical current, then the power must be off. But the power is not off, so the problem must not be in the electrical current."

(ii) SUFFICIENT CAUSE (CONDITION)

Kemp: "If you have the power to continue life, and do not, then you are a murderer." (Chapter V)

If a certain condition is asserted as sufficient for another condition to follow, that first condition is called a "sufficient condition." It is a sufficient condition, according to Kemp, if the Templars have the power to continue life, and do not, for it also to be true that the Templars are murderers. Similarly, if an effect (E) must occur when a cause (C) is present, C is called a "sufficient cause" for the occurrence of the effect E. Being submerged under water for ten minutes without the opportunity to breathe is sufficient to cause death, that is, is a "sufficient cause" for death. We can represent:

"C is a sufficient cause (condition) for E"

by the schema: $(C \supset E)$

It should now be evident that (a) to identify a cause or condition as a necessary cause or condition is not also necessarily to identify it as a sufficient condition, and (b) vice versa. (a) An electrical current is a necessary, but not a sufficient condition for the operation of the standard automobile. And vice versa, (b) being submerged under water without the opportunity to breathe is sufficient to cause death, but not necessary to cause death — falling from a twenty story building to a concrete walk below is quite sufficient too.

(iii) UNIQUE CAUSE (CONDITION)

"Fine! Splendid!" said Kemp, a bit distressed and impatient, glancing in the direction of Sherlock, who was only partly successful in restraining a grin. Kemp took hold of the French doors, which were slightly ajar, and opened them slowly. They emitted a definite grating, scratching sound of metal on metal."

"Oh! That's the French doors." Miss Ellie spoke out again quite proudly.

When we say that "C caused E" we sometimes mean not only that

274

"C is a condition sufficient to cause E," but also that "C is the only condition sufficient to cause E," at least in the instance to which we wish to refer. In other words, we sometimes believe that the presence of some cause C is not only sufficient but also necessary for the occurrence of a particular effect. Wherever a cause or condition is both sufficient and necessary for an effect E to occur, we will call it a "unique cause" or "unique condition." And we will, therefore, translate:

"C is a unique cause (or condition) for E"

by the schema: $(C \equiv E)$

Let us recall that this schema, which can also be read,

"C if, and only if, E," is equivalent to:

$(C \supset E) \bullet (E \supset C)$

(C only if E) and (C, if E)

SECTION II

DIFFERENT PATTERNS OF CAUSAL REASONING

Before we analyze some of the more important patterns of causal reasoning in detail, let us be reminded, with a brief outline, of their variety.

First of all, let us recall that we have already treated, (i) arguing from an unusual effect to an unusual cause, (ii) reasoning by analogy, which is often employed to determine a cause, and (iii) reasoning by induction to a causal generalization, with its allied fallacy "Post Hoc, Ergo Propter Hoc."

It is important also to be reminded of the fact that causal reasoning not uncommonly employs (iv) various patterns of deductive reasoning. For example, if we have narrowed the likely causes of some effect to two, say c_1 and c_2, and we now eliminate c_1, we can deduce, by disjunctive syllogism, that c_2 is the likely cause. Or suppose that on the hypothesis that either c_1 or c_2 is the likely cause of some effect, there follows a certain consequence which can be tested, and which when tested, proves to be false. It follows by Modus Tollens that neither C_1 nor C_2 is the likely cause.

The use of Modus Tollens reminds us of the importance of the role of disconfirming hypotheses. In a later section we will distinguish between

(v) disconfirming a necessary cause or condition, and (vi) disconfirming a sufficient cause or condition. In the upcoming section we will analyze (vii) The Method of Agreement, a particular pattern of causal reasoning used to identify a likely cause from among a group of possible causes. We will also analyze (viii) The Method of Difference, another pattern of reasoning for identifying causes. And finally, (ix) we will illustrate the use of the Method of Agreement and the Method of Difference in combination together.

A list of the patterns of causal reasoning which are surveyed in our study of logic, is therefore the following:

  (i)   Unusual Effect — Unusual Cause

  (ii) Analogical Reasoning

  (iii) Induction to a Causal Generalization

  (iv) Patterns of Deductive Reasoning

  (v)   Disconfirming a Necessary Cause or Condition

  (vi) Disconfirming a Sufficient Cause or Condition

  (vii) The Method of Agreement

  (viii) The Method of Difference

  (ix) The Method of Agreement and Difference Combined

SECTION III

THE METHOD OF AGREEMENT
(FOR THE CONFIRMATION OF A CAUSE)

"The answer, my dear Watson, is the convincing case you yourself made supporting the hypothesis that Laura Anderson's murderer must be someone from within the Anderson home."

. . . .

"So the murderer is not Miss Ellie. . .And it is not Richards either?"

"No."

"Then it must be either Louise-Phillipe or Dr. Anderson."

"Exactly."

"But since Dr. Anderson was in Torquay at the time of his wife's murder, then it must be Louise-Phillipe."

The above is an example of an (extended) use of Disjunctive Syllogism, or the elimination of alternatives. There is an interesting variant of this method of reasoning which is commonly called, "The Method of Agreement," following the terminology of the 19th Century Philosopher John Stuart Mill. (In fact, this and several other methods ordinarily attributed to Mill were advanced earlier by J. F. W. Herschel in a work entitled, *Preliminary Discourse on the Study of Natural Philosophy*, (1830).) [10]

If a group of possible causes for a certain effect is given, by utilizing the Method of Agreement the actual cause can sometimes be identified by determining which of the possible causes were, and which were not, present when the effect occurred. Consider, for example, the following case in which the perpetrator of a murder is easily identified by a simple application of this method of reasoning about causes.

Three brothers and a sister have resided for some time in a country mansion with a Butler, a Chauffeur, and a Gardener. Unfortunately, the three brothers were murdered on each of three successive days. Because of the nature of the murders, it is reasonable to assume that they were all committed by some one person within the household. We know, moreover, that; (I) everyone was at home during the time of the first murder except for the gardener, who was exhibiting roses at a Garden Show. (ii) Only the chauffeur, who was re-fueling the family limousine in the local village, was absent during the time of the second murder. And (iii), everyone was present at the mansion during the third murder except for the chauffeur and butler, who were out shopping for groceries for the household.

Since only the sister was invariantly present at all of the murders, and since we have assumed that all of the murders were committed by only one person, we can conclude that the sister is the murderer. Schematically we can represent the information in this case as follows:

1st MURDER		2nd MURDER		3rd MURDER	
Sister:	present	Sister:	present	Sister:	present
Gardener:	_____	Gardener:	present	Gardener:	present
Chauffeur:	present	Chauffeur:	_____	Chauffeur:	_____
Butler:	present	Butler:	present	Butler:	_____

As we can see, there is an invariant agreement of the sister's presence on the occasion of each of the murders. On the assumption that there is only one cause (perpetrator) of all of the murders, and that the perpetrator

277

is either the sister, the gardener, the chauffeur, or the butler, it is reasonable to conclude, by The Method of Agreement, that the sister is the murderer.

It is important to observe that although the person who caused the crimes has been identified, no further explanation of the crimes themselves — of their motive or their circumstance — has been advanced. This observation applies to many uses of the Method of Agreement, as the next example will vividly illustrate.

Let us suppose that you have suffered from an allergic reaction immediately following your evening meal at home on Monday, Wednesday, and Friday of the past week, and that you wish to determine the origin of these reactions, on the hypothesis that they were caused by some food that you consumed during those meals. You catalogue your diet as follows:

Monday: Chicken, baked potato, butter, salt, tomatoes, lettuce, olive oil, and vinegar.

Wednesday: Steak, lettuce, onions, olive oil, corn on the cob, butter and salt.

Friday: Haddock, tomatoes, onions, vinegar, rolls and butter.

Now, from this information it is reasonable to conclude that butter is the likely culprit, since it alone is invariant in your diet in all of the three meals preceding your allergic reaction. Let us be clear, that in this application of the Method of Agreement, the conclusion is not deduced, but is at best highly probable. For we have assumed that a food caused the allergic reactions, which may be false. We have also assumed that our memory of our diet is correct, which may also be false. Perhaps we overlooked a liquid, and this liquid is the cause. Moreover, it is even possible that two or more foods are the cause, and that butter is not one of them; for example, that tomatoes caused the reaction on Monday and Friday, and steak on Wednesday. And although this possibility may seem unrealistic, it is not; there are persons who develop allergic syndromes for whom most foods cause allergic reactions.

It is also important to record the fact that even if the correct cause, butter, has been identified by the Method of Agreement, no further account has been advanced to explain "how the butter caused the allergic effect." At one level the allergic effect is explained "as a reaction to the food product butter," and that identification is significant in itself. But at another level, no explanation is given of the process by which the butter had this effect.

278

THE DISCONFIRMATION OF A CAUSE

DISCONFIRMING A NECESSARY CAUSE (CONDITION)

Let us suppose, utilizing the example we have just reviewed, that we had first hypothesized olive oil to be the cause of the allergic effect, having observed its presence in our diet on Monday and Wednesday evenings.

Now, however, we recall that it was not present during our dinner on Friday, even though, on Friday, we did suffer the allergic effect.

We would naturally treat this newly remembered fact as disconfirming the hypothesis that olive oil caused the allergic effect. To be more precise:

(i) We would conclude that olive oil was disconfirmed as a necessary cause, for to assert that olive oil (O) is a necessary cause of the allergic effect (E), is to assert that the allergic effect can be present only if the olive oil is present, that is, $(E \supset O)$. But on Friday the allergic effect was present and the olive oil absent, i.e. $(E \cdot \sim O)$. In other words, it was not true that when the effect was present, so also was the olive oil, i.e. $\sim (E \supset O)$. (Note that $(E \cdot \sim O)$ and $\sim (E \supset O)$ are equivalent.)

(ii) We would conclude that the olive oil could not be the unique cause, that is, both a necessary and sufficient cause, since it was not a necessary cause. $(E \equiv O)$ cannot be true, since $\sim (E \supset O)$.

(iii) We could not altogether rule out the possibility that olive oil was one of two or more sufficient causes, even if we judged that to be very unlikely. It is possible, for example, that the allergic effect was caused by olive oil on Monday and Wednesday, and that it was caused by Haddock on Friday.

To summarize:

AN INSTANCE IN WHICH THE EFFECT TO BE EXPLAINED IS PRESENT, BUT THE HYPOTHESIZED CAUSE IS ABSENT, DISCONFIRMS THAT HYPOTHESIZED CAUSE AS: (i) A NECESSARY CAUSE, AND THEREFORE AS, (ii) A UNIQUE CAUSE.

DISCONFIRMING A SUFFICIENT CAUSE

Now, given a different form of evidence, it is also possible to disconfirm olive oil as a sufficient cause of the allergic effect. We merely need a case in which the olive oil is present and the allergic effect is not. For example, suppose once again that we have hypothesized olive oil to be the unique cause of the allergic effect, having observed its presence in our diet on Monday and Wednesday evenings when we did suffer the allergic effect. And now suppose we recall that olive oil was present in our diet on Tuesday, and yet on Tuesday we did not suffer the allergic effect. We would naturally treat this newly remembered fact as disconfirming the hypothesis that olive oil caused the allergic effect. To be more precise:

(i) We would conclude that olive oil was disconfirmed as a sufficient cause, since we have an instance in which olive oil was present and the allergic effect absent ($O \cdot {\sim}E$), which is equivalent to ${\sim}(O \supset E)$.

(ii) We would conclude that olive oil could not be the unique cause, that is, both a necesssary and sufficient cause ($O \equiv E$), since it was not a sufficient cause, that is, ${\sim}(O \supset E)$.

(iii) From the evidence of our diet on Monday, Tuesday and Wednesday, we could not altogether rule out the possibility that olive oil was a necessary cause, even if we judged that to be very unlikely.

To summarize:

AN INSTANCE IN WHICH THE HYPOTHESIZED CAUSE IS PRESENT, AND YET THE EFFECT TO BE EXPLAINED IS ABSENT, DISCONFIRMS THAT HYPOTHESIZED CAUSE AS A SUFFICIENT CAUSE, AND THEREFORE AS (ii) A UNIQUE CAUSE.

V.   THE METHOD OF DIFFERENCE

There is another form of reasoning, in addition to the Method of Agreement, which we commonly employ to identify a cause. Suppose that we observe that our automobile is suddenly running better, with a marked increase of power in acceleration. We note that our driving in previous weeks is no different from our driving now, except for the fact that we have shifted to a different brand of gasoline. We recall that our new brand costs a few cents more and has a higher octane. In no other respects have we changed our driving habits in the past few weeks, nor have we recently had any mechanical work done to our car. Given this scenario, we would naturally suspect the higher octane gas to be the cause of our automobile's improved performance. And we would be led to this hypothesis by the Method of Difference. We were originally concerned to identify the cause of a phenomenon in a particular situation. This particular situation was similar in all relevant respects, except for one, to another situation in which the phenomenon in question did not occur. We therefore hypothesized that the one respect in which the two situations differed—the brand of gasoline—was the likely cause of the phenomenon.

Let us consider another example of the Method of Difference, returning to our earlier illustration where we were concerned to identify the cause of an allergic effect. Let us suppose that our diets on Monday and Tuesday evenings are identically similar except in one respect: butter is present in our diet on Monday, but missing in our diet on Tuesday, and we experience the allergic effect on Moday, but not on Tuesday. Using our original example, this information can be represented as follows:

Monday: Allergic Effect	Tuesday: No Allergic Effect
Chicken	Chicken
Baked potato	Baked potato
Butter	———————
Salt	Salt
Tomatoes	Tomatoes
Lettuce	Lettuce
Olive oil	Olive oil
Vinegar	Vinegar

On the basis of this data, it is reasonable to identify butter as the likely cause by the Method of Difference. Given the hypothesis that some food ingested during the Monday evening meal caused the allergic effect, the additional evidence from Tuesday's meal eliminates all of the foods with the exception of butter. To be precise, all of the foods with the exception of butter are eliminated as a sufficient cause, and therefore as a unique cause, since they were all present on Tuesday but without the attendant allergic effect being present too. Olive oil, for example, cannot be a sufficient cause, since $(O \cdot \sim E)$ or $\sim (O \supset E)$. In contrast, butter

281

is not only partially confirmed as a sufficient and necessary cause by its presence in our diet on Monday, but its absence on Tuesday, along with the absence of the allergic effect ($\sim B \supset \sim E$), counts as an additional confirmation of it as a necessary cause ($E \supset B$). And, to turn this around, the absence of the allergic effect, along with its (butter's) absence ($\sim E \supset \sim B$), counts as an additional confirmation of it as a sufficient cause ($B \supset E$).

It is interesting to observe that we can combine the two methods of Agreement and Difference in some instances to successfully identify a cause. Suppose, for example, that we have identified either butter or oil as the cause of the allergic effect on Monday, Wednesday, and Friday by the Method of Agreement, because only butter and olive oil were invariantly present in our diets on those evenings. And suppose that on Tuesday and Thursday when we did not suffer the allergic effect, butter was again part of our diet but olive oil was not. By a variation on the Method of Difference we can now eliminate butter as a sufficient cause, and identify olive oil as the likely cause of the allergic effect.

I. In the following exercises, identify:

NC: The assertion or hypothesis of a *necessary cause*

SC: The assertion or hypothesis of a *sufficient cause*

UC: The assertion or hypothesis of a *unique cause*

DNC: The *disconfirmation of a necessary cause*

DSC: The *disconfirmation of a sufficient cause*

MA: The *Method of Agreement*

MD: The *Method of Difference*

ARC: *Analogical Reasoning* to a cause

(i) When the radiator overheats, this does not necessarily mean that the liquid in the radiator is low. For it is possible that the fan belt is broken and not supplying its usual assistance in cooling the liquid as it passes through the radiator. Alternatively, the radiator cap may not fit properly, or there could even be a malfunctioning of the thermostat. Worst of all, the radiator itself may be old and inefficient, and may need to be replaced or at least rebuilt. Of couse, although these several alternatives exist, we should not for that reason completely neglect the level of liquid in the radiator. For if it gets too low, you can be certain that the radiator will overheat.

(ii) I'm convinced that you must run as a Democrat in order to win as a congressman from Natchez county. When I studied the record of elections over the past forty years it was obvious. I first thought that the main pre-requisite for election was membership in the legal profession, since the past three members of congress, two men and a woman, were all practicing attorneys. However, even though attorneys constitute the majority in the past forty year history, I discovered that there were businessmen, and even one farmer, who had been elected too. On the other hand, even though there were a number of popular republican contenders for the office, not a single one was ever elected. A democrat always won. I am now turning eighteen and must register to vote. I plan to run for city council at twenty-two and for congress before I'm thirty. You can be sure that I'm going to register as a democrat.

(iii)   My car would not start in a terrible storm yesterday, and I
        had to walk in the rain all of the way home. I thought for
        sure the problem was the battery. I don't remember leaving
        my lights on, but I know that if your battery is low, then
        there's not sufficient electricity to turn over the starter, and if
        the starter won't turn over, there's no chance that the car will
        start.   I also know that if your battery is low, if you use
        jumper cables from someone else's battery, then you can
        start your car. But when I tried this with a friend of mine who
        has jumper cables, it didn't work. The starter was certainly
        turning over fast, but the engine still would not start. I then
        remembered a fishing trip I had taken with my uncle. We had
        planned to take his boat out fishing after a night of a very
        heavy rainfall, and his outboard motor would not start. He
        said that it was probably moisture on the spark plugs, and after
        wiping the plugs off, the outboard motor started right up. So I
        thought that might be the cause of my problem too. I dried
        around the top of the plugs, and to my great delight, my car
        started right away.

(iv)   Person A: You can only be a legal candidate for the presi-
                  dency if you are a U.S. citizen.

        Person B: That's certainly true.   You wouldn't want a
                  foreigner running your country would you?
                  Moreover, as you must know, being a citizen is not
                  enough.   You must also be a natural born citizen
                  too.

        Person A: Yes. I know. In fact, I believe you have to be a
                  natural born citizen even to hold a cabinet post
                  in the federal government, for example, to be
                  Secretary of State.

        Person B: No. That can't be true. Henry Kissinger was the
                  Secretary of State under Richard Nixon, and his
                  birthplace was Germany.

(v)   I planted two small separate plots of tomato plants in my
        back yard two summers ago. One produced excellent plants
        and tomatoes, but the other did not. I couldn't figure it out,
        and was extremely puzzled, because I used seeds from the same
        packet, I watered both plots equally, I didn't apply fertilizer
        to either, and as far as I could tell, the soil in the two plots,
        which were not at a great distance from one another, was
        similar.   Then I realized that during the first month of the

plants' growth, the second plot, for part of the day, was in the shade of a tree I have in my back yard, whereas the first plot that fared so well was in the sun all day long. I naturally hypothesized that insufficient sunlight was the cause of the less desirable plant growth. I couldn't be certain of this hypothesis. For all I knew there was some other explanation. For example, perhaps there was a difference in the drainage of the two plots. I had heard somewhere that drainage can make a lot of difference in the growth of certain kinds of plants. But I thought my hypothesis was sufficiently likely to be tested out, and so last summer when I planted these two plots again with tomatoes, I made a point of pruning back my tree so that it did not shade the troublesome plot. And this time the second plot produced just as excellent plants and tomatoes as the first. I, of course, was extremely happy. If I can now just figure out how my neighbour grows even bigger and better tomatoes just on the other side of my fence, I'll be even happier.

(vi) A friend of mine who knows a great deal about automotive maintenance pointed out to me that my tires were wearing erratically. Both of my two front tires were wearing very rapidly on the inside edge. She explained that there was only one explanation as to why that would occur: my tires must be tilted at an angle outwards. She insisted that if my tires were wearing on the inside edge and only the inside edge, the tilt had to be the problem, and that I needed to have my front tires re-aligned. We also checked my rear tires, and although my left rear tire was fine, my right rear tire was curiously wearing rapidly on both the inside edge and the outside edge too. I was a bit frustrated because I knew I had replaced that tire not too long ago. My mechanical minded friend pointed out that my tire must not be properly inflated. She explained that if the air in the tire is low, then the tire wears on the outer two edges. I asked whether wear like this could be caused in any other way. She said she didn't think so, and in fact, when we checked that tire it was just as she had predicted. It only had about eighteen pounds of pressure, far below what is normally recommended. I learned a few lessons that day on what causes what, lessons I'm sure that will save me money in the future.

(vii) As a student of animal behaviour encamped in the Sierras for the purpose of studying a species of ground squirrel, I observed right away that sometimes when I approached the vicinity of one of these squirrels it would sit up and emit a distinctive chirp, which I assumed was an alarm call to others. I was uncertain of this interpretation, however, because on other occasions when approaching one of these squirrels, it would not emit this distinctive chirp at all, but would quickly scurry down into a burrow. If the chirping was a call of alarm announcing a dangerous intruder, why was it sometimes present and sometimes absent?

These reflections prodded me to explore two further questions. First of all, if the chirping behaviour was an alarm call, then I ought to find it exhibited, characteristically, upon the approach of any dangerous intruder. And, indeed, it was. In each of several instances over a period of the next several weeks, whenever a coyote came into the vicinity, one of the squirrels would sit up and emit the distinctive chirping sound. Secondly, although these observations seemed to constitute a pretty definitive corroboration of my first interpretation, I continued to be plagued by the question as to why this response behaviour was sometimes exhibited and sometimes not. I was determined to find out what distinguished those occasions when in the presence of an intruder the chirping behaviour was exhibited, and when in the presence of an intruder it was not. It was not long before I ascertained that it was only adult male squirrels who merely scurried into their burrows upon an intruder's approach. The adult males lived away from the main female nesting area, each on his own. I thought: "They have no one to warn but themselves, and so warning behaviour is inappropriate. The females of one family, on the contrary, nest in an area together."

These last observations led me to raise a still further question. If I was correct in my interpretation of the chirping behaviour as a call of alarm, then it was reasonable to presume that it was an effective alarm. I should be able to observe that more females survived the threat of predators than males. However, much to my dismay, in a study that covered the next several months, I discovered that it was exactly those females who emitted the alarm call who were most likely to be killed! Apparently the alarm call signaled the presence of the squirrel to an approaching predator, and even guided the predator directly to its prey. Of course, I was not only dismayed, but also quite excited over the discovery. For it seemed to be clear counter-evidence to my and many other biologists' understanding of the survival of certain behavioural traits. If the alarm call response was not only ineffective, but even directly facilitated the killing of those who exhibited it, then why had it not been eliminated altogether in this species' behaviour?

Feeling confident that I had sufficient evidence to communicate my results, and fantasizing myself at the center of a controversy in Biology as either famous or infamous, I broke the news of my discovery to a friend who was a student of animal behaviour too. However, instead of being impressed, my friend pointed out that I had committed an error in my reasoning. Certainly, he insisted, I must have observed that the other female family members in the nesting area of the alarm–calling female, her sisters and daughters, for example, were effectively warned, and did take appropriate protective behaviour which enhanced their survival. I had to admit that this was true. "It follows then," he continued, "that the alarm call is actually effective in promoting the survival of that genetic group. Your error was in assuming that animal behaviour must be seen as exclusively egoistic. And just because you're an egoist it doesn't mean that squirrels are too." Naturally, I was sufficiently chastised, and returned somewhat more humbled to my investigative work. Although I hasten to add that I couldn't help but chuckle on the evening when a bear ripped open the side of my friend's tent, and he ran out of it in a panic. [11]

FOOTNOTES

CHAPTER II:

(1) It is important to qualify these comments on the logical form of partial confirmation. According to the analysis we have given, even an hypothesis we know to be false is amenable to partial confirmation. For example, we know — within the story — that if the chambermaid committed the murder, then she must have been present in the Anderson home when the murder occurred. That she was, indeed, in the Anderson home at that time, therefore constitutes a partial confirmation of the hypothesis that she committed the murder, an hypothesis we know to be false. This observation points up the necessity of introducing the following qualification: We continue to understand the logical form of the partial confirmation of an hypothesis to be:

(i) If H_1, then C_1

(ii) C_1

C_1 is a partial confirmation of H_1

But we add the following qualification that not every chain of reasoning of the logical form:

(i) If A, then B

(ii) B

A

constitutes the partial confirmation of an hypothesis.

(2) *The Republic of Plato*, Translator: Francis M. Cornford, Oxford University Press, reprint 1979, Chapter IX, pp. 72-73.

CHAPTER IV:

(3) John Stuart Mill, *A System of Logic* (Collected Works), University of Toronto Press, Routledge & Kegan Paul, Toronto & Buffalo, 1974, Vol. VIII, Chapter V, p. 785.

(4) Ludwig Wittgenstein, *Philosophical Investigations*, The MacMillan

Company, New York 1957 (Second Printing) and *The Blue and Brown Books*, Harper Colophon Books, Harper & Row, Second Edition, 1960.

(5)   John Stuart Mill, *A System of Logic*, Vol. VII, p. 312.

(6)   *Ibid,* p. 312.

(7)   *Ibid,* p. 788.

CHAPTER V:

(8)   David Hume, *Dialogues Concerning Natural Religion*, Hafner Library of Classics, Ed: Henry Aiken, Hafner Publishing Co., N.Y. & London, 1969, Part V.

CHAPTER VI:

(9)   George Orwell, "Politics and the English Language," *The Collected Essays, Journalism, and Letters of George Orwell*, Harcourt & Brace, 1968, Volume IV, p. 135.

CHAPTER VIII:

(10)   Herschel, John Frederic William, *A Preliminary Discourse on the Study of Natural Philosophy*, London, Longman, Rees, Orme, Brown, and Green, 1831.

(11)   This problem is a fictitious reconstruction of some observations made by Paul Sherman of Cornell University and Martin Morton of Occidental College, in their studies of ground squirrel behaviour in the Sierras of California.